Intermediate Sanctions in Corrections

GAIL A. CAPUTO

Number 4 in the North Texas Crime and
Criminal Justice Series

University of North Texas Press
Denton, Texas

Permissions:
University of North Texas Press
P.O. Box 311336
Denton, TX 76203-1336

The paper used in this book meets the minimum requirements of the
American National Standard for Permanence of Paper for Printed
Library Materials, z39.48.1984. Binding materials have been chosen for
durability.

Library of Congress Cataloging-in-Publication Data

Caputo, Gail A., 1965-
Intermediate sanctions in corrections / Gail A. Caputo.
p. cm. — (North Texas crime and criminal justice series ; no. 4)
Includes bibliographical references and index.
ISBN 1-57441-182-9 (cloth : alk. paper) — ISBN 1-57441-186-1
(pbk. : alk. paper)
1. Alternatives to imprisonment—United States.
2. Corrections—United States. I. Title. II. Series.
HV9304.C32 2004
364.6'8'0973—dc22
2004011388

Intermediate Sanctions in Corrections is Number 4 in the
North Texas Crime and Criminal Justice Series

Design by Angela Schmitt

For my family: Kathleen, Anthony, Betty, Theresa, Susan, Howie, Chris, Annie, and Lily

 # CONTENTS

PREFACE

In the past two decades, states and the federal government have developed and implemented new correctional options in an attempt to reduce correctional crowding and costs, better manage higher-risk offenders in the community, reduce crime, and achieve greater fairness and effectiveness in criminal sentencing for adults. These innovations are referred to as intermediate sanctions programs and are the subject of this book.

This book provides a simple but comprehensive description of the intermediate sanctions system and meaningful analysis of the individual programs. The book is organized into three parts. Part I presents to the reader a background and context for understanding the role of intermediate sanctions in the criminal justice system. It explains the history and development of intermediate sanctions, including philosophies of punishment and an overview of sentencing processes. The key issues for evaluating the effectiveness of intermediate sanctions are outlined in Part I. In Part II, each of the seven chapters focuses on a specific intermediate sanction: intensive supervision programs, boot camps, day reporting centers, home confinement with electronic monitoring, monetary penalties, community service, and halfway houses. Each chapter traces the history of the intermediate sanction, provides statistics on its extent and scope, and describes target populations, program characteristics, and research findings. Program examples are a main feature of each chapter. Part III summarizes the research related to intermediate sanctions and provides recommendations for the future.

In writing this book I was assisted with the work and support of Dana Nurge of San Diego State University who reviewed and edited early versions of this book. Jon'a Meyer of Rutgers University in Camden, New Jersey, has contributed to this book by authoring the chapter on home confinement with electronic monitoring. I would also like to thank Michael S. Vigorita and Bradley Stewart Chilton for their thoughtful reviews and Paula Oates of the University of North Texas Press for her commitment to this project.

PART I

Background and Foundation of Intermediate Sanctions Programs

 **CHAPTER 1**

Overview and Theoretical Foundations of Corrections

THE CRIMINAL JUSTICE SYSTEM

Criminal justice in the United States involves three interdependent agencies—law enforcement, courts, and corrections—operating at the federal, state, and local levels. Together, these agencies represent the criminal justice system. Although with distinct lines of funding, rules, standards, procedures, and organizational structures, these agencies must work together in the processing of criminal cases. This process is traditionally characterized by a model developed by the President's Commission on Law Enforcement and the Administration of Justice (LEAA) (President's Commission on Law Enforcement and Administration of Justice, 1967). The model portrays a rational, systematic assembly line-like processing of criminal cases through the three agencies. Law enforcement agencies are formally charged with the prevention and control of crime. To this end, they respond to reports of criminal activity, investigate these reports, and make arrests when appropriate. Then, courts determine criminal charges, decide guilt of the accused, and impose criminal sanctions. Finally, correctional agencies administer these penalties through control, custody, and supervision.

COMPONENTS OF CORRECTIONS

Corrections refers to the myriad policies, programming, services, organizations, and facilities designed for individuals who are accused and convicted of crimes. Correctional programs are administered by all levels of government—local, state, and federal. Common correctional options and other restrictions placed on offenders are illustrated in Figure 1.1. Very minor offenders may lose driving privileges as a punishment measure. First-time shoplifters may be ordered to probation for one year, pay court costs, pay a fee for probation supervision, and report face-to-face to a probation officer monthly. The probation department would monitor the offender's criminal activity, his or her payment of fees, and so on. Felons may be placed under home confinement with electronic monitoring, perform community service, and serve weekends in jail. These sanctions and restrictions can be used in any number of different combinations and judges have considerable discretion in their application.

The most commonly used correctional options are illustrated in Figure 1.2. These options are classified into three categories: incarceration, community corrections, and intermediate sanctions programs. Incarceration refers to jails and prisons. The term community corrections refers to a variety of programs that are outside of jails and prisons. These are most notably probation and parole and can include community-based treatment programs. The third category is the subject of this text. Intermediate sanctions are designed for persons who require more supervision and control than community corrections but less supervision and control than incarceration. Although it can be argued that many community correctional programs are intermediate sanctions because they are designed to divert offenders from more intrusive penalties, there is general agreement that intermediate sanctions are made up of a set of eight correctional options falling between probation and incarceration. Figure 1.2 illustrates the correctional options on a continuum, because they vary in the type and amount of control placed over an offender's behavior. Options to the left, such as probation, offer the least amount of control over offenders and are considered the least severe sanctions. Moving toward the right side, the options become more punitive. Incarceration, for example, is typically reserved for the serious or repeat offender. The continuum of sanctions enables judges to choose punishments that fit the crime and offender.

Especially for adults, incarceration, community corrections, and intermediate sanctions are being used more now than ever before. The number of offenders involved in these programs has increased dramati-

Type		Example
Restrictions on the offender's behavior		Limits on travel (e.g. outside of county; to specific places; at certain times) Limits on social interaction with people (e.g. gang members, convicted offenders, other known offenders) Loss of driving privileges for a certain length of time or during certain hours Limits on the possession of weapons Limits on the use of alcohol
Monetary Penalties		Restitution Fines Forfeitures Support payments Court costs Supervision fees
Work-Related Measures		Community service Requirement to remain gainfully employed
Education-Related Measures		Enrollment in academic program (e.g., basic literacy, GED, English as second language) Enrollment in vocational training
Treatment Measures		Enrollment in substance abuse treatment Enrollment in psychological or psychiatric counseling
Physical Confinement Measures	Partial/Intermittent Confinement	Split sentences, intermittent confinement Home curfew Day reporting center Halfway house Restitution center Outpatient treatment facility (e.g., mental health, drug)
	Full/Continuous Confinement	Home confinement (i.e., full curfew) Other residential treatment (e.g., drug/alcohol) Boot camp (i.e., shock incarceration) Jail/Prison
Compliance and Monitoring Measures	Required of offender	Mail reporting Phone reporting Face-to-face reporting Urine analysis (random; routine)
	Required of agency	Criminal records checks Sentence compliance checks (payment of monetary penalties; attendance/participation/performance at treatment, work, or educational sites) Third-party checks (family, employer, service/treatment provider) Direct surveillance/observation (random/routine visits) Electronic monitoring (active, passive)

Adapted from Hartland, 1998

Figure 1.1. Various Restrictions and Sanctions for Criminal Offenders

cally over the past three decades. According to the Bureau of Justice Statistics, more than 6.5 million adults were incarcerated, on probation, or on parole at the end of 2001: about 63,240 in jails, just over 1.3 million in prisons, 732,351 on parole, and more than 3.9 million on probation (Glaze, 2002). These figures are the best estimates of the adult correctional populations in the United States but do not accurately account for the thousands of offenders in intermediate sanctions. The following section reviews the three correctional options beginning with incarceration, the most punitive and restrictive.

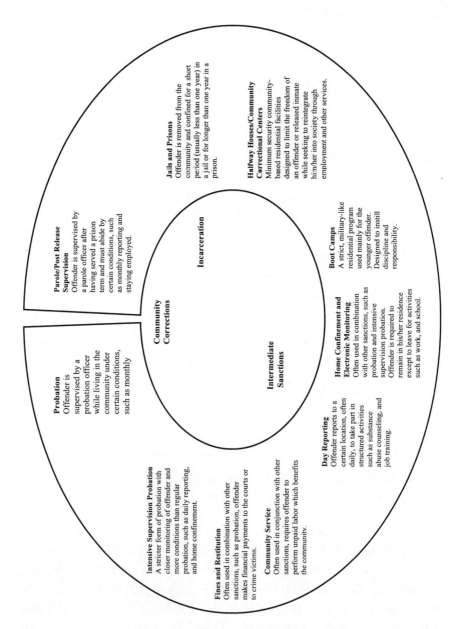

Figure 1.2. Varieties of Correctional Options

Incarceration: Jail and Prison

Incarceration requires that a criminal offender remain housed in a secure facility for a certain length of time and with certain requirements and restrictions. Aside from temporary detention facilities and police lockups, the two options for incarceration include jail and prison. Jails and prisons differ according to inmate populations and administrative jurisdiction.

Jails are short-term confinement facilities typically housing convicted misdemeanants and unconvicted defendants during court processing. At midyear 2001, jails housed 631,240 people (Beck, Karberg, & Harrison, 2002). More than half (59%) had not been convicted of crimes. They were awaiting court action on their current charge. Officially these inmates are detainees. Persons are detained during court proceedings for two main reasons: (1) they cannot afford bail; or (2) they pose a danger to society and a risk of fleeing the jurisdiction while their case is being tried. The remaining 41% of jail inmates were serving a sentence, usually for a misdemeanor, or were awaiting sentencing for a crime. Misdemeanants usually serve jail terms of less than one year. A variety of persons are housed in jails and include:

- Persons awaiting arraignment, trial, or sentencing;
- Convicted felons awaiting transfer to state and federal prisons;
- Probation and parole violators proceeding through revocation hearings;
- Bail bond violators;
- Persons awaiting transfer to federal, medical, juvenile, military, and other correctional facilities;
- Persons held for protective custody, for contempt of courts, and crime witnesses;
- Convicted felons from federal and state facilities due to crowding;
- Persons sentenced for misdemeanors generally under one year; and
- Persons sentenced to a short jail term for a felony (a split sentence).

The sheriff's department runs the majority of jails at the county level. Jails also operate at the city and regional levels. There is no equivalent to the local jail at the federal level. Private agencies play a small role in jail administration. In very rural areas and where correctional populations are very low, two adjoining counties might decide to pool resources for the operation of a regional jail that would serve both counties. There are more than 3300 jails in the United States (Stephan, 2001).

Prisons are long-term confinement facilities housing felony offenders and parole violators serving sentences of greater than one year. At midyear 2001 there were 1,334,255 men and women in state and federal prisons (Beck, Karberg, & Harrison, 2002). By design, prisons are intended for offenders who have been convicted of felonies and who are serving sentences of more than one year. A small number of prison inmates are serving sentences of less than one year because of overcrowding in local jails.

A common misconception is that prisons are filled with dangerous and violent offenders. According to recent statistics (Beck & Harrison, 2001), violent offenders make up less than half (about 48%) of all prisoners in state jails. These offenders are serving time for crimes such as robbery, assault, and murder. The remaining 52% of sentenced prisoners are primarily property, drug, and public order offenders. Common property offenses include burglary, larceny, motor vehicle theft, possession and sale of stolen property, trespassing, and vandalism. Public-order offenses include such crimes as drunk driving, escape, obstruction of justice, weapons-related offenses, and liquor law violations. A fair number of newly admitted prisoners are persons who were released from prison on parole and who were returned to prison as a result of a parole violation, such as a new crime.

The federal government and state government operate prisons. Private companies also operate prisons for the federal government and the state governments. Federal prisons house offenders convicted or accused of federal offenses. According to the Bureau of Justice Statistics (Beck, Karberg, & Harrison, 2002), federal prisoners represent about 11% of all prisoners. More than one million people, (about 89% of all prisoners) are housed in state facilities. Compared to jails, prisons are typically larger and range in custody level from minimum security to super maximum security where the nation's most dangerous offenders are confined. At the end of 2000, there were 1,558 state facilities and 84 federal facilities operating in the United States (Beck & Harrison, 2001).

Community Corrections: Probation and Parole

Probation refers to the action of suspending a sentence and allowing the offender to serve the sanctions imposed by the court while living in the community. It involves supervision by probation departments and is the most commonly used correctional option. During the period of community supervision, probationers are required to abide by certain court-imposed conditions, such as maintaining employment and reporting to a probation officer. An array of other conditions may be imposed, including community service and restitution. A probationer who violates conditions may have the sentence revoked and be subject to imprisonment. A judge decides revocation after conducting a hearing.

Probation is mainly used for convicted offenders and less frequently as a means to supervise offenders who have not yet been convicted of crimes. Often, defendants proceeding through court who are not detained in jail are subject to probation supervision as a condition of their pretrial release. Though not technically criminal offenders because they are still unconvicted, they would be required to abide by many of the same restrictions and conditions as convicted offenders. Probation can also be used with incarceration in different ways: split sentences and intermittent sentences. An offender given a split sentence would be incarcerated for a short period (usually six months) before beginning the probation supervision. Intermittent incarceration requires offenders on probation to spend nights or weekends in jail.

More than 3.9 million adults were on probation at the end of 2001 (Glaze, 2002). Before the 1980s, probationers were typically misdemeanor offenders seen as posing little risk to public safety. Now, supervision of offenders with lengthier criminal histories and felony-level offenses is the norm. In 1986, probation was granted to 46% of all convicted felons (Petersilia, 1998) At the end of 2001, according to Glaze, 53% of all probationers had been convicted of a felony.

The administration of probation is not as clear-cut as the administration of prisons and jails. There are three models for the administration of probation in the states: state-administered, local-administered, and mixed models. According to McCarthy, McCarthy, and Leone (2001) in the most states (25) probation administration rests with the state government. Nineteen states follow the mixed model, where probation administration is a function of some combination of state, county, and city governments. In nine states, county governments operate probation in the local-administered model. The Federal Probation Service supervises federal probationers.

Parole refers to the conditional release of a prisoner after some portion of the prison sentence has been served. Parole is also referred to as community or supervised release, which involves a period of supervision following a prison term. After being released from prison, parolees are placed on community supervision and must abide by certain conditions and restrictions, much like probationers. Prisoners who have completed their entire prison terms are not normally subject to parole supervision. Most prisoners are released from prison early and subject to community supervision; at yearend 2001, 732, 351 offenders were on parole (Glaze, 2002). Inmates are released early from prison to parole in one of two ways: discretionary release and mandatory supervised release. With discretionary release, the parole board makes the decision to release a prisoner early to community supervision. Only about 37% of parolees were released in this way in 2001. The remaining 63% of parolees were released from prison under supervised mandatory release. This involves a legislative rule allowing early release for prisoners who have completed a certain proportion of their sentences (usually 85%). With changes in sentencing policy, many states have eliminated or restricted discretionary release. According to a recent federal report, 14 states have abolished discretionary release for all offenders (Ditton & Wilson, 1999), and several others, such as New York and Virginia, have abolished early release of certain violent felony offenders. In addition to diminishing or eliminating the release powers of the parole board, recent laws restrict or abolish the practice of crediting inmates with "good time" to reduce their time spent under custody.

Following release from prison, the amount of time a parolee must serve on parole varies and may be for the period remaining on the original sentence. An offender sentenced to five years in prison and released on parole after three years might serve the two years remaining on his or her sentence under parole supervision.

Parole operates much like probation but is administered at the state level. The primary difference is that all parolees have served a prison term and that nearly all parolees had been convicted of a felony. Like probation, parole involves an array of conditions over an offender's behavior, such as drug treatment and fines. Intermediate sanctions, such as home confinement, are also used for parolees. When a parolee fails to abide by conditions or commits a new crime, the parole authority has the power to revoke parole after conducting a hearing. Revocation of parole could lead to reincarceration. At yearend 2001, less than half (46%) of adults leaving parole had successfully completed parole, 40% were revoked from parole and returned to prison, and the remainder had not completed parole for other reasons, such as having absconded or died (Glaze, 2002).

Intermediate Sanction Programs

Intermediate sanctions include a range of punishment options between probation and imprisonment. These programs are also referred to as intermediate penalties and intermediate punishments. The principal forms of intermediate sanctions include: intensive supervision programs (ISP); boot camps; day reporting centers; home confinement (with or without electronic monitoring); monetary penalties (fines and restitution); compulsory labor in the form of community service; and halfway houses.

Intensive Supervision Programs (ISP) provide for the intensive monitoring and surveillance of criminal offenders usually by a probation or parole supervision officer. ISP is used by probation and parole agencies. Is often referred to as Intensive Supervision Probation and Intensive Supervision Parole. ISP is a more restrictive form of probation and parole for the higher risk offender. While on ISP, offenders are required to abide by strict rules such as refraining from drinking alcohol, and regulations such as reporting to a probation officer weekly. Fines and other intermediate sanctions are usually added to this sanction.

Boot Camps represent a residential intermediate sanction program. Typically used for young offenders, boot camps provide for very structured and military-like activities focusing on discipline, physical labor, and education.

Day Reporting Centers combine high levels of control with intensive delivery of services. They require offenders to report to a specific location on a routine, prearranged basis, usually daily, where they participate in structured activities such as counseling and job training.

Home Confinement/House Arrest requires offenders to remain under curfew usually in their homes for a specified number of hours per day or week. They may be permitted to leave for approved activities such as employment and religious services.

Electronic Monitoring is not a criminal sanction. Rather, it is a means to monitor the offenders' presence in a proscribed location and is used with home confinement and other intermediate sanctions, such as ISP.

Fines are financial penalties requiring offenders to make payments to the court. Fines are usually based on the seriousness of the crime committed but can also be based on the offender's income.

Restitution refers to compensation for financial, physical, or emotional loss suffered by a crime victim. The compensation is usually financial whereby an offender makes payments, usually through the court, to the victim.

Community Service is compulsory, free, or donated labor on the part of an offender as punishment for a crime. An offender under a community service order would perform labor for a certain length of time at charitable not-for-profit agencies, such as domestic violence shelters, or governmental offices, such as courthouses.

Halfway Houses/Community Correctional Centers are community-based, minimum-security residential facilities that provide offenders and released inmates with housing, some treatment services, and access to community resources for employment and education.

Each of these programs can be used on its own as a penalty or in conjunction with other correctional options, mainly probation and parole. Typically, offenders given intermediate sanctions are under some form of probation supervision, whether it is regular probation or intensive supervision probation. They are assigned conditions that include home confinement, electronic monitoring, and other intermediate sanctions. For instance, an offender on ISP may also be required to pay restitution and perform community service when he or she is financially able to make restitution and can perform the types of labor that could benefit the community.

Traditionally, intermediate sanctions are designed for offenders who require a correctional option that is more punitive and restrictive than routine probation but less severe than imprisonment. But, intermediate sanctions are used for a variety of offenders:

- Persons accused of crimes and released into the community during court proceedings;
- Persons convicted of misdemeanors and felonies directly sentenced to an intermediate sanction;
- Persons on probation;
- Jail inmates;
- Prison inmates; and
- Persons on parole.

Unlike probation and parole where statistics are readily available, it is difficult to accurately determine the number of offenders involved in intermediate sanctions or even the number of intermediate sanctions that exist in different areas. This is because the intermediate sanctions system is varied, complex, and dynamic. Suffice it to say, there are thousands of offenders involved in intermediate sanctions on any given day. According to the Bureau of Justice Statistics (Beck, Karberg, & Harrison, 2002), 25% of the adults supervised by jail staff who were not housed in jails were participating in required community service (17,561 adults) and 14% were under electronic monitoring (10,017 adults).

The administration of prisons, jails, probation, and parole is clearly designated in each state as a local or state agency responsibility. For instance, adult probation in Texas is operated by 122 Community Supervision and Corrections Departments (CSCDs) at the county level and administered by the Criminal Justice Assistance Division of the Texas Department of Criminal Justice at the state level. Jails in Texas are normally operated at the county level and prisons are administered by the state. The administration of intermediate sanctions is not as clearly defined and involves all levels of government. Since ISP is the most commonly used intermediate sanction program and is usually administered by probation departments, we could assume that probation departments play the major role in the administration of intermediate sanctions. Despite the lack of uniform information, it appears that every state incorporates intermediate sanctions and that the use of such programs has been expanding rapidly since the 1980s.

THEORETICAL FOUNDATIONS OF CORRECTIONS

Rationales for the punishment of criminal offenders have been debated throughout history. Today, four popular approaches, commonly referred to as philosophies, justifications, rationales, or goals, guide the use of correctional options: retribution, deterrence, incapacitation, and rehabilitation. Each outlines a specific correctional aim to be achieved, a justification for imposing punishment, and a basic assumption about what types of correctional options would further the specific purpose. It is important to understand the rationales because correctional programs, programs, and practices are based on them. Figure 1.3 illustrates the four rationales.

	Retribution	Deterrence	Incapacitation	Rehabilitation
Reason for Imposing Criminal Sanction	To show blame and show disapproval	To prevent future crime through fear of punishment	To prevent continued crime by restricting the offender's criminal opportunities	To assist the offender in becoming law-abiding through treatment and services
Assumption about Crime Causation	None	Crime results from offender's rational decision to commit crime based on expected utility	Crime results from offender's rational decision to commit crime; crime results from influence of treatable conditions attributed to offender	Crime results from influence of treatable conditions attributed to offender
Basis for Choosing Sanctions	Offense characteristics	Offender and Offense characteristics	Offender and Offense characteristics	Offender characteristics
Appropriate Criminal Sanctions	Any; depends on seriousness of harm	Any	Any; tradition is incarceration	Community Corrections and Intermediate Sanctions

Figure 1.3. Theoretical Foundations of Corrections

Retribution

Thought of as revenge throughout much of history, retribution aims to impose punishment upon offenders simply because they have committed a wrong and deserve to be punished. According to the most popular retributive theory, just deserts theory (von Hirsch, 1976) the purpose of corrections is to assign blame to the offender for the harm caused by the crime. Preventing future crime is not the objective. For retribution, the reasons that people engage in crime are unimportant. Regardless of conditions or limitations in people's lives, such as drug abuse or poverty, all offenders should face blame. The basis for choosing appropriate sanctions rests with the nature of the offense. Very simply, the amount of punishment should be proportionate to the harm caused. The seriousness of the crime determines the severity of the punishment—a fair penalty is one that reflects the blameworthiness of the criminal conduct.

Any correctional option would serve the retributive function as long as it matches the severity of the crime. For illustration, think of a scale. On one side of the scale is the harm an offense has caused and on the other is the weight of the penalty. The penalty should be only as severe as to balance the scale. A fine of $50 might befit an offender who has stolen a $50 pair of jeans. Thus, less serious crime would be deserving of less severe penalties and more serious crimes would be deserving of more severe penalties. It is important to note, however, that most retributivists would not support the death penalty since more than "an eye for an eye" is considered, such as assuring fairness and equity.

Deterrence

Deterrence aims to prevent crime through the application and fear of punishment. Two forms of deterrence are distinguished: general and specific. General deterrence seeks to dissuade the general population from engaging in criminal conduct by witnessing punishment imposed on a criminal offender. In our early history, punishments were inflicted in public. In part, this was done to set an example to would-be offenders that criminal offenders would not escape punishment. Specific deterrence (also called special deterrence) seeks to change the future behavior of people who have been convicted of crimes. It assumes that criminal offenders will be dissuaded from committing future crimes for fear of being punished again. Offenders have experienced the punishment first hand, should never forget the experience, and should fear it so much that they conform.

A contemporary example of deterrence is the "scared straight" program, which brings youth face-to-face with prisoners who vividly present the pains of prison life in order to discourage the youth from committing crime: to "scare them straight" (See Finckenauer, 1982). Deterrence rests on the belief that potential offenders are knowledgeable, rational, and calculating and would abandon committing a criminal act for fear of punishment. Theoretically, punishments should be certain, swift, and often severe. Any sanction would fit the idea of deterrence as long as the punishments are perceived to outweigh the benefits of criminal behavior.

Incapacitation

Incapacitation aims only to render offenders unable to commit crime by restricting access to criminal opportunities for the period of their sentence. It involves controlling their actions so that they are unable to harm society. Incarcerating a habitual offender is a means to achieve this incapacitation, because while behind bars, the offender is unable to harm society.

Two types of incapacitation strategies are distinguished: selective and collective. (See Spelman, 1994.) Selective incapacitation is geared toward habitual or high-risk offenders in an attempt to limit the number of crimes they commit. Generally referred to as career criminals, this group represents a small segment of the offender population thought to commit crimes at a high rate throughout their lives (Greenwood & Abrahamse, 1982). Policies such as "three strikes and you're out" represent one such approach. Collective incapacitation targets offenders who commit a particularly sensitive crime, such as driving while intoxicated (DWI) or drug sales.

The reasons that people engage in crime are not important to this goal of corrections, since the objective is to constrain the offender. Any combination of correctional options can facilitate incapacitation. Capital punishment is the most extreme form of incapacitation. Typically, restraint through incarceration has been the dominant approach in the United States.

Rehabilitation

Rehabilitation seeks to assist the offender in becoming law-abiding through treatment and services designed to address the problems that are thought to contribute to his or her criminality. As a goal of corrections, its purpose is to enhance community protection by addressing the treatment needs of people who engage in criminal acts because it is assumed that their decisions, thoughts, and actions are influenced by certain events or conditions in their lives. Poverty, neglect, poor social skills, inadequate education, substance abuse, and mental health are all examples of potential contributors to criminal behavior.

For rehabilitation, punishment alone has little utility (Andrews, 1994; Gendreau, 1993). Sentences for people who commit criminal acts should be designed according to the specific treatment needs of the offender (drugs or attitudes, values, and behaviors for instance) rather than exclusively on the crime. Though a very popular approach to corrections throughout the 1900s, rehabilitation came under attack in the 1970s. However, research has shown that effective treatment can be achieved through carefully designed correctional strategies. Most proponents of rehabilitation argue against the uniform use of incarceration, because the punitive environment is thought to contaminate treatment. Non-incarcerative, community-based sanctions (such as drug treatment programs, community service, or intensive probation) are thought to be more appropriate than incarceration.

KEY ISSUES IN CORRECTIONS

Before beginning our exploration of intermediate sanctions, it is important to understand how the effectiveness of correctional programs can be judged. Today, correctional programs are judged using a variety of measures including: recidivism, net widening, cost effectiveness, program completion, and behavioral change/treatment effectiveness. Throughout the book I refer to these key issues when discussing the effectiveness of the various types of intermediate sanctions. Figure 1.4 illustrates the measures of program effectiveness.

	Definition	How Concept is Usually Measured	Typical Indicators of Program Effectiveness
Recidivism	The recurrence of criminal behavior on the part of an offender	Documenting rates of rearrest, reconviction, and reincarceration of offenders completing a program; and/or a comparison of these rates for different programs	Rearrest, reconviction, and reincarceration rates are low; and/or similar to or lower than other programs
Net Widening	The sentencing of offenders to more restrictive sanctions than their offenses warrant	Estimating if offenders in a particular program would have otherwise been sent to a more severe program, such as incarceration	Net Widening is absent or minimized. Offenders are diverted from a more severe program
Cost Effectiveness	The immediate and long-term financial benefits and costs associated with a correctional program	Comparing the cost of administering various correctional programs	Total costs or daily operating costs associated with a program are lower than other programs
Program Completion	The compliance on the part of an offender with the rules, activities, and conditions set forth in a correctional program	Documenting the number of offenders who complete a program successfully and the number who violate rules (technical violations), commit new crimes during the program (criminal violations), and fail to complete the program (revocation)	Technical violations, criminal violations, and revocations (program failure rates) are low; and/or similar to or lower than other programs
Behavioral Change/ Treatment Effectiveness	The development and sustenance of positive and prosocial attitudes and behaviors	Assessing whether behaviors being targeted by treatment are modified as desired; such as remaining drug/alcohol free	Offenders exhibit positive and prosocial attitudes and behaviors; such as remaining drug/alcohol free

Figure 1.4. Measures of Correctional Program Effectiveness

Recidivism

Recidivism refers to the recurrence of criminal behavior on the part of an offender. Recidivism has been the most common and usually the only measure of program effectiveness. Return to criminal behavior (recidivism) is measured in three main ways: rearrest, reconviction, and reincarceration. Rearrest has been the most-often-used measure of recidivism and is based on official police reports. Most research judges program effectiveness in this way by considering whether an offender was rearrested after having participated in a correctional program. Some researchers consider the length of time that has passed between completion of a program and the first arrest as well as the number and type of crimes committed. Rearrest can also refer to the arrest of an offender while he or she is still participating in a correctional program. Other research uses reconviction as a measure of recidivism. Research on programs for released prisoners may incorporate return to prison (reincarceration) as a way to judge recidivism.

Net Widening

The problem of net widening refers to the placement of offenders into more restrictive controls (i.e. sanctions) when the offenders would function well without the additional controls. Net widening increases the number of offenders who are plaed in more restrictive levels of supervision. A person who commits a minor offense and has never before been arrested might normally be sentenced to a short term of probation. If this offender is instead sentenced to a more restrictive sanction, such as incarceration, net widening has occurred. Net widening, or "widening the net" has three main negative effects: increasing the burden of punishment on an offender, increasing rather than decreasing the cost of corrections, and failing to reduce jail and prison crowding. The key to avoiding the problem of net widening is in the proper selection of offenders into correctional programs.

Cost Effectiveness

Cost effectiveness deals with the immediate and long-term financial benefits and costs associated with a correctional program. Correctional costs vary for different correctional programs. Prisons are the most expensive to administer and account for about 80% of all state correctional dollars spent. The nation's prisons cost $2.45 billion in 1996 (Stephan, 1999). Within community corrections and intermediate sanctions especially, cost varies with such factors including the organizational structure and size of a particular program, the number of offenders participating, the duration of the program, whether the program is located in a high dollar real estate area, and the number of staff. For programs to have a practical value they must be cost-effective.

Assessing whether a correctional program is cost effective can be done in various ways (See Cohen, 2000). The simplest way is to compare average daily costs associated with different penalties, such as community service and jail. Costs include what may be called day-rates and represent the accumulated daily cost of the various forms of correction. Subsequent costs encompass the post-program criminal justice processing of offenders (from arrest through resentencing). For illustration, assume the costs associated with participation in a community service program are less than costs associated with an alternative period of confinement. The diversion of an offender from confinement to a community service program should then immediately "displace" jail bed days for a measurable period of time and in turn would reduce front-end correctional costs. Depending on how well the participant does in the program and after program completion, additional correctional costs would also be counted. If the participant completes the program and is not rearrested, reprocessed, and resentenced over a certain time period, the system has benefited at the back end as well. Conversely, if the participant is rearrested, reprocessed, and incarcerated, the system may face a greater cost by making the initial placement than it would have had the participant been incarcerated at the outset. On the other hand, if the placement was not made at the outset and the offender was incarcerated, released, and then reprocessed for a new crime, the system should incur an even greater cost.

When thinking about cost effectiveness, it is also helpful to consider the benefits to offenders and communities of different programs in light of their costs. For programs such as fines, restitution, and community service, effectiveness can also be understood as the financial and tangible benefits to victims, criminal justice systems, and communities.

Program Completion

Program completion deals with compliance on the part of an offender with the rules, activities, and conditions set forth in a correctional program. Depending on the type of correctional option and the nature of the research, program completion is judged in different ways: technical violations, criminal violations, and revocation. Technical violations occur when offenders fail to abide by any conditions attached to the sanction. Criminal violations are more serious and involve the commission of new crimes during supervision. Depending on various factors, such as the type of correctional program and the offender's behavior, these violations do not necessarily result in a revocation. Often, offenders are given a second chance and remain involved in the program. For serious or repeat violations, an offender may have the sanction revoked and be subject to incarceration or another penalty. Generally, research on program completion compares the proportion of offenders who complete a program successfully with the proportion of offenders who are revoked. Successful programs show high completion and compliance rates.

Behavioral Change/Treatment Effectiveness

Many programs include treatment and services to facilitate behavioral change. Behavioral change refers to increasing prosocial behaviors and attitudes and reducing the risk that offenders will again become involved in destructive behaviors. Treatment effectiveness is a related idea. It refers to the success of a specific treatment for participants of a program. Many intermediate sanctions aim to assist offenders in developing positive attitudes, better social skills, and practical employment skills. They target behaviors that are thought to contribute to criminal behavior, such as drug and alcohol abuse. Though not commonly used in all research, since not all correctional programs are geared toward behavioral change, assessment of behavioral change can tell a good deal about the usefulness of a correctional program. Good programs meet their stated behavioral change objectives.

SUMMARY

Corrections is a crucial component of the criminal justice system and involves programs, services, and facilities operated by all levels of government. Many different types of offenders are involved in correctional programs. Serious and repeat offenders are usually incarcerated in jails and prison. Community corrections—probation and parole—promote rehabilitation by enabling offenders to remain in their communities while under correctional supervision. A relatively new breed of correctional programs referred to as intermediate sanctions serves many different types of offenders. Fines, restitution, community service, intensive supervision programs, boot camps, home confinement, halfway houses, and day reporting centers are intermediate sanctions that combine high levels of control over offenders. Rationales for various punishments have changed over time and include retribution, deterrence, incapacitation, and rehabilitation. For correctional programs to succeed, they must be effective at meeting key correctional goals. They should limit recidivism; limit net widening through the proper diversion of offenders from incarceration; be cost effective and economically beneficial; result in acceptable of completion; and meet any goals designed to facilitate behavioral change on the part of the offender.

**CHAPTER 2**

Development, Goals, and Structure of Intermediate Sanctions Programs

THE EMERGENCE OF INTERMEDIATE SANCTIONS

Prior to the 1980s, the standard sentencing options for judges consisted of probation or incarceration. Although community-based programs, such as probation, restitution, community service, and halfway houses, were available in the 1960s and 1970s, they lost credibility and support mainly because they were shown to be ineffective in a number of ways (Tonry, 1997). It was not until the early 1980s as correctional crowding became a serious problem that alternatives to incarceration, or intermediate sanctions, were formally organized into state correctional options (Lurigio & Petersilia, 1992). Boot camps and intensive supervision probation and parole emerged in the middle 1980s and the other, fragmented assortment of programs, such as community service and home confinement, were "repackaged" and formally implemented as intermediate sanctions. Three main correctional issues prompted the need for change in corrections and led to the formal development of intermediate sanctions in the middle 1980s: a lack of success with felony probationers and to a lesser extent, parolees, severe overcrowding in prisons and jails, and inadequate sentencing choices.

Problems with Felony Probation

High revocation and recidivism rates of felons on probation as well as the inadequate supervision and limited treatment for adults on probation and parole contributed to the development of intermediate sanctions (Petersilia, 1998, 1999). During the 1960s and 1970s when rehabilitation and reintegration were the guiding philosophies of corrections, probation was a popular sanction. Probation officer caseloads were relatively low at this time, which enabled probation officers to individualize treatment and service programming to meet the specific needs of each probationer. Officers were expected to deliver important services, such as counseling, encouragement, and job placement assistance while also providing control and supervision over the probationer. Probation departments experienced dramatic changes in the 1980s, which led to the call for an increased focus on supervision/ surveillance over offenders sentenced to probation.

First, the type of offenders being sentenced to probation changed (Petersilia, et al., 1985). Given the increasing problem of prison overcrowding in the 1980s, more serious and "high risk" offenders were being placed on probation. These more serious (felony) offenders posed a potential risk to public safety. According to Petersilia (1998), nationally in 1986, probation was granted to 46% of all convicted felons, and 30% all offenders ordered to probation were also required to serve some jail time. About six percent of offenders convicted of homicide, 20% convicted of rape, 20% convicted of robbery, and 40% convicted of burglary were sentenced to probation.

At the same time that probation caseloads were changing in nature and becoming more "high-risk" (Byrne, Lurigio, & Baird, 1989), and thereby requiring more supervision, probation departments were experiencing significant budget cuts, resulting in the reduction or elimination of probation officers and limitations on the treatment and services offered. While probation department cuts led to larger caseload sizes and fewer treatment options, probationers were presenting greater supervision and treatment needs. As such, the frequency of contacts between probationers and their probation officers was reduced. It was estimated that during the late 1980s, most offenders who were on probation for felony offenses were meeting with their probation officers at most only once each month (Langan & Cunniff, 1992). The low levels of officer/probationer contact, lack of services, and inadequate supervision contributed to high failure and recidivism rates among probationers, particularly felony probationers. These factors, coupled with general shifts in the political climate to "get tough on crime" and public dissatisfaction with the rehabilitative ideal, led to a greater focus on crime control through incapacitation and deterrence. The focus of probation began to change from one-on-one offender contact and "service-delivery" to "risk management" with enforcement-centered supervision and minimal treatment delivery.

The RAND Study

A 1985 study conducted by the RAND Corporation highlighted the problems of failure and recidivism among felons on probation (Petersilia, et al., 1985). The research revealed that many states were forced to rely on probation for serious felony offenders and other "high-risk" groups (such as drug users) due to increasing prison populations and prison crowding. The research also suggested that these offenders were being supervised inadequately. In terms of public safety, about 75% of the 2,000 probationers tracked in the research were rearrested within three years, most for serious offenses. Not only did this present serious public safety issues, it exacerbated the existing prison crowding problem; many offenders who failed on probation were incarcerated in the already burdened prison system. The RAND project emphasized the need for sanctions falling in between prison and probation: punishments that could effectively supervise felony offenders who would otherwise be sent to jail/prison, if this option did not exist. This research suggested that through the creation of a continuum of middle-range sanctions, prison and probation populations could be relieved without compromising public safety.

Byrne, Lurigio, and Baird (1989) also point to the problem of parole crowding; between 1979 and 1984, the adult parole population increased by more than 20%. This was due in part to pressures to relieve prison crowding, which resulted in an increase in the early release of prison inmates to parole. Similar to probation crowding, parole departments experienced increased caseloads, as well as a growing population of higher risk offenders who were more difficult to supervise under regular parole. According to the research, 10% to 15% of the parolees could be identified as high risk and approximately 60% of parolees could be expected to return to prison after three years.

Prison and Jail Crowding

For alleviating prison crowding and finding new ways to manage felons in the community, the need for punitive, noncustodial sanctions became apparent. Most state prisons were experiencing extreme overcrowding (it was not unusual for cells designed for one person to hold three), which resulted in a variety of problems, including increased prison violence and assaults, and reduced programming/services. In many states the federal courts intervened on prisoners' behalf, and through consent decree, required the states to reduce their correctional populations (Petersilia, 1999). Because southern states, in particular, could not afford prison construction costs, they sought to find alternative ways through which offenders could be effectively punished without being incarcerated. As such, Georgia became the first state to develop an intermediate sanction program, which was designed to serve as a cost-effective punishment falling in between probation and prison.

Among the first new wave of intermediate sanctions programs was Georgia's intensive supervision probation program developed in 1982 (Morris & Tonry, 1990). Twenty-five offenders were assigned to a team of two probation officers. One officer acted in the surveillance role and the other provided counseling and had legal authority over the case. Each offender was required to visit face-to-face with the team a minimum of five times a week, perform community service, pay a supervision fee, and either maintain legitimate employment or be enrolled in an educational program. An evaluation showed a very low failure (rearrest) rate and most offenders complied with the requirements. Supervision fees made the program virtually self-supporting. Publicity quickly led to development of projects in other states, including Massachusetts and New Jersey.

Inadequate Sentencing Choices

The United Sates experienced an increase in the overall crime rate, which began in the mid-1960s and continued to escalate during the early 1970s. Politicians reacted to the public's fear of crime and victimization by promising tougher approaches to crime and punishment. The traditionally guiding correctional goal of crime prevention through offender rehabilitation was replaced by the philosophy of "just deserts" (imposing deserved punishment by fitting penalty to the seriousness of the criminal act), and a renewed interest in incapacitation and deterrence. The aim of criminal sanctioning shifted to public safety and crime control. Indeterminate sentencing (where judges impose a minimum and maximum prison sentence), which allowed for individualized sentencing and consideration of treatment needs, came under attack in the 1970s. It was criticized for permitting too much judicial discretion, which was believed to lead to bias and disparity. In response to these concerns and the increased emphasis on punishment rather than treatment, sentencing reforms that focused on guiding and restricting judicial discretion took place in the 1980s.

The conservative desire to "get tough" and the liberal argument against sentencing disparities, especially in terms of racial and class bias, created increasing support for sentencing standards based on the severity of the offender's crimes and past behavior. Sentencing guidelines and commissions were developed during this time to guide judicial decision-making, and many statutory mandatory sentences (particularly for drug and weapons offenses) accompanied the guidelines. The desire for toughness and proportionality in sentencing contributed to the development of intermediate sanctions, ranging in punitiveness between prison and traditional probation. For conservatives, intermediate sanctions could reduce the strain on correctional institutions and through their graduated structure and control, could punish and incapacitate the less serious offenders. For liberals, community-based sanctions rather than institutional confinement were seen as promising approaches to the rehabilitation of offenders.

GOALS OF INTERMEDIATE SANCTIONS

There is no single objective for intermediate sanctions. Like most criminal sanctions, intermediate sanctions have multiple goals and these goals often conflict. Goals of intermediate sanctions vary from one program to another and from similar programs in different jurisdictions. These goals fall into three broad categories: offender-based goals, community-based goals, and system-based goals.

Offender-Based Goals

- Rehabilitate offenders through mandated and voluntary treatment;
- Allow offenders to remain in the community so they may continue in their work, family, and social responsibilities and activities; and
- To avoid the stigma of incarceration.

Community-Based Goals

- Save taxpayer dollars by providing cost-effective alternatives to jail and prison;
- Deter offenders specifically and the public generally from engaging in criminal conduct;
- Protect the community through graduated control systems; and
- Respond to the needs of communities.

System-Based Goals

- Reduce the flow of offenders into jails and prisons (and limit their duration in jails and prisons);
- Provide flexible and fair penalties scaled according to crime seriousness and offender need; and
- Provide effective alternatives to incarceration for probation and parole violators.

TARGET POPULATIONS FOR INTERMEDIATE SANCTIONS

An intermediate sanction's target population refers to the types of offenders who are eligible and who should be selected for participation in a given program. The reader should recognize that there is no one type of offender who participates in intermediate sanctions. Target populations for intermediate sanctions include male and female juvenile and adult offenders, misdemeanor and felony offenders, violent and non-violent offenders, first time and repeat offenders, offenders who have never been incarcerated and those who are in jails and prisons, and offenders on probation or parole. In general, most intermediate sanctions exclude the high-risk violent offenders, but this is not always the case.

Target populations usually vary from one type of intermediate sanction to another. For instance, boot camps are designed for the younger offender because physical fitness is crucial to program performance. Target populations may also be different for the same type of intermediate sanctions program. Some boot camp prisons, for instance, are designed exclusively as an alternative to imprisonment whereby offenders are sent to this type of "shock incarceration" program rather than prisons. Other boot camps draw offenders already serving prison terms and allow them to shorten their term through participation in a boot camp. Most community service programs do not allow chronic and repeat offenders to participate, but the Community Service Sentencing Project in New York targets such a group for participation (Caputo, 2000). Individual chapters in this book that are dedicated to specific intermediate sanctions will describe the relevant target populations in greater detail.

STRUCTURE OF INTERMEDIATE SANCTIONS

Intermediate sanctions are used in various ways at different points in the criminal justice system. Figure 2.1 illustrates five common intermediate sanctions models. Some draw participants from prisons and some receive participants from regular probation or parole populations. Intermediate sanctions are often used in combination. For example: community service may be coupled with restitution, home confinement may be supervised through electronic monitoring supervision, and residency in a halfway house may be a requirement of an intensive supervision probation or parole program. The differences between diversion programs and enhancement programs, and stand-alone programs and program components, are highlighted in the sections to follow.

Front-End and Back-End Diversion Programs

To better understand the types of offenders participating in intermediate sanctions, it is important to distinguish between "front-end" and "back-end" diversion.

Front-end programs target offenders who would normally be sentenced to jail or prison terms and divert these offenders from incarceration into intermediate sanctions. Box 2 in Figure 2.1 illustrates the use of intermediate sanctions as a front-end diversion program. As the illustration suggests, the offender is diverted from incarceration into an intermediate sanctions program by the judge at sentencing. This offender may be a person who has come before the judge as a result of a new crime or a person who has come before a judge as a result of a probation violation. In either case, the offender is diverted from incarceration into an intermediate sanctions program.

Back-end programs are designed specifically for the supervision of offenders who are released from prison or jail after a portion of the

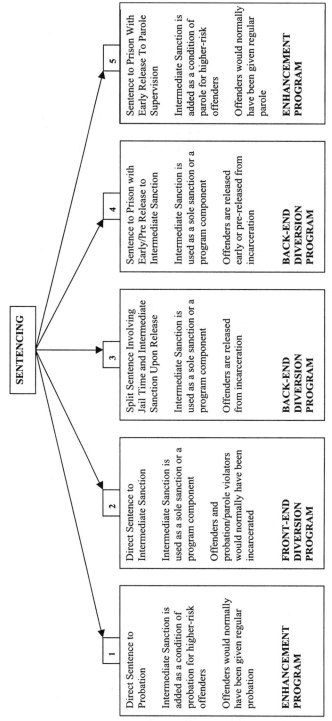

Figure 2.1. Various Models for the Use of Intermediate Sanctions

sentence of confinement is served. Boxes 3 and 4 in Figure 2.1 illustrate back-end diversion. Intermediate sanctions are often used in conjunction with jail incarceration, whereby offenders receive a split sentence of jail incarceration followed by participation in an intermediate sanction (Box 3). Box 4 illustrates the use of intermediate sanctions as back-end diversions from prison. In this model, an offender is sentenced to prison, but is released from imprisonment early into an intermediate sanctions program. This model is also used for parolees who have violated their parole conditions. Rather than being reincarcerated for the violation, parolees are placed into intermediate sanctions.

Enhancement Programs

Enhancement programs are designed to "enhance" a regular probation sentence or parole term, such as with increased contacts (as with ISP) and greater control and surveillance (such as with electronic monitoring and home confinement). An enhancement type of intermediate sanction does not necessarily aim to divert offenders from incarceration. Instead, offenders who are selected for participation are already on probation or parole. Their probation or parole supervision is simply "enhanced" by the addition of intermediate sanctions as required conditions of their probation or parole. Boxes 1 and 5 in Figure 2.1 illustrate the use of intermediate sanctions as enhancement programs. Providing enhanced supervision (and perhaps services) to the highest risk segment of the probation population is intended to reduce such offenders' threat to public safety. As described in Box 1, intermediate sanctions are used as enhancement programs and not diversion programs when probation officials decide to "enhance" a probationer's supervision by adding an intermediate sanction as a required condition of a probationer's sentence. Box 5 illustrates the use of intermediate sanctions as enhancement programs for parolees.

Stand Alone Programs and Program Components

Intermediate sanctions, whether used at the front-end or back-end of the system, may be stand-alone programs or components of probation and parole. An intermediate sanction is a stand-alone program when the program exists on its own without probation or parole supervision. When offenders are sentenced to community service without probation or parole supervision, we say that community service is used as a stand-alone program. More typically, intermediate sanctions are used in conjunction with other programs, including probation and parole supervision.

An intermediate sanction is a program component when it is used as part of probation and parole supervision. For example, an offender may be sentenced by a judge to probation with the addition of various intermediate sanctions, such as community service, restitution, and home confinement.

PLACEMENT OF OFFENDERS INTO INTERMEDIATE SANCTIONS

Offenders are placed into programs in different ways, depending on the target population for an intermediate sanction. Some offenders are placed directly into intermediate sanctions by a judge at sentencing. This is referred to as a direct sentence (Boxes 2 and 3 of Figure 2.1). When intermediate sanctions are used as enhancement programs for probationers (Box 1 of Figure 2.1), probation officials and judges make the placement decision. The decision to use intermediate sanctions as enhancement programs for parolees (Box 5 of Figure 2.1) or back-end diversion (Box 4 of Figure 2.1) is typically made by parole authorities.

Structuring Selection of Offenders Into Intermediate Sanctions

Typically, judges and paroling authorities have wide discretion in deciding which offenders are placed into intermediate sanctions and which offenders are not. Some states have devised ways to structure these decisions, including the use of sentencing guidelines (Morris & Tonry, 1990; Tonry, 1997). The simplest guidelines take the form of a two dimensional grid which includes offense-specific information (such as offense level) on one side and offender-specific information (such as criminal history) on the other. When using the guidelines, a judge locates the appropriate cell in the grid, which provides the presumptive sentence for that offense and offender. The presumptive sentence is the "typical" sentence to be given for a particular offense.

In some states, guidelines incorporate intermediate sanctions, guiding judges' decisions about when an intermediate sanctions program is an appropriate sentence and enabling them to choose between a jail or prison sentence and an intermediate sanction (Tonry, 1997). The guideline systems do not necessarily dictate which intermediate sanction ought to be imposed, however. The State of Washington uses a guideline structure that includes intermediate sanctions. For example, an offense calling for nine months of confinement in jail can be "exchanged" for five months of jail time, three months of partial confinement, and one month of community service. The North Carolina, Pennsylvania, and proposed Massachusetts guidelines use "zones of discretion" that allow judicial departure from confinement penalties, but do not identify appropriate non-custodial penalties. No survey of state legislation is currently available to distinguish states with such sentencing structures from states without structures.

SUMMARY

Intermediate sanctions were developed to provide a cost-effective and safe alternative to incarceration. Their creation and rapid expansion through the 1980s was spawned by prison overcrowding, increasing correctional costs, the low success rates of felony probation, and concerns about public safety and being "tough" on offenders. These programs are used and accessed in three main ways. First, they are used at the front end as a diversionary sentence for offenders who otherwise would go to jail or prison. Second, they are used at the back end whereby prison inmates are released from jail/prison early in order to participate in the program. Third, they are used as enhancement programs, providing greater supervision over offenders already on probation or parole. Programs can stand alone as sanctions in their own right or be used as components of other sentences. The major forms of intermediate sanctions are discussed in the chapters to follow.

PART II

Intermediate Sanctions Programs: Descriptions and Research

**CHAPTER 3**

Intensive Supervision Programs

BACKGROUND

Intensive Supervision Programs, the most popular intermediate sanctions in the United States, provide for closer monitoring and surveillance of offenders than is possible with regular probation and parole. An intensive supervision program (ISP) is a more enhanced and restrictive form of probation or parole intended to protect the public.

Probation departments experimented with intensive forms of probation as early as the 1950s. These early programs emphasized low caseloads to afford probation officers better control of offenders under supervision. In the late 1970s there were as many as 46 ISPs. These programs were used for offenders on probation and provided for smaller caseloads and increased officer-offender contacts (Byrne, Lurigio, & Baird, 1989).

It was not until the mid-1980s, however, that intensive supervision programs emerged in their present forms. Like other intermediate sanctions, intensive supervision programs were created to reduce reliance on prisons and to fill the gap between traditional probation and incarceration by serving as tougher punishments with stricter controls over offenders than traditional probation could provide. The impetus behind this new generation of programs was to alleviate crowding in prisons, to more effectively supervise higher-risk offenders on probation, to save money, and to control crime (See Petersilia, 1999; Haas & Latessa,

1995). The "new" ISPs also aimed to prevent the negative and stigmatizing effects of incarceration by diverting offenders away from prison (Byrne, Lurigio, & Baird, 1989).

During the 1980s, many corrections departments were experiencing the problem of having little or no space for housing new admissions. Consequently, a higher proportion of felony offenders began receiving probationary sentences. As probation caseloads grew, many probation departments also experienced budget cuts (Petersilia et al., 1985). This naturally led to reduced staffing and services, and subsequently larger caseloads (for example, the number of probationers in California increased by 50% while the number of probation officers decreased by 20%) (Lurigio & Petersilia, 1992) and less supervision of higher risk and higher need offenders. All of this is thought to have contributed to high rearrest, reconviction, and return-to-prison rates (Byrne, Lurigio, & Baird, 1989). According to Lurigio and Petersilia, a study conducted by RAND in 1985 revealed that felons were not faring well on probation: 65% were rearrested during their supervision. Clear and Hardyman (1990) point out that the combination of high risk/high need offenders and less than necessary levels of supervision and services increases the likelihood that the higher risk/need offender would again become involved in criminal behavior. The RAND study received much attention and helped to propel the proliferation of "tougher" intensified probation programs. These problems in probation were also experienced at the parole level (Byrne, Lurigio, & Baird, 1989) and it became apparent that ISPs may be an effective way to divert lower-risk felons from prison to a more structured probation or parole supervision program.

Early reports from Georgia's program implemented in 1982, which was the first new generation program, and New Jersey's program implemented a year later, as well as the ISP in Texas, showed great promise. This contributed to the rapid proliferation of intensive supervision programs throughout the country. Between 1980 and 1990 every state and the federal system implemented some form of intensive supervision program (Petersilia & Turner, 1993). Today, the overriding goal of ISPs is to better provide community protection through enhanced monitoring and stringent restrictions of offenders. ISPs also aim to reduce correctional costs and crowding through the diversion of offenders from incarceration.

Across the nation in the late 1980s, about three percent of all probationers were assigned to ISPs (Byrne, Lurigio, & Baird, 1989). Although intensive supervision is a popular form of probation and parole (Haas & Latessa, 1995), a relatively small proportion of criminal offenders are supervised in these programs. According to a recent survey by the Criminal Justice Institute, Inc. (Camp & Camp, 2000), 122,938 individuals were in ISP at the start of 2000. This represents about five percent of the total population of individuals identified as being on active probation or parole in the selected jurisdictions (Figure 3.1). Applying this five percent figure to probation and parole populations at yearend 2001 (Glaze, 2002) identified by the Bureau of Justice Statistics (3,932,751 on probation and 732,351 on parole), we could estimate the number of adults on ISP to be about 233,225 (196,637 probationers and 36,617 parolees). According to these figures, ISP may be the most commonly used intermediate sanctions program in the United States.

Probation	Regular	Intensive	Electronic	Special
States and D.C.	1,496,586	47,012	59,443	66,943
Federal	69,135	0	3,648	25,680
Total	1,565,721	47,012	63,091	92,623

Parole	Regular	Intensive	Electronic	Special
States and D.C.	334,349	57,509	4,681	12,907
Federal	2,902	309	6	430
Total	347,251	57,818	4,687	13,337

Probation & Parole	Regular	Intensive	Electronic	Special
States	251,755	18,108	1,638	301
Total	251,755	18,108	1,638	301

Summary	Regular	Intensive	Electronic	Special
Probation	1,565,721	47,012	63,091	92,623
Parole	347,251	57,818	4,687	13,337
Probation & Parole	251,755	18,108	1,638	301
Grand Total	2,164,727	122,938	69,416	106,261

Source: Adapted from Camp & Camp, 2000.

Figure 3.1. Probationers and Parolees by Case Type, January 1, 2000

TARGET POPULATIONS

The target populations for whom ISPs are designed vary from state to state and typically include drug offenders, non-violent offenders, and property offenders, as well as probation and parole violators. In Colorado, participants of the ISP in 1993 were more likely than regular probationers to have a current probation revocation, a violent arrest as a juvenile, or a current violent offense (English, Pullen, & Colling-Chadwick, 1996). A Wisconsin ISP program is designed exclusively for adult sex offenders (Roberts-Van Cuick, 2000). Offenders with histories of violence may be participating in ISPs; however the serious violent offenders are normally excluded. For instance, the New Jersey program excludes offenders convicted of homicide, robbery, or sex offenses. The typical caseload in New Jersey is composed of relatively low-risk, nonviolent felons (Pearson & Harper, 1990). Ohio's Clermont County ISP excluded offenders who commit a violent offense and show patterns of violent behavior (Haas & Latessa, 1995).

While acknowledging the assorted target populations for different jurisdictions, one can generally say that ISPs are usually used for offenders who have not committed violent crimes or sex offenses and who do not suffer from mental disorders (Bennett, 1995). Additionally, they are generally designed for the higher-risk felony offender who could not be effectively supervised on regular probation or parole and who requires a greater level of supervision and controls over his or her behavior.

Another way to understand the target populations for ISPs is to consider the three models for ISP use. The models illustrate how intensive supervision programs are designed to draw participants from three pools: offenders headed for jail or prison, prison inmates eligible for early release, and high-risk offenders who are on probation or parole. These three models also illustrate three different goals of ISPs: to prevent offenders from entering prison, to permit the early release of offenders who are in prison, and to enhance the supervision of an offender who is already being supervised in the community (Lurigio & Petersilia, 1992). Figure 3.2 shows how intensive supervision programs are used in these three different ways: as a front-end diversion from incarceration, as a back-end diversion (early release) from incarceration, and as a probation or parole enhancement mechanism.

ISP MODEL 1	ISP MODEL 2	ISP MODEL 3
ISP is a front-end diversion from incarceration	ISP is a back-end diversion from incarceration/ early release mechanism	ISP is a probation enhancement tool
ISP is a form of probation and may be referred to as *Intensive Supervision Probation*	ISP is a form of parole and may be referred to as *Intensive Supervision Parole*	ISP is a form of probation and may be referred to as *Intensive Supervision Probation*
THE GEORGIA INTENSIVE SUPERVISION PROGRAM **Program Description** Implemented in 1982, ISP targets adult non-violent felony offenders and probation violators who would otherwise be sent to prison. Participants are supervised in the community in ISP in lieu of serving prison terms. **Three Phase Program** Offenders usually spend 6-12 months in the program. The program is structured according to three phases in which restrictions and requirements are greatest at Phase One. Offenders serve a minimum of three months in Phase One and three months in Phase Two before enrollment in Phase Three or placement on regular probation. Offenders must abide by a set of conditions at each phase. Participants who complete the program successfully are released to regular probation for a period of one year. Participants may be removed for a new arrest or a technical violation and be sent to prison or to a more restrictive placement. **Supervision of Participants** Teams of two probation officers are used to supervise the ISP participants. Each team is made up of a probation officer and a surveillance officer and supervises 25 participants. The supervision officers oversee all aspects of supervision, treatment programming, and services while surveillance officers enforce the conditions of probation and oversee compliance and enforcement functions. **Program Requirements** In addition to reporting to the probation office and submitting to home and collateral visits by officer teams, participants must abide by conditions including: ▫ Maintaining multiple weekly contacts with officer teams (up to 7 contacts weekly) ▫ Performing community service ▫ Abiding by a mandatory curfew ▫ Paying a supervision fee ▫ Maintaining employment or school attendance ▫ Participating in treatment ▫ Submitting to random urinalysis ▫ Home confinement as ordered	**THE NEW JERSEY INTENSIVE SUPERVISION PROGRAM** **Program Description** Implemented in 1983, ISP targets state prison inmates, usually non-violent felony offenders, who are motivated to improve their lives. Offenders convicted of a homicide, robbery, or sex offense are ineligible. Eligible inmates who apply and who are selected are placed in ISP for two 90-day trial periods and if successful, are officially placed in ISP. **Stringent Selection Process** Offenders who have recently been sentenced to prison (within 30-60 days) apply for ISP in writing. An ISP Screening Board interviews eligible candidates in order to ascertain their motivation for change and interest in the program. An ISP Resentencing Panel made of state judges then releases selected offenders from prison to ISP for a 90-day trial period. When offenders successfully complete the trial period, they are again sentenced to a 90-day period after which they are formally resentenced to ISP. The ISP resentencing panel reviews violations of ISP conditions and applies sanctions upon participants when appropriate. **Supervision of Participants** Individual probation officers handle small caseloads of ISP participants. The officers are available 24-hours each day and are involved in the selection of offenders into the program as well as all aspects of ISP supervision. The program also involves the community in the supervision of offenders. Each ISP participant works with a "community sponsor" who encourages participants to reach their supervision goals and plans. **Program Requirements** Participants must meet the following conditions: ▫ Perform 16 hours of community service each month ▫ Mandatory drug testing ▫ Home detention if necessary ▫ Maintain employment or school attendance ▫ Mandatory curfew ▫ Maintain 20 hours of contacts with probation officer monthly ▫ Participate in treatment	**THE MASSACHUSETTS INTENSIVE SUPERVISION PROGRAM** **Program Description** Implemented in 1985, ISP targets high-risk probationers. High-risk offenders who are sentenced to probation are placed in ISP, the highest supervision level available for probationers in Massachusetts. **Selection of Offenders to ISP** Offenders on probation are assessed according to their risk for reoffending and their need for treatment and services. This is done through interviews and standardized risk assessment and needs assessment instruments commonly used in probation departments throughout the country. Various factors are considered when assessing need and risk, such as criminal history, education and employment history, relationship stability, vocational skills, and drug and alcohol use. Once assessed according to risk and need, offenders are placed into one of four supervision levels. ISP being the highest level of supervision. **Program Requirements** In addition to having to report to the probation office and to submit to home visits and visits to employers and even family members, participants are also required to abide by the following conditions: ▫ Perform 16 hours of community service each month ▫ Mandatory drug testing ▫ Home detention ▫ Maintain employment or school attendance ▫ Mandatory curfew ▫ Maintain 10 contacts per month with probation officer ▫ Participate in treatment programming, particularly related to substance abuse, employment, and counseling

Sources: Georgia Department of Corrections, 2001; Harper, 1997; McCarthy et al, 2001; Pearson & Harper, 1990.

Figure 3.2. Three Common ISP Models

Front-End Intensive Supervision Programs

Some intensive supervision programs are designed to divert offenders from prison before the offenders ever spend time behind bars (Byrne, Lurigio, & Baird, 1989). In these programs, convicted offenders or probation and parole violators are usually identified and diverted to the ISP at sentencing. Referred to as front-end intensive supervision programs, these types of programs have the greatest potential of saving prison space and money. When used as an alternative to prison in this way, the ISP is technically a form of probation and is often termed Intensive Supervision Probation or Intensive Probation Supervision. Such front-end ISPs are administered usually by probation departments.

Georgia implemented the first front-end diversion program in 1982. There, offenders convicted of non-violent felonies and probation violators are ordered by judges to participate in ISP in lieu of serving prison sentences (Morris & Tonry, 1990). It is a "direct sentence option" (Georgia Department of Corrections, 2001:5). The idea was to provide a tougher and more surveillance-oriented sanction than regular probation, which was more cost effective than prison. Offenders are put in ISP at three different points: as an initial sentence, instead of probation revocation, or through post-sentencing modifications. Once placed in ISP, offenders must abide by strict conditions and proceed through a phased program. Probation officers are available 24 hours per day to make contact with the offenders in ISP and to ensure compliance. According to the Georgia Department of Corrections statistics in fiscal year 2000, an average of 4,150 probationers participated in ISP each month. Georgia's program serves as the model for prison diversion ISPs (Petersilia, 1990b).

Back -End Intensive Supervision Programs

In 1983, New Jersey developed an intensive supervision program that targets offenders who are incarcerated (See Pearson & Harper, 1990). It is a back-end diversion from incarceration whereby offenders are released early from prison into the ISP, a diversion to continued confinement. The objective of such early release programs is to cut the amount of time an offender serves in prison, thereby lowering correctional costs and reducing crowding (Harper, 1997). By design, the program includes an element of shock incarceration; its participants would have served a minimum of 60 days in prison. The median prison time served before release into intensive supervision is about three-and-a-half months (Pearson & Harper, 1990). New Jersey relies on a stringent selection and placement process. Eligible offenders are those who are sentenced to prison by judges and who are actually committed to prison. The offenders (inmates) would apply to the ISP, and if selected would be placed into the ISP for a 90-day trial period. If successful, they are again given a 90-day trial and are then officially released from prison (resentenced) into the program by a panel of judges appointed by the Chief Justice. The ISP is about 18 months in duration. According to Harper (1997), more than 5400 inmates have been released into ISP during its first 13 years.

Back-end ISP programs, such as in the case of New Jersey, are usually administered by corrections and parole departments. The programs usually target low-risk felons who are more suited to community supervision than serious, violent, and high-risk inmates. Intensive supervision programs targeting prison inmates are also termed intensive supervision parole programs. According to recent statistics (See Figure 3.1) most ISP participants are parolees.

Intensive Supervision as Probation and Parole Enhancement Mechanisms

Most intensive supervision programs draw offenders from regular probation and parole populations. The overriding goal of the enhancement intensive supervision programs is to control the risks that some offenders pose to the community. While on probation or parole, more serious or high-risk offenders are moved to an ISP caseload, usually after a risk and needs assessment. Risk and needs assessment instruments are commonly used in probation and parole departments throughout the country. These instruments help estimate the likelihood an offender is to commit new crimes and take into account such factors as age at first offending, prior criminal history, number of probation and prison terms served in the past, substance abuse, and employment history.

The Massachusetts intensive supervision program is an enhancement program designed to provide better supervision to offenders who have been sentenced to probation and who require closer, more stringent surveillance (Morris & Tonry, 1990). There, offenders are moved to an

ISP caseload when assessments by probation officers reveal a high risk for reoffending.

In the late 1980s, Texas developed an intensive supervision parole program to alleviate prison crowding. The ISP was designed for the intensive supervision of parolees who were currently under parole supervision and who were performing poorly on regular parole and who had the highest probability of returning to prison (Turner & Petersilia, 1992). The program was designed to supervise offenders for up to 12 months and required 10 face-to-face contacts each month between offenders and supervision officers. For those offenders not enrolled in school or employed full-time, the program also required verification of job search efforts on the part of offenders and enrollment in job training programs.

Probation and parole enhancement models are also used for probation and parole violators who do not require incarceration, but who require a higher, more restrictive level of supervision. In ISP, where caseloads are smaller and conditions more restrictive, the offenders are subject to greater surveillance and control. Used in this way, ISP is a case management tool to afford better protection to the community. Intensive supervision for probationers is usually administered by probation departments while programs that draw from inmates or parolees are administered by parole departments.

PROGRAM CHARACTERISTICS

The primary difference between intensive supervision programs and traditional probation or parole rests with the level of surveillance. Intensive supervision programs provide an increased number of contacts, smaller caseloads, random drug testing, and more stringent enforcement of conditions such as curfews, employment, and treatment (Haas & Latessa, 1995). ISPs are geared more toward community safety and crime control than treatment. According to Byrne, Lurigio, and Baird, (1989) ISPs are intensive because:

- Supervision is extensive—offender-officer contacts are frequent and collateral contacts with employers as well as arrest checks are common.
- Supervision is focused—offenders must abide by stringent regulations, rules, and conditions.

- Supervision is ubiquitous—offenders are usually required to submit to random and unannounced drug testing.
- Supervision is graduated—offenders commonly proceed through graduated phases of supervision.
- Supervision is strictly enforced—penalties for noncompliance are severe and swift.
- Supervision is coordinated—specially trained officers in specialized units monitor offenders.

Small Caseloads

Intensive supervision caseloads are generally much smaller than regular probation or parole caseloads. A recent national survey of probation and parole caseloads (Camp & Camp, 2000) found that on average, intensive supervision probation caseloads are 29 offenders per officer compared to the regular supervision caseload of 139 offenders per officer. For parole, ISP caseloads were 25 parolees for each officer compared to 66 parolees per officer for regular parole supervision. The rationale for low caseloads is simple: lower caseloads should enable supervision officers to maintain effective controls over the higher risk offender and thereby afford greater protection to the community. It is recommended that ISP caseloads range from 20 to 30 offenders (Fulton & Stone, 1995). Lower caseloads should also allow officers to better assist in the rehabilitation of offenders, but officers themselves must be skilled and supervision and surveillance techniques must also be effective.

Specialized Supervision

Probation and parole departments have developed two models for the supervision of ISP participants: individual ISP officers who handle all aspects of supervision and teams of two officers who share supervision and enforcement duties. The use of teams minimizes role conflict, which is inherent in offender supervision. Traditionally, probation and parole officers maintained two roles: enforcing laws and assisting the offender. In order to perform their jobs effectively, officers must find a balance between each important and necessary function. The use of teams minimizes the conflict. With teams, one officer may specialize in enforcement and the other may concentrate on supervision and the provision of services. The team model was introduced in Georgia, the state with the first intensive supervision program. Georgia's program relies on teams of two officers (one probation officer and one surveillance officer), which supervise 25 offenders. Probation officers oversee all aspects of supervision, treatment, and services while surveillance officers enforce conditions of probation and oversee compliance and enforcement. The programs in Montana and Florida also use two-officer teams. In the late 1980s, it was estimated that nearly 60% of intensive supervision programs in 31 states relied on team supervision (Byrne, Lurigio, & Baird, 1989).

Surveillance and Supervision Techniques

Surveillance of ISP participants involves activities on the part of supervision officers, teams of officers, and correctional agencies designed to monitor offender activity, compliance with rules and regulations, and the social environment of the offenders. Surveillance activities are directed foremost at community protection (Fulton & Stone, 1995).

The surveillance and supervision of ISP participants are often varied. The most common supervision technique is face-to-face contacts at the probation or parole office. The number of face-to-face contacts required is one of the distinguishing characteristics of ISP. According to a recent survey (Camp & Camp, 2000), offenders on regular probation in 1999 met face-to-face with officers 12 times during the year on average whereas offenders supervised in intensive supervision probation met with officers 83 times on average. Parolees on regular supervision in 1999 met with officers an average of 21 times, while intensive supervision parolees met with officers an average of 102 times over the year. Alabama, Missouri, North Carolina, and other jurisdictions that combine probation and parole supervision reported higher rates of offender and officer contact for ISP participants—an average of 102 contacts during 1999. In addition to the face-to-face visits, ISP officers rely on telephone contacts and home visits, often unannounced and especially during curfew. Officers ascertain information about offenders through contacts with the offenders' employers, family members, significant others, and treatment providers.

Conditions of Supervision

A hallmark of intensive supervision programs is the variety of strict conditions placed on participants. Conditions of supervision are the rules and regulations that prohibit certain behaviors and require others. Conditions of supervision can be grouped into three types: standard, punitive, and treatment. Typically, ISP participants enter into a contract with the supervising agency acknowledging their understanding and willingness to comply with conditions.

Standard ISP Conditions

Standard conditions are general requirements applied to all ISP participants. Standard conditions include the requirement to refrain from drug and alcohol use, obey all laws, restrict travel to within the jurisdiction, meet with probation officers (usually weekly), maintain employment or attendance in school or vocational programs, and to pay supervision fees. Drug and alcohol testing is a main component of ISP and is usually standard for all participants. Some jurisdictions, for instance North Carolina, have added the additional condition of participation in a day reporting center as a condition of ISP (Marciniak, 2000).

Treatment ISP Conditions

A focus on the provision of treatment and services is advocated. Treatment conditions are special requirements designed to address the treatment needs of each ISP participant, such as mandated participation in drug and alcohol treatment, individual and family counseling, anger management classes, and so on. Most intensive supervision programs are surveillance and control oriented, with treatment as a supplemental focus, and other ISPs are heavily geared toward treatment.

According to the literature, the provision of treatment and services to address the needs of offenders is a means of control and reformation (Fulton & Stone, 1995). To be effective, according to Gendreau (1993), treatment must target offenders' criminogenic need factors, such as antisocial attitudes and values. Identifying the needs of offenders is common with ISP supervision and involves standardized and an often quite simple and straightforward process whereby probation supervision officers acquire information from offenders or their case files and complete an assessment that identifies the nature and extent of each offender's treatment needs. According to Harper (1997), New Jersey's ISP is treatment-oriented. Nearly all of its participants are required to participate in treatment, such as Alcoholics Anonymous, Narcotics

Anonymous, and Gamblers Anonymous, out-patient and in-patient drug and alcohol treatment programs, mental health treatment, education and training programs, as well as workshops on parenting, and addiction and relapse prevention.

Punitive ISP Conditions

Punitive conditions are additional sanctions required of the offender. They address the need for accountability. Accountability refers to measures taken to ensure that criminal offenders are held accountable and responsible for the harms (damages, injury, loss) they have caused as a result of their criminal behavior (Fulton & Stone, 1995). They include being required to pay fines, make restitution to crime victims, and perform community service. Offenders may be ordered to home confinement. A period of incarceration may also be required as part of the ISP.

Most ISPs incorporate a mix of these three types of conditions. New Jersey's program requires 16 hours of community service each month, drug testing, mandatory employment, mandatory curfew, 20 hours of contacts with an ISP officer each month, treatment participation, and often, home detention (See Harper, 1997). Participants are also required to work with an individual in the community; this "community sponsor" encourages and supports participants in reaching their program goals. Depending on the type and characteristics of the offense and the behavior of the offender in ISP, restrictions and requirements are gradually reduced over the 18-month program (Pearson & Harper, 1990). According to Petersilia (1990a) many of New Jersey's ISP participants retract their agreement to participate as a result of the strict conditions and instead serve their terms in prisons.

Georgia's conditions include multiple weekly contacts between probation officers and offenders (up to 7 contacts each week), more than 96 hours of community service, a mandatory curfew, mandatory employment or school attendance, treatment participation, and random urinalysis (McCarthy, et al., 2001). Colorado's program was developed in the middle 1980s as a front-end prison diversion program. It requires a minimum of two scheduled contacts with an ISP officer per week, random contacts, prohibited alcohol and drug use, participation in treatment, and payment of a $20 monthly supervision fee (Bureau of Justice Assistance, 1997).

In addition to standard conditions of probation, participants of the sex offender ISP in Wisconsin are required to comply with the following conditions (Roberts-Van Cuick, 2000):

- Have no contact with any person under the age of 18 unless a preapproved supervising adult is present. Do not establish a dating, intimate, sexual relationship with an adult without prior approval of the probation/parole agent and/or treatment clinician.
- Do not consume or ingest alcoholic beverages, illegal or nonprescription drugs unless permitted by the agent (supervision officer).
- Enter and successfully complete sex offender programming as recommended by agent at an approved treatment facility. Pay for the programming as ordered.
- Participate in sex offender testing, evaluation, and assessment as directed by agent.
- Do not reside near, visit or be in or about parks, schools, day care centers, swimming pools, beaches, theaters or other places where children congregate without advanced approval of agent and a preapproved supervising adult. Incidental contact with children must be reported within 24 hours.
- Have no contact with any adult or child victims or their families without prior agent approval.
- Do not be in or near any establishment whose sole purpose is the sale of alcohol.
- Do not possess any sexually explicit or erotic materials or be in or about the parking lot of any establishment whose primary business is the sale of sexually explicit or erotic materials. Do not reside overnight in any residence other than your designated residence without prior approval from agent. Be present in your approved residence from 11 p.m. to 5 a.m. unless you have prior agent approval.
- Face-to-Face Registration: Report to and register with the local police department and county sheriff's office within 10 calendar days of any temporary or permanent change in residence, or as directed by agent.

- Registration Change of Information: In accordance with Wisconsin ss.301.45, report any changes, whether temporary or permanent, in residence, employment, school enrollment, use of vehicle or name immediately, or no later than within 10 calendar days of the change.
- Permit no juvenile or adult to reside or stay overnight in your designated residence at any time without prior agent approval.
- Do not purchase, possess or use a home-based computer, software, hardware or modem without prior agent approval.
- Do not possess any instrument that can be used to subdue or restrain another person, including, but not limited to, handcuffs or any other restraints unless approved by your agent.
- Do not work or socialize in any capacity that will put you in contact with any vulnerable population including children, psychologically impaired persons, the elderly, developmentally disabled, non-English speaking, etc.
- Do not alter your identity in any manner whatsoever, including but not limited to, changing your name, wearing a law enforcement officer's badge, wearing a disguise or changing your physical appearance without prior agent approval.

Strict Enforcement of Supervision Conditions

When a participant violates conditions of ISP supervision, correctional officials may modify the supervision plan or revoke the offender to a more restrictive placement, such as prison. Minor technical violations, such as a missed curfew, may be overlooked or resolved with modifications to supervision. Multiple or more serious technical violations, such as routinely missing treatment appointments or failing drug tests, and especially the commission of crimes, usually result in revocation, but not before a revocation hearing.

Graduated Supervision

Intensive supervision programs vary in duration from about 6 to 18 months. Following successful completion of ISP, participants may be released completely from correctional supervision or more likely, transferred to a regular probation or parole caseload where conditions and officer contacts are less rigorous (Byrne, et al., 1989). During the period of ISP supervision, most programs are comprised of graduated phases that vary in levels of intensity and restriction for the offender. Progression through phases is based on time and program compliance. In Georgia, for instance, offenders serve a minimum of three months in Phase One, which may include home confinement, three months in Phase Two, and finally enrollment in Phase Three or placement on regular probation. In New Jersey, offenders serve a minimum of 180 days in Phase One. Montana's ISP is a good example of a program with graduated supervision (Figure 3.3).

THE MONTANA INTENSIVE SUPERVISION PROGRAM

Program Description

ISP is a 9 month (270 day) nonresidential alternative to incarceration for adult felony offenders who would otherwise be sent to prison for a new crime or probation/parole revocation, and for inmates who are eligible for release on parole but who are too high a risk for regular parole. Essentially, the program operates as a front-end diversion from prison (Intensive Supervision Probation) and a back-end diversion from prison (Intensive Supervision Parole).

Three Phase Program

Participants progress through three phases of supervision spending a minimum of 90 days in each phase. Treatment, services, and supervision vary at each phase. Phase I is the most restrictive phase with the most intense surveillance, including electronic monitoring. A handbook for participants is included at orientation to the program so that participants are clear about the rules, activities, and expectations of the program. Participants who violate any requirement may be extended in a phase, restart a phase, or be returned to a phase already completed.

Weekly Schedule of Activities

Activities of participants are highly structured. Each participant submits a schedule of activities he or she plans for the upcoming week. The schedule is detailed, containing the times and locations of any planned activities such as going to school, performing community service, working, attending treatment, recreation, and doing laundry. Once accepted by a supervision officer, the schedules become part of the supervision plan for participants.

Supervision of Participants

Several teams of two officers supervise caseloads of 25 participants. Teams use electronic monitoring, scheduled and unscheduled home visits and collateral visits to the participant's employers, family members, and counselors. These visits are performed weekly in Phase I of the program and biweekly or on another schedule in Phases II and III. At each phase, however, participants are required to visit the probation office weekly.

Program Requirements

In addition to reporting to the probation office and submitting to home and collateral visits by officer teams, participants are also required to:

- Establish and maintain a residence
- Maintain employment or enrollment in an educational/vocational program
- Submit to regular and random searches of residences and vehicles
- Avoid bars, casinos, or other gambling establishments
- Remain in the county of jurisdiction
- Obtain officer approval for visitors or new persons in residence
- Perform at least 70 hours of community service
- Pay fines, restitution, and supervision fees
- Submit to regular drug and alcohol testing
- Participate in treatment programs
- Submit to electronic monitoring
- Submit to unannounced home, work, and collateral visits
- Report weekly to the probation department

Status Upon Release

Once participants complete the three phases of the program successfully, they are released to regular probation or parole. Participants may be removed for a new arrest or a technical violation and be sent to prison or to a more restrictive placement.

Program Performance

A review of the program indicates a rather high completion rate of 72% for the probationers studied and a lower completion rate (52%) for the parolees. Most failures were a result of technical violations, such as failing a drug test, and not the commission of new crimes.

Source: Montana Department of Corrections, 1998.

Figure 3.3. The Montana ISP

RESEARCH ON INTENSIVE SUPERVISION PROGRAMS

Program Completion

Offenders who participate in intensive supervision programs finish successfully at similar or slightly lower rates than offenders on probation and parole; approximately 50% of participants complete ISP. Research on Colorado's program (English, et al., 1996) reported no statistical difference in the completion rates between ISP participants and regular probationers, which indicates that ISP participants did no worse than regular probationers. However, according to the U.S. General Accounting Office (1993c), the Arizona program was more effective in controlling criminal behavior while offenders were under supervision than probation. Fewer ISP participants were arrested for new crimes during supervision than probationers.

Most ISP failures result from technical violations. This means that ISP participants fail to abide by conditions of supervision more often than they commit new crimes. The largest program evaluation was a 14-site study conducted between 1986 and 1991 (Petersilia, 1999). The research used a strong design in that it provided random assignment of offenders into either ISP or traditional supervision, thereby making it possible to compare the effects of different sanctions on offender outcomes. Published results indicate that ISPs do provide enhanced surveillance, which should explain higher technical violations. Two-thirds (65%) of the ISP group had technical violations as compared to 38% of traditional probationers. Additionally, ISP participants violating a condition were more likely than regular probationers to be revoked to prison. Increased surveillance leads to increased detection of program violations and revocation.

Research on a Texas ISP (Jones, 1995), used for high-risk probationers and probation violators, documents a failure rate of 50%, with 35% revoked for technical violations. According to the Montana Department of Corrections (1998), 53% of ISP participants studied completed successfully and 47% failed mainly for technical violations. Similar findings were reported on a sample of offenders in Colorado's program; 49% completed, 10% failed due to the commission of a new crime, 32% committed a technical violation, and 9% absconded (English, Pullen, & Colling-Chadwick, 1996). Research of an ISP in Ohio (Haas & Latessa, 1995) also indicates that participants more frequently violated

for technical violations, rather than for the commission of new crimes. It was pointed out that this appears to be a function of the higher level of supervision in ISPs compared to regular supervision probation (and parole) as well as greater demands on the offender.

Recidivism

Early evaluations of intensive supervision programs indicated that ISP was reducing recidivism among offenders who participated, but more recent research indicates that intensive supervision programs do not reduce reoffending (Petersilia, 1999). Although the ISPs and offenders participating are very diverse and it is somewhat difficult to make accurate generalizations across programs, available research suggests that participants commit new crimes after their ISP supervision at about the same rates as offenders who are placed on regular probation or parole. According to Petersilia, a study of 14 ISPs in nine states showed similar one-year rearrest rates for ISP participants (38%) and regular probationers (36%). Reports from Arizona indicate that participants in the ISP recidivated at higher rates than probationers but at rates no different than parolees. According to a U.S. General Accounting Office report (1993c), intensive supervision parole (back-end ISP) does not eliminate crime, but it is more effective at controlling reoffending for a longer period of time than incarceration followed by regular parole.

Increased contact alone is not sufficient to reduce recidivism rates (Fulton, Latessa, et al., 1997). Based upon existing research, it appears that treatment programming and the provision of service impacts reoffending rates. According to the literature, effective programs address criminogenic need factors (such as antisocial attitudes and values) and use treatment models (such as cognitive behavioral) that have demonstrated effectiveness in reducing recidivism. (See Andrews, 1994; Andrews, Bonta, & Hoge, 1990; Bonta, 1997; Gendreau, 1993.) The National Institute of Corrections (2000) reports that the most successful types of treatment models include (1) social learning (ex. anti-criminal modeling and skills development); (2) cognitive behavioral (ex. problem solving, self-control skills, anger management, personal responsibility, attitudinal change, moral reasoning, social perspective taking); (3) radical behavior (ex. classical and operant conditioning); (4) family based therapies; and (5) the provision of intensive services. With respect to ISPs, it was reported in the 14-site study of intensive supervision programs previously discussed (Petersilia, 1999), that ISP participants involved in treatment and employment programs had recidivism rates up to 20% lower than those who did not participate. According to Harper (1997), a 1995 evaluation of the New Jersey program, which is focused on treatment, also reported favorable recidivism rates. There, only 6.8% of participants who had successfully completed the program and who were out of the program for about six years were convicted of a serious new offense.

When ISPs incorporate the provision of intensive services and focus less intently on surveillance, it is anticipated that recidivism should be affected favorably (Turner & Petersilia, 1992). In fact, according to research on ISP for drug offenders, Turner, Petersilia, and Deschenes (1992, p. 553), the surveillance-oriented ISPs will "almost certainly increase the number of technical violations brought to the court's attention and, depending on the sanction imposed, may increase significantly the number of offenders incarcerated, particularly in local jails."

Net Widening

Net widening occurs when offenders are placed in more restrictive sanctions than their offenses warrant. Net widening has three main negative effects: increasing the burden of punishment on an offender, increasing rather than decreasing the cost of corrections, and failing to reduce jail and prison crowding.

Probation Enhancement ISPs

Intensive supervision programs that enhance probation or parole widen the net because offenders who are moved to ISP caseloads come from the regular probation and parole populations. Given that probation enhancement is the most common form of ISP, most ISP participants have not been diverted from prison. The key to reducing the problem of net widening and therefore freeing up prison beds and saving correctional dollars is the proper selection of offenders into intensive supervision programs.

Front-End ISPs

ISPs that target prison-bound offenders are most subject to net widening. Net widening would occur in these cases if the ISP participants were not diverted from prison but were instead drawn from probation or another less restrictive sanction. There is no certain measure of net widening in the case of front-end programs, because one could never know with certainty whether an offender who was sentenced for the ISP would have otherwise been sentenced to prison had the ISP been unavailable.

Researchers in Colorado estimated the extent to which offenders in the ISP were diverted from prison by comparing criminal history characteristics of ISP participants with the characteristics of offenders on regular probation and prisoners. They concluded that ISP participants had much more serious criminal histories than regular probationers and were most similar to prisoners and therefore were probably diverted from prison to the ISP (Bureau of Justice Assistance, 1997). Research of a Tennessee ISP (Whitehead, Miller, & Myers, 1995), reports that the program is meeting part of its objective. The program did divert some offenders from prison terms, but the program was also being used for offenders who would not normally have been sent to prison and therefore some net widening had occurred. On the whole, intensive supervision programs doubtfully reduce prison populations through front-end diversion and are subject to varying levels of net widening (Fulton & Stone, 1995). In fact, Tonry (1990) points out that net widening and high failure (revocation) rates for front-end programs may actually increase prison populations.

Back-End ISPs
Intensive supervision programs designed to divert offenders from prison at the back end are the least subject to net widening, since offenders are already in a more restrictive sanction (prison) and would be released to a less restrictive sanction (ISP). These programs are true diversions from incarceration when the offenders who are placed into ISP would not have been released from prison (for instance to regular parole) had ISP not been available. Back-end intensive supervision programs therefore have the potential of reducing correctional costs and crowding especially when the beds are not again filled simply because they are available.

Cost Effectiveness

The simplest way to assess cost effectiveness is to compare average daily costs associated with different penalties, such as intensive supervision and prison. Using this method, intensive supervision programs are less costly than incarceration but more costly than regular probation or parole. A national survey of ISPs (Camp & Camp, 2000) indicates that prison costs an average of $57.92 per day for each inmate, regular probation and parole costs $3.35 per offender per day, and ISP costs $9.73 per day for each offender. In Montana, for example, the Montana Department of Corrections (1998) estimates that its ISP program costs an average of $14.04 per day, regular probation and parole costs $3.33, and incarceration costs $49.42. In Florida, ISP costs $6.49 per day and jail costs $19.52 (Wagner & Baird, 1993).

ISPs that divert offenders from incarceration at the front and back ends have the potential of saving money. The probation enhancement model, which is the most common form of ISP, does not. On average, expenditures for probation departments using ISP for purposes of enhancing supervision for their regular population cost twice as much as regular probation.

A more rigorous cost assessment takes into account marginal or incidental costs, for instance the additional cost of reprocessing offenders who are revoked from a program. As Petersilia & Turner (1993, p. 99) noted in their multi-site evaluation programs: "Our cost analysis estimated the total criminal-justice dollars spent on each offender during the one-year follow-up period, including the costs of correctional supervision and the court costs associated with reprocessing recidivists. In no instance did ISPs result in cost savings. At most sites, ISP resulted in more technical violations, more court appearances, and more incarcerations than did the conventional program—resulting in costs up to twice as high as for routine supervision. The principal variation in program costs is related to what the ISP does about violations. If violations were ignored, program costs were lower; if not, costs were higher." Similar findings were reported on ISP programs in Arizona. According to the U.S. General Accounting Office (1993a), revocations increase the overall cost of the punishment, because the cost of supervision following revocation from ISP to prison includes the original cost of ISP and the subsequent prison costs. In one county, ISP costs increased by $11,306 for each revocation.

Costs for ISP should be higher, perhaps reaching the costs for incarceration when the costs take into account the reprocessing of offenders who have failed ISP as a result of technical and other violations

(Fulton, Latessa, et al., 1997). Based on these and other research projects, it appears that ISP is not currently meeting its goals of cost savings.

Behavioral Change/Treatment Effectiveness

Intensive supervision treatment components appear to facilitate successful completion of ISP on the part of participants and contribute to a reduction in their recidivism as we have discussed. For example, a report on Colorado's ISP indicates that 70% of ISP participants who received individual counseling, 68% who received group counseling, and 73% who attended Alcoholics Anonymous completed ISP successfully (Bureau of Justice Assistance, 1997). Programs that incorporate treatment report reductions of recidivism by 20%–30% compared to programs that focus exclusively on surveillance (See Petersilia & Turner, 1993). Petersilia (1999) reported recidivism rates for ISP participants involved in treatment, community service, and employment programs that were as much as 20% less than the rates for ISP participants not involved in these programs. Additionally, such treatment-focused programs appear to have a positive effect on offenders' quality of life after successful completion. For example, the New Jersey program reported an employment rate for its graduates of 95% (Harper, 1997). According to Fulton, Latessa, et al. (1997) treatment for offenders, especially cognitive treatment, employment services and drug treatment, appear to be effective at behavioral change and social stability following participation in ISP

SUMMARY

Intensive supervision programs allow for the closer monitoring of high-risk offenders than is provided by regular probation and parole. Although every state now uses some form of ISP, it is estimated that fewer than six percent of all adult probationers and parolees participate (Petersilia, 1999). Intensive supervision programs are used mainly as case management tools, or probation and parole enhancement mechanisms. In such programs, probationers and parolees who are deemed high risks for reoffending receive an enhanced level of supervision and are subject to restrictive conditions in an effort to manage the risk they pose to the community. Front-end intensive supervision programs target offenders who are headed for prison, but research suggests that most offenders placed were not actually prison-bound. Net widening occurs in these cases and has negative effects, such as increasing the costs of corrections. To accomplish true prison diversion, offenders need to be assigned to ISPs after a sentence of imprisonment; ISPs should operate as back-end programs. Back-end programs are designed to supervise inmates who are released early from incarceration and have the greatest potential for cost savings and alleviating prison crowding. ISP participants tend to fail as a result of technical violations and when incarcerated as a result, costs of punishment tend to increase. Research has shown that programs with treatment components more effectively facilitate successful completion and reduce reoffending than programs that focus heavily on surveillance and control. Intensive supervision programs remain the foundation of intermediate sanctions.

Based upon research findings, current efforts are being made to improve intensive supervision programs, such as to enhance their treatment aspects and to reconsider sanctions for technical violations. Three important recommendations have been offered (Fulton, Latessa, et al., 1997). First, clarify ISP goals. ISPs aim to reduce prison crowding, reduce costs, provide an intermediate punishment, protect the public, and rehabilitate offenders, but achieving all of these goals may be impossible. Second, focus on understanding and addressing offenders' criminogenic needs. Third, concentrate on improving ISP program integrity, by implementing theoretically and empirically based treatment and by ensuring that programs are implemented as designed, such as diverting offenders from prison when programs are so designed.

**CHAPTER 4**

Boot Camps

BACKGROUND

Boot camps are highly popular residential intermediate sanctions typically used for young offenders and provide for very structured and military-like activities such as strict discipline, physical training and labor, drill, and a regimented schedule of daily activities. Boot camps differ from other intermediate sanctions in that participants are incarcerated, albeit for short and intensive terms, participants are often under the jurisdiction of state or county correctional departments and therefore considered inmates, and many boot camps are located on or near prison grounds.

Although the term boot camp is often used synonymously with shock incarceration, boot camps are actually only one form of shock incarceration. Shock incarceration programs vary, but the common feature is that an offender is confined for some period; this incarceration experience is typically brief but intense. As the term suggests, the idea behind shock incarceration is to provide a deterrent shock or jolt to the offender. To achieve this sense of shock, boot camps are structured and emphasize discipline and rigorous physical training. Boot camps differ from other forms of shock incarceration in that participants are separated from other inmates, participate in physical training drill, and the atmosphere of the program is militaristic in nature with a strict daily structure of activities (MacKenzie & Shaw, 1993).

The first boot camp programs were implemented in Georgia and Oklahoma in 1983 to help relieve prison and jail crowding. They were first developed in the adult system and then expanded to the juvenile system (MacKenzie, Wilson, & Kider, 2001). The concept behind the boot camp was to revive the military-style incarceration experience that was popular in some reformatories (such as Elmira in New York) from the late 1800s through the early 1900s. The emphases on strict discipline and other elements of current shock incarceration models eventually faded out in these reformatories due to abuses and a shift towards rehabilitation efforts. So, the creation of boot camps in the 1980s was more of a revival and return to familiar themes than a correctional innovation (MacKenzie & Parent, 1992). During the 1980s, boot camps quickly became a popular intermediate sanction. An important factor in this popularity was their public appeal; boot camps presented conservatives with a tough and punitive sanction, while liberals were appeased by the potential for rehabilitation and reduction in prison overcrowding.

Since the development of the first boot camps in the 1980s, there has been tremendous growth in this intermediate sanction. In 1990, most states operated one or two boot camp programs with capacity for about 100 to 250 participants (MacKenzie, 1990). By 1994 there were at least 59 programs in 29 states that could accommodate more than 10,000 offenders (Cronin, 1994). The Bureau of Prisons operates two boot camps for federal offenders. Boot camps are also used for jail inmates; in 1992, there were 10 jail-based programs (Austin, Jones, & Bolyard, 1993). According to a recent survey (Camp & Camp, 2000), there were 51 prison boot camps operating in 30 states and the federal system in 1999.

States also operate boot camps at the probation and parole levels. For example, according to Camp & Camp (2000), Texas probation departments operated three boot camps in which 572 adults were participating on January 1, 2000. Mississippi also operated three boot camps at the probation level. North Carolina operated the most boot camps (16). In total, the 19 states responding to the survey reported the use of 32 boot camp programs in operation at the probation and parole levels.

Although there are no national statistics available on the total number of offenders participating in boot camps, research by the

Criminal Justice Institute (Camp & Camp, 2000) indicates that on January 1, 2000, there were at least 6,983 inmates in boot camp programs. The survey did not account for all states. As to the number of inmates participating in boot camp annually, New York has continued to lead the nation in 1999, with at least 2,741 offenders placed in boot camps. Illinois placed the second largest number (2,224) followed by Georgia (1,523) and North Carolina (1,184). These figures refer to boot camp programs operated by state correctional agencies (prisons) and not jail boot camps or those operated by probation agencies and parole departments.

Boot camps aim to achieve several goals. Most importantly, it is argued that prison overcrowding could be alleviated if certain offenders who are or who would be sentenced to a prison term (e.g., two to four years) are diverted to a shorter, yet equally punitive and effective boot camp sentence (e.g., 90 to 180 days). Deterrence (both specific and general) is inherent in the concept of shock incarceration. The theory behind the boot camp model is that the shock experience and extremely regimented period of incarceration will produce a strong disincentive for an individual to reoffend. At the same time, the strict discipline and grueling and tiresome exercise and drill and ceremony are intended to serve as a threat to discourage others from offending (general deterrence). Boot camps, or at least certain components of them, may be viewed, and are often promoted, as rehabilitative. Advocates, for instance, argue that the strict discipline and military-like atmosphere instill discipline, responsibility, and self-esteem. In addition to the correctional goals of deterrence and rehabilitation, it can be argued that boot camps meet the other two correctional goals of retribution and incapacitation. Whereas prisoners and jail inmates often sit idle in their cells, boot camps require rigorous physical activity, which may better satisfy the public's demand for punitive sanctions. The goal of incapacitation is also addressed, albeit for a shorter amount of time.

TARGET POPULATIONS

Most boot camps are designed for first time and nonviolent offenders. Many target drug offenders. Some boot camps do allow repeat offenders, those with prior prison terms, and offenders convicted of violent offenses to enter programs. In fact, of the 14 states with boot camps in 1990 according to MacKenzie and Parent (1992), half allowed violent offenders to enter programs. Given the heavy emphasis on physical training and labor, boot camps are reserved for relatively young offenders (usually under age 35), although states differ in their age limits for participation. Kansas and Oklahoma set the upper age limit at 25, while California allows participants up to 40 years of age to enter boot camps. Most boot camps (upwards of 90%) appear to be predominately male programs. Additionally, programs require participants to volunteer for participation.

In most states and in the federal government, boot camps are designed to reduce reliance on prison and jail incarceration. To that end, many states and the federal government designate boot camp placements to two populations of offenders: those who are directly sentenced by the court as a front-end alternative to traditional incarceration and those who are already serving terms of incarceration and who are diverted to boot camp incarceration. Figure 4.1 illustrates these two main boot camp models.

BOOT CAMP MODEL 1	BOOT CAMP MODEL 2
The boot camp is a front-end diversion from incarceration	The boot camp is a back-end diversion from incarceration
Participants are directly sentenced by the courts to the boot camp usually as a condition of probation. Probation and parole violators may be sent to the boot camp in lieu of jail or prison for violating conditions of their supervision.	Participants are selected from newly admitted jail or prison inmates and volunteer for participation in exchange for a shorter sentence. Participants may also be required to spend a significant period of their sentence in jail and prison before they are released to the boot camp. Participants of back-end programs are usually placed on parole or probation supervision.

Figure 4.1 Two Main Boot Camp Models

Front-End Boot Camp Models

Some states, counties, and the federal government operate boot camps for offenders who are directly sentenced by the court as punishment for their crimes. In some cases, boot camps are also used for probation and parole violators as an alternative to confinement. Figure 4.2 illustrates a front-end boot camp program in Texas.

Figure 4.2. Tarrant County (Texas) Shock Incarceration Facility (SIF)
A Front-End Alternative to Incarceration

PROGRAM DESCRIPTION

The Shock Incarceration Facility (SIF) is a 120-bed boot camp program developed in 1992 and operated by the Tarrant County Community Supervision and Corrections Department (probation). It is a highly structured boot camp for adult male and female offenders who are on community supervision (probation) and who have been directly sentenced to the SIF as a condition of probation. The primary staff of the boot camp includes a Boot Camp Commander, two Drill Lieutenants, two Drill Sergeants, and six Drill Instructors.

ELIGIBILITY CRITERIA

Offenders are eligible for sentencing to the boot camp if their current offense involves no bodily injury or weapons, if they have no chronic medical ailments, if they are in reasonably good physical and mental health, and if they are aged 17-25. Participants spend six months in the program.

BOOT CAMP PROGRAMMING

During the six-month program, participants receive orientation for up to one month and then participate in a variety of required and need-based programming for the remaining five months. During the orientation phase, participants are exposed to the rules and requirements of the program, issued clothing, and given bed assignments. This orientation lasts eight hours each day. Following orientation, participants are exposed to programming, which includes:

- **Group Counseling:** All participants are required to attend substance abuse education for one hour daily and for 24 weeks. Based upon a standardized substance abuse screening instrument, individual treatment plans are devised for each participant.
- **Family Counseling:** Aftercare programming begins three weeks before discharge from the boot camp and includes family counseling. The SIF uses a family counseling and aftercare program to assist the participant in his or her reintegration into the community.
- **Personal Living Skills:** Participants are taught proper hygiene and attire and how to properly launder and press clothing. Ten hours each week are devoted to personal living skills programming.
- **Daily Household Duties:** Participants are assigned to daily chores, such as cleaning personal space, restroom facilities, and work detail in surrounding areas. Participants work in platoons and spend at least 20 hours a week on these tasks.
- **Educational Program:** The boot camp requires GED classes for all participants who have not received a high school diploma or GED. Participants who speak English as a second language must participate in English as a Second Language classes. A private contractor teaches these courses at the facility for two hours each day over 12 weeks.
- **Drill and Ceremony:** All participants must take part in physical drill and training. Military-style activities include marching in formation, reveille, learning military routine, and inspection. Marching in formation takes place at least one hour each day.
- **Life Skills Training:** The life skills program provides programming in decision-making, anger management, employment readiness, and cultural diversity awareness. Participants are required to participate in at least five hours of life skills training each week.
- **Vocational Training:** Participants who have attained a GED or high school diploma are required to attend vocational training classes for two hours weekly. Participants are assessed as to their need for vocational training and then participate in training appropriate to them and at his or her own pace.
- **Physical Education:** Daily physical training is required and includes push-ups, sit-ups, and running. Participants must spend at least 18 hours weekly involved in physical training.
- **Recreation:** Participants are allowed four hours of recreation time during the week and on weekends.
- **Individual Counseling:** Participants who require more intensive treatment are offered one hour of counseling weekly.
- **Chaplaincy:** Participants may opt to attend religious services and participate in bible study.

Aftercare: All participants who successfully complete the program are placed on community supervision. Most are initially transitioned to a Shock Incarceration Transition Aftercare Program for up to 12 weeks before placement on probation.

Source: Adapted from Martin, Choate, Johnson, and Willett, 1998

Figure 4.2. Tarrant County (Texas) Shock Incarceration Facility (SIF)

The Bureau of Prisons operates boot camps referred to as Intensive Confinement Centers. Most participants (90%) are directly sentenced to the boot camps as an alternative to traditional prison confinement (Klein-Saffran, 1996). The primary goal is to change offenders' behavior through hard work and discipline as well as programming in the form of substance abuse counseling, education, life skills, and health. The program emphasizes treatment components over military-style activities. Participants spend about six months in a period of incarceration at a boot camp followed by residential stays in halfway houses and then in home confinement.

Georgia's boot camp began as a highly militaristic program stressing discipline and hard work. Based upon research, the Comprehensive Correctional Boot Camp Program has been redesigned to include several treatment components, such as mandatory substance abuse education and aftercare (Keenan, 1996). The state operates boot camps designed as back-end alternatives to prison as well as programs designed as front-end alternatives. Participants placed into the front-end programs are directly sentenced by judges to the boot camps as a condition of probation and spend an average of 90 days at the boot camps. These probation-based programs provide room for 437 offenders at any given time. Participants are typically young felony property, drug, and DWI offenders. In addition to the rigid schedule and punitive atmosphere, the boot camp provides drug and alcohol abuse treatment. Participants move through the boot camp in four phases: intake, work and discipline, programming, and prerelease. They are oriented to the programs during their first week and then participate in physical training (ceremony and drill) and work for the next four weeks. After completing the work and discipline phase, participants are exposed to the treatment for four weeks, although work and discipline continues. The final phase is designed to transition participants out of the program through programming related to job readiness and planning and housing preparation. Georgia boasts a 95% completion rate for its front-end programs.

Back-End Boot Camp Models

Boot camp programs that select participants from prison or jail populations are considered back-end boot camp models because they choose offenders who are already imprisoned and are designed, in large part, to reduce the length of time an inmate spends in prison or jail. Some boot camps select participants when they are newly admitted to prisons and jails or in the early stages of their terms, usually if they have received relatively short sentences (e.g. six months or two years). For instance, Georgia selects participants while they are involved in the prison classification process. Other states select participants when they are nearing the end of their prison terms. Boot camp participants who volunteer for back-end programs are still considered inmates in most cases and are therefore still under the custody of the state correctional department. Programs operated by the state prison system would normally release participants who successfully complete the boot camp to parole supervision.

New York operates the largest boot camp program in the country. In the mid-1990s, New York's "Shock inmates" accounted for about one-fifth of all prisoners in state and federal boot camps nationally. The state created its first of four boot camp programs in 1987 in hopes of reducing prison crowding by releasing select inmates from prison terms to the Shock incarceration facilities for six months followed by intensive parole. The program is illustrated in Figure 4.3. Male and female inmates who are serving their first term of adult incarceration and who have no histories of violent crimes are eligible if they are in good physical and mental condition and have a minimum sentence of three years or less. Prison officials screen inmates who have applied for the program and proceed through an orientation process to weed out inmates who are not fully committed to volunteering for the alternative placement. All Shock graduates return to the community under intensive parole supervision. Shock "platoons" returning to New York City participate in an Aftershock program that includes substance abuse and vocational services, and a program designed to maintain group spirit. In addition to the usual emphasis on discipline, physical work, regimentation, and other military-style activities, the program is treatment-focused and provides substance abuse treatment and educational services during the boot camp phase and the aftercare phase. At any one time, 1,390 men and 180 women inmates are in the program: about two percent of all state prisoners. By the end of 1997, about 29,500 inmates had been admitted (New York State Department of Correctional Services & Division of Parole, 1998).

Figure 4.3. New York's Shock Incarceration Programs
A Back-End Alternative to Prison

PROGRAM DESCRIPTION
New York began shock incarceration in 1987 and by 1994 was operating four programs with a total capacity of 1,570. The boot camps are used to provide an early release from prison for adult males and females in order to reduce prison space. The boot camp programs incorporates military-style activities, such as physical training, drill, and ceremony with substance abuse treatment and education to instill personal responsibility, character, and promote a positive self image.

ELIGIBILITY CRITERIA AND SELECTION
The boot camps are not used as a direct sentence, but rather a back-end alternative to prison. Nonviolent male and female inmates younger than 35 years of age who are eligible for parole release within three years and who have not served prison terms in the past are eligible for the program. Candidates deemed eligible are moved to a central screening center where they are oriented to the program. Candidates are assessed as to their mental and physical capabilities and any other problems that would prevent them from completing the program. Once oriented, eligible inmates who then volunteer to participate in the program in place of serving out their prison terms are then placed into one of the four boot camp facilities. Female participants are assigned to a facility that stresses hard outdoor labor in a remote wooded area. Males enter shock programs monthly in platoons of up to 60 inmates.

TWO PROGRAM PHASES
Phase One: Boot Camp Participation
The first six months of participation involves the boot camp experience. During the first two weeks, participants are exposed to the rules and discipline and learn how to perform physical training and military drill and ceremony. This period is referred to as "zero weeks" because it is intended to reduce early dropouts in its emphasis on orientation activities. During the entire boot camp phase, participants arise at 5:30 am and are involved in activities until lights out, which is at 9:30 p.m. Inmates have no free time, receive no mail, do not have access to commissary, no radios television, newspapers, or magazines. Phase One activities include:

- **Physical Training:** drill and ceremony: 26% of the inmates' time. Each morning participants perform calisthenics and run. Inmates march in platoon or squads to and from activities throughout the day. Formal company formations of platoons assemble three times daily.
- **Network:** The Network program is best characterized as a therapeutic approach. The objective of Network is to promote problem solving and building self-esteem. It emphasizes responsibility for the self, for others, and for one's quality of life. Network is a five-step model taught in 12 sessions and is required of all inmates. In support of this approach, inmates are grouped in platoons during the day and in the evenings. Network meetings are used to resolve problems and promote group cohesion, socialization, critical thinking skills, and communication.
- **Substance Abuse Treatment and Education:** 28% of the inmates' time. All inmates take part in at least six hours of alcohol and substance abuse treatment in the form of education and group counseling.
- **Academic Education:** 13% of the inmates' time. All participants must spend at least 12 hours engaged in academic programming. The education offered includes remedial education, basic adult education classes, and GED preparation, and a volunteer program for inmates who have attained a GED.
- **Hard labor:** 33% of the inmates' time. Inmates perform six hours of hard labor each day in two three-hour periods before and after lunch. Inmates work on the ground of the facility and in nearby conservation land. Inmates also perform unpaid community service.
- **Evaluation of Inmate Performance:** Staff evaluate inmates each day as to their progress in work assignments, Network, and physical training as well as weekly evaluations of participation in substance abuse treatment and academic education. Inmates who commit violations may be subject to removal and incarceration.

Phase Two: Intensive Community Supervision
Once inmates have completed the boot camp phase of the program, they receive graduation certificates at a ceremony and enter phase two of the program. Phase two is referred to as "AfterShock" and consists of six months community supervision under the administration of parole. Parole officers assigned to AfterShock are expected to maintain a high level of supervision over participants and do so through home visits, curfew checks, and drug testing. Shock graduates have priority access to community services for employment, counseling, substance abuse, and educational/vocational training.

Evaluation Outcomes
About 37% of participants drop out of the boot camp phases; this is attributed to the program's rigor. In terms of cost, the Department of Correctional Services estimate savings of $2 million for every 100 graduates of the boot camps. Additionally, research indicates that participants improved in their educational abilities.

Source: Adapted from Clark, Aziz, and MacKenzie, 1994

Figure 4.3. New York's Shock Incarceration Programs

PROGRAM CHARACTERISTICS

A Brief Period of Confinement

Built around the concept of shock incarceration, boot camp programs are designed to provide a punitive and deterrent shock to offenders. Therefore, participants spend brief but intense periods of confinement in boot camp programs. On average, participants spend between 90 to 120 days in boot camps across the country, although some programs, such as New York's, require longer stays (MacKenzie & Parent, 1992). As a show of intensity, boot camps are generally located on or around prison grounds. During this period of confinement, participants are subject to a strict daily schedule during which they are engaged in a variety of activities, namely physical training, and subject to strict rules.

A Strict and Complete Daily Schedule

A main characteristic of boot camp programs is strict adherence to a prearranged and demanding daily schedule. Participants arise early in the mornings and participate in activities and treatments, if offered, throughout the day until lights out. They march in platoons or other groups to and from activities. Figure 4.4 illustrates the daily schedule for all participants in the New York boot camp programs. As the figure shows, participants are engaged in training, drill, and activities throughout the

A.M.	
5:30	Wake up and standing count
5:45-6:30	Calisthenics and drill
6:30-7:00	Run
7:00-8:00	Mandatory breakfast and cleanup
8:15	Standing count and company formation
8:30-11:55	Work and school schedules
P.M.	
12:00-12:30	Mandatory lunch and standing count
12:30-3:30	Afternoon work or school schedule
3:30-4:00	Shower
4:00-4:45	Network community meeting
4:45-5:45	Mandatory dinner, prepare for evening
6:00-9:00	School, group counseling, drug counseling, prerelease counseling, decision-making classes
8:00	Count while in programs
9:15-9:30	Squad bay, prepare for bed
9:30	Standing count, lights out

Source: Clark, et al., 1994

Figure 4.4. Daily Schedules for Offenders in New York Boot Camps

day and evening with no free time. Every minute is structured and prearranged. Programs vary considerably in the types of activities required of participants in a typical day as well as the number of hours devoted to these activities, such as physical training and education.

Military-Style Components

The original boot camps developed in the early 1980s were highly militaristic in structure, focusing on physical drill and other military-like activities thought to instill discipline, responsibility, accomplishment, and respect. Many of the newer boot camp programs have incorporated treatment programming designed to address problems in the lives of participants, such as substance abuse programming. In some cases, these newer programs have placed the therapeutic focus above the military atmosphere. Most boot camp programs that exist today contain elements of each approach.

Military Centered Boot Camps

Most boot camps are based on a military environment, although programs vary widely with regard to the emphasis on the military-style activities and atmosphere. Programs incorporate military activities in some degree with regard to the use of strict rules and discipline, military style uniforms, military titles for staff, drill instructors, barracks housing, rigorous physical training and drill, and references to participants as platoons and platoon members. A U.S. General Accounting Office survey of boot camps (Cronin, 1994) found that all of the adult boot camps included in the survey (29) could be characterized as militaristic. Ninety percent of the programs used barracks-style housing for participants and more than 75% incorporated drill instructors, military-style uniforms for staff, grouping of participants in platoons, and summary or group punishments. In other research, Keenan and Barry (1994) developed measures of the military atmosphere of boot camp programs and reported that back-end programs were much more militaristic than probation-based or front-end boot camp programs. In the back-end programs, participants were more often required to use the word "sir," come to attention, wear a uniform properly, have close-cropped hair, march in step and in straight lines, chant during march, and follow drill instructions exactly.

The National Council on Crime and Delinquency has characterized the Maricopa County Aftershock program, otherwise known as Shock, as a military model boot camp program (Austin, Camp-Blair, et al., 2000). Shock was created in 1988 as a direct court sentence for offenders who could be helped by rigid structure and discipline. Offenders eligible for sentencing to the program are between the ages of 18 and 25 who have never been incarcerated in adult prisons and who have no mental disorders or physical impairments that would limit physical activity. Offenders sentenced to the program are granted intensive supervision probation and required to participate in the boot camp for four months as a condition of their probation. The program emphasizes military activities of hard work, physical training, drill, and ceremony. It does not offer treatment, such as life skills, counseling, or vocational programming, but does provide 32 hours of academic training.

The military environment is designed not only to deter and punish, but also to transform participants into law-abiding and self respecting citizens. The idea is that the discipline and regimented lifestyle imposed in the boot camp will create habits that can be transferred to life on the outside. Self-esteem, self-control, responsibility, and the ability to cope with stress are some of the habits that boot camp programs aim to instill. Advocates support the punitive environment as a credible way to transform offenders and to deliver a tough and necessary punishment. Some critics (for example Lutze & Brody, 1999) contend that the harsh and militaristic environment of boot camps creates a potential for abuse. Practices such as verbal confrontation and summary punishments are present in many boot camp programs (Morash & Rucker, 1990; Parent, 1989) and are thought by critics to be humiliating and publicly demeaning and therefore considered forms of abuse.

Treatment Centered Boot Camps

In the past few years, many boot camps have begun to move away from a primarily military emphasis towards a combined military/treatment model and have incorporated strategies found to be effective in treating offenders. Provisions of the 1994 Crime Bill requiring boot camps to have treatment and aftercare programming to be eligible for federal funding may have contributed to this shift. Today, boot camps may provide educational and vocational classes and counseling, job readiness, substance abuse treatment, as well as cognitive-based approaches that aim to help offenders develop more prosocial attitudes, values, and behaviors. Life skills classes, anger management, problem solving, and communication are offered by many boot camp programs. Substance abuse treatment and education has become a popular form of treatment. According to research by Cowles and Castellano (1996) all of the boot camp programs surveyed in 29 states and the federal system reported that they provide substance abuse education to participants. The amount of time dedicated to any type of rehabilitation differs from program to program, but generally, boot camps do appear to provide more rehabilitative activities than traditional prisons and jails. The variability in emphasis on treatment is apparent, however. For example, Georgia boot camp participants spend the least amount of their daily routine in rehabilitative activities (less than a half-hour per day), while in New York offenders spend nearly six hours a day in rehabilitative activities (MacKenzie & Souryal, 1994).

The Oregon Adult SUMMIT program is one example of a boot camp that has stressed a therapeutic model (See Figure 4.5). SUMMIT was established in 1994 as a back-end alternative to prison for adults. Participants are selected from among adult inmates who volunteer to participate and who have no more than three years remaining on their sentences, who are assigned minimum custody, and who are not serious or violent offenders. In the boot camp phase, participants are exposed to education, cognitive retraining, substance abuse treatment, and work squads. They are also required to perform military drill and ceremony as well as physical training. Participation is required seven days each week and follows a strict and regimented daily schedule. The boot camp stresses treatment in the form of cognitive retraining, which addresses thinking patterns, attitudes, behaviors, and decision-making. Anger management, problem solving, and communication programming are also addressed. The goal is to help participants develop more positive attitudes, values, and belief systems so that they are better prepared to act responsibly.

Aftercare Provisions

States have begun to devise aftercare components for boot camp graduates. According to Zachariah (1996), most boot camp programs now provide aftercare for participants who have successfully completed

Figure 4.5 Oregon's Adult SUMMIT Program
A Treatment-Focused Boot Camp

PROGRAM DESCRIPTION

The Oregon Adult Summit program was established in 1994 as a back-end alternative to prison for adult offenders. It operates within a military framework, but stresses a therapeutic model.

ELIGIBILITY CRITERIA AND SELECTION

Participants are selected from among adult inmates who volunteer to participate and who meet the following eligibility criteria: assigned to minimum custody, have less than 36 months to serve on their sentences, and have no serious or violent offenses. Inmates nearing the end of their prison terms are given priority. Inmates are admitted in platoons of 60 and are referred to as inmates throughout their participation, since they are still under the custody of state corrections.

TWO PROGRAM PHASES

Phase One: Boot Camp Participation

In the boot camp phase, which is 26 weeks in duration, participation is required seven days each week and follows a strict and regimented daily schedule with programming beginning at 5:30 am and ending at 9:30 p.m. The boot camp stresses treatment in the form of cognitive retraining, which addresses thinking patterns, attitudes, behaviors, and decision-making. Anger management, problem solving, and communication programming are also addressed. The goal is to help participants develop more positive attitudes, values, and belief systems so that they are better prepared to act responsibly. Other programming includes:

- ❑ **Physical Training.** Inmates participate in physical training daily. The assumption is that physical exercise and training can lead to a sense of achievement
- ❑ **Community Service Work.** Platoons perform unpaid work in the community three days each week wile supervised by staff. The assumption behind this component is that inmates learn how to work with others, develop work experience, learn to manage time, and develop a sense of pride in the accomplished work.
- ❑ **Education.** Inmates are offered educational classes 13 hours each week. Each inmate is assigned to certain classes depending on his educational level and ability. Basic education, computer skills, and GED classes are offered.
- ❑ **Substance Abuse Treatment.** The program stresses the treatment of substance abuse. Inmates are offered 12 hours of classes, discussion, and self help meetings weekly.
- ❑ **Community Meetings.** Inmates participate in community meetings each day. Staff leads the meetings and inmates take turns in leading discussions about the boot camp experience and issues that affect inmates as a whole.
- ❑ **Drill and Ceremony.** The daily drill and ceremony characterize the militaristic component of this boot camp. Inmates are required to move about in squads or platoons, in formation, and in military cadence.

Phase Two: Transitional Aftercare

Inmates who do not successfully complete the boot camp phase are returned to prison to serve out their sentences. Inmates who successfully complete 120 days of boot camp participation are assigned to a 90-day period of intensive supervision in the community. While on community supervision the inmate is still considered a participant of the boot camp program and is returned to the boot camp for violations. Inmates who complete the 90-day period are released to parole supervision. Those who successfully complete receive an average reduction of 311 days off their original sentence.

Source: Adapted from Austin, Camp-Blair, Camp, Castellano, Adams-Fuller, Jones, Kerr, Lewis, and Plant, 2000

Figure 4.5 Oregon's Adult SUMMIT Program

boot camp. This aftercare usually comes in the form of community supervision (probation or parole) and can also include other intermediate sanctions, such as day reporting and halfway house placement. Aftercare tends to be designed into the boot camp as a final phase of participation.

An inventory of 34 adult boot camp programs (National Institute of Justice, 1996) showed the variety in aftercare programming for boot camp graduates. In Pennsylvania, offenders are directly sentenced to the Quehanna Boot Camp program for six months as an alternative to incarceration and are then released to intensive probation or parole for between 1.5 and 4.5 years. While on intensive community supervision, participants receive substance abuse treatment, stress and anger management, vocational training, employment placement, and physical training. They may also be placed in a halfway house or be electronically monitored. The Harris County (Texas) Boot Camp Program, which is used for adults on probation who need a more structured level of supervision, contains a three-to-four month boot camp phase followed by probation supervision and participation in a day reporting program. During the initial aftercare phase, participants attend life skills programming twice weekly, a boot camp support group weekly, and are assisted with job placement. Finally, in Michigan, the Special Alternative Incarceration Program provides for several aftercare components depending on the needs of boot camp graduates. After spending 90 days in the boot camp, participants may be released to a residential program in the community for up to 120 days followed by another 120 days on intensive supervision or proceed directly to a 120-day period of intensive supervision.

RESEARCH ON BOOT CAMPS

Program Completion

Boot camp programs are demanding intermediate sanctions, as evidenced by failure rates of about 30% to 40% (Parent, 1996). Boot camp failures tend to occur in the early stages of boot camp participation (Poole & Slavick, 1995). Discharges are nearly always technical in nature, such as for disciplinary infractions, rather than terminations resulting from the commission of new crimes, so public safety is not at issue. What is problematic with failure rates in general, especially given the overriding goal of reducing prison crowding, is the likelihood that participants who do not complete are sent to or are returned to prison or jail.

Recidivism

The most comprehensive research on boot camps was sponsored by the National Institute of Justice and undertaken by Doris MacKenzie. This research involved a multi-site evaluation of boot camp programs in Georgia, New York, Oklahoma, Florida, Texas, Louisiana, South Carolina, and Illinois (See for example MacKenzie, 1994; MacKenzie, Shaw, & Gowdy, 1993; MacKenzie & Souryal, 1994; MacKenzie, Brame, et al., 1995) and follow-up research (MacKenzie, Wilson, & Kider, 2001). According to findings from these studies and other research (See Austin, Camp-Blair, et al., 2000; Flowers, Carr & Ruback 1991; Stinchcomb & Terry, 2001; U.S. General Accounting Office, 1993d) boot camps are no more effective in reducing recidivism than traditional sanctions.

The research has shown that recidivism rates of boot camp graduates are similar to comparison groups (typically comprised of eligible offenders who served their lengthier term in prison). However, the multi-site evaluation found lower recidivism rates for boot camp graduates in New York and Louisiana, which are programs geared toward rehabilitation. Perhaps the lower recidivism rate for graduates of these programs is due, in part, to the treatment offered in these programs or, as MacKenzie and Souryal have suggested, the aftercare provided to participants. In a further exploratory analysis examining program differences and recidivism rates, MacKenzie, Brame, et al. (1995) reported that boot camps devoting more than three hours each day to treatment, such as therapy, counseling, substance abuse treatment, and education, were more successful in reducing recidivism among participants. Additionally, the research showed that recidivism rates for those who completed successfully were significantly lower than the rates for those who were dismissed. Based upon a meta-analysis of research on boot camp programs, Mackenzie, Wilson, and Kider (2001) the following conclusions can be drawn:
- The military atmosphere, structure and discipline of correctional boot camps is not alone effective to reduce recidivism; and
- Programs incorporating components such as therapeutic activities during the boot camp and follow-up in the community (aftercare) may be successful in reducing recidivism.

Net Widening

The issue of net widening does not appear to be as problematic with boot camps as with other intermediate sanctions, since most states take boot camp volunteers directly from the prison population and these are offenders who would otherwise be serving a longer sentence. In some jurisdictions, judges may sentence offenders directly to boot camps, which means that net widening may be more apparent. For instance, sentencing offenders who would have otherwise received probation or another less severe sanction to boot camp will not result in prison bed or cost savings. A boot camp program can produce bed-savings or reduce prison crowding if it draws participants who would otherwise be incarcerated, offers significant reductions in prison terms in exchange for boot camp participation, minimizes the number of dropouts and returns to prison, and is adequately large (Parent, 1996). Presently, dropout rates are probably too high and most boot camps are not large enough to make a dent in the overcrowding problem.

Cost Effectiveness

Boot camp programs are still too small to see significant cost savings. According to MacKenzie and Souryal (1994), boot camp programs have the potential to reduce costs if they are large enough, target offenders who would otherwise serve longer sentences, and ensure that enough participants do not return to prison for a new arrest. While many states fail to meet these caveats, some, including New York and Louisiana, may not.

New York's program is the largest in the country and is a back-end program. Evaluations suggest it does result in some cost savings, at least in the short term (New York State Department of Correctional Services & Division of Parole, 1998). The research reported average savings of 11.7 months of prison time for each Shock graduate. For every 100 Shock inmates, the state has estimated savings of $2.55 million and between 1987 and October 1997 these savings amounted to $458.6 million. This research did not take into account the cost of Aftershock (the aftercare component). To see any significant savings, as MacKenzie and Souryal (1994) suggest, an important characteristic of cost effective programs is a low rate of return to prison. To its benefit, New York has consistently found the same or lower rates of return to prison for Shock graduates compared to prison inmates who were eligible for Shock placement. However, the research did not assess cost savings when including participants who did not complete Shock and who returned to prison. The findings do suggest that the boot camp programs in New York do reduce prison stays for a small proportion of inmates and do result in some initial cost savings, at least for those who graduated the program.

Behavioral Change/Treatment Effectiveness

The multi-site evaluation of boot camps previously discussed (See MacKenzie & Brame, 1995; MacKenzie & Souryal, 1994) assessed participants' attitude change in boot camp programs and their positive adjustment to the community upon release. Results showed that many boot camp participants consider the experience a positive and helpful one, despite its rigors, and many individuals report rehabilitative gains. While many offenders deem the experience a positive one, these feelings do not guarantee that they will be able to make it in the community. One of the goals of boot camp programs is to reform offenders. The tough and demanding experience and the educational and treatment components are intended to address problems that make participants at risk for future offending. As to the extent to which graduates of boot camp programs experienced a positive adjustment to community life upon completion, findings indicated that graduates of boot camps did not adjust more positively than boot camp failures, inmates released to parole, or probationers. Boot camp graduates were no more successful in terms of employment stability, education, or residential and financial stability. That is, the incarceration phase of boot camp programs had little, if any impact on behavioral change or community adjustment. This and other research suggests that the militaristic environment alone is not enough, but strong aftercare programs may play a crucial role in helping offenders make a successful transition from boot camp back to the community, and that this in turn, may lead to reduced recidivism. As a result of research, many jurisdictions have begun to bolster this post-release component of the boot camp program.

SUMMARY

Boot camp programs are arguably the toughest intermediate sanctions that currently exist. They are the most popular form of shock incarceration, requiring a brief but intense and physically demanding period of confinement. Boot camp programs usually target younger and nonviolent offenders in order to reduce prison and jail crowding and recidivism. Most programs are designed as back-end alternatives to incarceration and draw participants from inmates in prisons in order to cut prison time for participants who successfully complete the boot camp incarceration. Boot camps that operate as front-end diversions from incarceration get participants directly from the courts. Probation and parole violators may also be sent to boot camp programs. Newer boot camp models have begun a trend toward treatment programming, although the military-style activities of physical activity, drill, and ceremony are still emphasized. Additionally, community supervision following the boot camp phase (aftercare) has become a central component of boot camps nationwide.

As to the debate about boot camps, advocates support the strict and militaristic atmosphere because it is assumed that these characteristics instill respect, responsibility, and positive growth. Opponents have claimed that the failure of boot camps to consistently lead to a reduction in recidivism is due to the focus on a military-style and punitive environment and that what is needed is a dedication to a therapeutic foundation. Although boot camps are very popular, the programs that currently exist are small in number and probably have little overall impact on prison crowding and correctional costs. Results of research show that many boot camps have failed to meet the goal of reducing recidivism, although treatment programming during the boot camp phase and through aftercare appears to have a positive effect. Despite the mixed results as to their effectiveness, boot camps remain very popular. It is easy to predict the continued expansion of boot camp programs because of their widespread public and political appeal to get tough with criminal offenders.

 **CHAPTER 5**

Day Reporting Centers

BACKGROUND

Day reporting centers are known by various names: Alternative to Incarceration Programs (ATIs) in New York City, Day Reporting and Day Resource Centers in Texas, Day/Night Reporting Centers in Utah, as well as Day Centers, Day Treatment, and Day Reporting Programs in other states. The day reporting center (DRC) combines high levels of controls over offenders to meet public safety needs with the intensive delivery of services to address rehabilitation needs. It is a highly structured non-residential program requiring frequent reporting to a specific location (e.g., the center) on a routine and prearranged basis, usually daily or in the evenings, where participants engage in activities such as substance abuse treatment, counseling, educational and vocational training, and employment services.

The day reporting concept originated in England in the 1970s. Day centers, as they were originally termed and now referred to as probation centers, are used primarily as a front-end diversion from incarceration for young, male, property offenders with prior terms of incarceration and employment problems (Mair, 1995). By 1985, there were more than 80 centers throughout England and Wales.

The first day reporting center in the United States was developed in Hampden County, Massachusetts, in 1986 to address the problem of prison crowding (Larivee & O'Leary, 1990; Larivee, 1995; McDevitt &

Miliano, 1992). Although officials there had a variety of existing intermediate sanctions to work with, such as home confinement and restitution, it was decided that a new sanction would be devised based on three potential strengths of the British day reporting concept:

(1) Day centers offer a unique locus. A single site could offer supervision and program services and serve as the broker for structured community sanctions and human service activities. Community service work, restitution programs, home confinement, victim/offender reconciliation, substance abuse services, and other activities could be coordinated from a central location.

(2) The centers offer structure appropriate to a number of correctional populations. The needs of probationers, parolees, and inmates were similar and included employment, substance abuse treatment, and education. Day reporting centers could be tailored to probation and parole and could meet the needs of each of their populations.

(3) The supervision, structure, surveillance, and support mechanisms used by the British as part of the day reporting center include restitution, intensive supervision, and home confinement, which are also used in the United States.

The Hampden County Day Reporting Center is publicly operated and draws participants from state prisons. It is different from the British model in that it was designed as a back-end diversion from incarceration. Eligible prisoners serving relatively short prison terms agree to a contract outlining terms of supervision in the Center, including treatment and educational programming. Participants attend the program while living in the community for up to 60 days before the completion of their sentences or their release on parole. They report in person daily, provide written plans for their activities each day, report by telephone when appropriate, submit to drug testing and to random checks of their whereabouts while not at the Center, comply with curfew in the evenings, and agree to electronic monitoring. They also make restitution or perform community service. The Center provides a variety of treatments and services in-house, such as substance abuse therapy, family and group counseling, education and vocational training, and assistance with locating employment. Participation requires 50–80 participant-staff contacts weekly and mandatory participation in a 21–day substance abuse program. Over the first two years of the program, 280 mostly male inmates entered the DRC.

Following the lead of Massachusetts, Connecticut opened the second DRC the same year (Parent, 1990) and other states developed centers throughout the late 1980s and 1990s. Unfortunately, no published literature pinpoints the number of offenders who participate in day reporting centers throughout the country or the number of centers in operation. This is due in part to the involvement of various agencies (jails, probation, and private agencies for example) overseeing day reporting centers and the lack of centralized data collection. Based upon the few surveys conducted, it is clear that the day reporting concept is becoming increasingly popular. For example, a 1989 National Institute of Justice survey located 22 day reporting centers in eight states (Parent, 1990). The same survey conducted five years later identified at least 114 in 22 states (Parent, Byrne, et al., 1995). Some centers are quite small, serving fewer than 14 participants, while others are much larger. The national average is about 85 participants at any one time.

According to Parent and Corbett (1996), two-thirds of the day reporting centers developed before 1992 were privately run. Today, day reporting centers also operate through a variety of public agencies, including probation, jail, prison, court, and parole systems. As to the use of day reporting for jail inmates, a Bureau of Justice Statistic report (Harrison & Karberg, 2003) shows that 1,283 persons were participating in day reporting centers while supervised by jails in 1995. That number more than doubled in 2000 and by 2002, more than 5,000 persons were participating in day reporting centers while under jail supervision. As to parole, a survey by the Criminal Justice Institute (Camp & Camp, 2000) showed 20,650 parolees across the nation were placed in day reporting centers as a diversion from incarceration in 1999. States with the highest numbers of participants were New Jersey (1,701), New York (1,658), Virginia (1,418), and Washington (1,000).

The goals of day reporting centers are varied (Parent, 1995; Parent, Byrne, et al., 1995; Marciniak, 1999). Most centers were established to reduce crowding in prisons and jails. A primary focus is on the rehabilitation of offenders, evident through the emphasis on treatment and services available to participants. Punishment appears to be a much less important goal. Other goals are to protect the public through strategies of incapacitation and control, build political support, and provide a cost effective criminal sanction. Programs usually seek to fulfill multiple goals. For example, the Harris County, Texas, day reporting program is used for offenders undergoing probation revocation hearings for which a jail or prison sanction is likely and also for offenders coming out of residential community-correctional programs (such as drug treatment programs and boot camps). So it serves as a punishment for some participants and as transitional aftercare for others.

TARGET POPULATIONS

Day reporting centers are arguably the most diverse intermediate sanctions program, particularly with respect to the types of offenders who participate. Depending on the programmatic design of the DRC and its goals and objectives, different types of offenders would be targeted for participation. Some centers are geared to high risk and felony offenders and others to misdemeanants. Programs can be gender-specific and many specialize in the treatment of substance abusers. It appears that the most serious and high-risk offenders, such as sex offenders and those with histories of violence, are excluded from participation because of the risks they pose to communities. However, not all programs exclude serious or violent offenders. In New York City, for example, certain violent offenders are eligible for participation, as are theft and drug offenders. In fact, one program (STEPS to End Family Violence) selects only female offenders who have committed a violent offense against their abusers and who are likely to receive prison terms upon conviction (Young, Porter, & Caputo, 1998). Eligibility criteria for day reporting centers vary by program and are usually based upon the offense for which a person is charged or convicted, gender, age, legal status, treatment needs, and prior criminal record (Diggs & Pieper, 1994). Figure 5.1 illustrates this diversity among day reporting centers geared toward women. As the figure shows, some programs target women who have substance abuse problems while others target women who have children who are at risk for crime, pregnant women, and women with sex offenses.

A simple method for understanding the diversity among day reporting centers is to consider the legal status of offenders who are targeted for participation. Figure 5.2 illustrates four models in the use of day reporting centers: (1) programs that divert defendants from pretrial detention; (2)

Program Name	State	Participant Legal Status	Target Population	Clients	Program Length	Program hours per week	Programming Available at Center	Other
Female Furlough Program	IL	Pretrial release	Substance abusing detainees with $100,000 bail who do not have a history of violence or felony offenses.	100+	14 days	20+	Substance abuse; current partner abuse; other abuse; mental health; HIV; cognitive/behavioral skills; parenting/child development; gang issues; work skills/employment; education/GED; life skills/personal development; mentoring; transportation; transitional services/aftercare	
Female Offender Day Reporting Program	IN	Pre-release or Post-custody	Non-violent felons	25-49	12 months	20+	Substance abuse; mental health; cognitive/behavioral skills; parenting/child development; work skills/employment; education/GED; life skills/personal development; transportation; transitional services/aftercare	Home detention; electronic monitoring
Rebound	MN	Probation	Women with at-risk children and chemical issues	25-49	18 months	4-10	Crime victim reconciliation; current partner abuse; other abuse; mental health; HIV; cognitive/behavioral skills; parenting/child development; child care/daycare; children's services; life skills/personal development; Mentoring; transportation; transitional services/aftercare	Restitution
Project Premie	CA	Probation Pre-release or post-custody	Pregnant women who have children 5 years and younger and who have drug/alcohol abuse	9 or fewer	12 months	4-10	Substance abuse; current partner abuse; other abuse; medical services; HIV; cognitive/behavioral skills; parenting/child development; child care/daycare; life skills/personal development; mentoring; transportation; transitional services/aftercare	
Women's Track at Community Corrections Centers	MA	Probation	Non-violent substance abusers; women involved in petty larceny/welfare fraud, prostitutes, HIV-positive women, and intensive supervision offenders	10-24	N/A	N/A	Substance abuse; other abuse; HIV; child care/daycare; work skills/employment; education/GED; life skills/personal development; transportation; transitional services/aftercare; housing	Home detention; electronic monitoring
Sex Offender Program Services	WI	Probation Pre-release or post-custody	Sex offenders; women with history of criminal and/or deviant sexual behavior	10-24	6 months	N/A	Cognitive/behavioral skills; life skills/personal development; transitional services/aftercare	

Source: Harding, 2000

Figure 5.1. Six Day Reporting Programs for Women

programs that divert offenders from incarceration at the front-end; (3) programs that enhance probation and parole supervision; and (4) programs that provide early release from jail and prison.

DRC MODEL 1	DRC MODEL 2	DRC MODEL 3	DRC MODEL 4
Day reporting center is a pretrial release option; an alternative to pretrial detention	Day reporting center is a front-end diversion from incarceration	Day reporting center is a probation/parole enhancement tool	Day reporting center is a back-end diversion from incarceration, an early release mechanism

Figure 5.2. Four Common Models for Day Reporting Centers

Day Reporting Centers as Pretrial Release Mechanisms

Day reporting centers are popularly being used as an option for pretrial release. Pretrial release refers to the temporary release from custody of a criminal defendant. When used in this way, defendants who cannot afford bail and who do not pose significant risks to the community are diverted from detention and released temporarily back into the community under the conditions that they participate in a DRC and return to court when scheduled. One benefit of the pretrial release day reporting center is to allow a criminal defendant the opportunity to remain in the community engaged in work, family, and other responsibilities while awaiting the outcome of his or her case.

One such program operates in Cook County, Illinois, through the Sheriff's Office (McBride & VanderWaal, 1997; Martin, Olson, & Lurigio, 2000). The Cook County Day Reporting Center (CCDRC) was developed in 1992. CCDRC is one of various alternatives to pretrial detention for male defendants developed in response to crowding in the local jail. Participants are selected from among defendants in the Electronic Monitoring Program, which is a pretrial release mechanism for non-violent offenders who do not pose threats to the community and who are ordered to home confinement. CCDRC was developed to increase court-appearance rates, reduce pretrial criminal activity, and initiate rehabilitation. By 1996 the average daily population was more than 400 participants, quite large compared to other day reporting programs. CCDRC provides its services to a population of young adults who have little education and who are typically unemployed, repeat offenders, and those charged with felony offenses related to substance abuse. Participants must report to the CCDRC Monday through Friday from 8:45 a.m. to 8:00 p.m., except for approved activities such as court appearances and job interviews. Lectures, support groups, counseling, and computer lab activities are offered daily. Participants are assessed as to their treatment needs, assigned to a "service track," and begin substance abuse treatment and drug testing. Most participants are assigned to "Track A" in which resistance, personal control, and responsibility are emphasized. "Track B" focuses on treatment. The third most popular track provides drug treatment during the evening hours. Participants generally complete successfully and do so when their criminal processing has been completed through conviction or dismissal. More than 10,000 defendants have entered the program since 1992 and evaluations show that participants have low rearrest rates, high court appearance rates, and decreases in drug use (all goals of the program).

Front-End Day Reporting Centers

Day reporting centers are also designed as alternatives to jail and prison to reduce crowding and correctional costs and provide rehabilitation services to offenders. Front-end centers target misdemeanor and felony offenders who would otherwise be given jail or prison terms.

Over the last several decades, New York City has developed a network of front-end day reporting centers. The Vera Institute of Justice has profiled and evaluated nine of these programs, which are privately operated and target various subgroups of offenders charged with rather serious felony offenses (usually robbery and drugs) and who face incarceration (See Young, Porter, & Caputo, 1998; Kramer & Porter, 2000; Porter, Lee, & Lutz, 2002). Two centers are geared toward youth, four target substance abusers, two serve women, and one is used for a general population of adult felony offenders. In total, the programs serve upwards of 1250 participants annually. Three of these centers are highlighted in Figure 5.3.

Participants are selected from the criminal courts using a methodology designed to increase the likelihood that only jail- and prison-bound offenders are chosen. Upon intake, participants' treatment needs are evaluated and these needs have included treatment for substance abuse, employment, education, as well as psychiatric and medical problems. The centers offer a similar set of services to meet these needs. Participants progress through three phases each lasting from two to six months. Movement from one phase to the next is based in part on progress in treatment. Phase I is the most highly structured and participants spend most of their time on-site. Phase II is dedicated to delivery of services. On average, participants have completed nine group-counseling sessions and 90 minutes of individual counseling weekly. In Phase III participants are often off-site and engaged in employment and education. In this last phase of the program, those who are nearing the end of their sentences help to orient newly entering participants. Participants who successfully complete may be sentenced to regular probation. The evaluation has suggested that the centers are probably operating as true alternatives to incarceration and therefore have the potential of achieving cost savings.

Back-End Day Reporting Centers

Day reporting centers are also used to replace jail or prison incarceration at the back end and represent early release mechanisms to assist in inmate transition back into the community and reduce jail and prison populations. Depending on the needs of correctional systems, some centers draw participants from jails while other centers select participants who are nearing the end of their prison terms.

A program targeting inmates is Arizona's Maricopa County Day Reporting Center (Jones & Lacey, 1999). It incorporates a strategy designed to help offenders who have been incarcerated effectively reintegrate into communities. The target population is limited to DWI felony offenders who have pleaded down to a misdemeanor and who are serving jail terms. Eligible offenders must also be motivated to change negative behavior, have no history of violence or sex offending, and have a verified residence. Participants who are selected are "furloughed" from jail and placed on probation while participating in the day reporting center. The center emphasizes strict supervision in the form of daily contacts, home confinement, drug and alcohol tests, as well as on-site and off-site (around the clock) surveillance by officer teams. Participants who commit technical violations that do not call for their removal from the program may be given more stringent conditions, increased surveillance, community service hours, and a temporary return to custody. Participants engage in hour-by-hour activities and programming at the center and in the community during the day. Employment in the community is mandatory; participants are given up to 10 days to gain employment before they are returned to jail. Assessment of participants' treatment needs is an ongoing process. The program is divided into three phases: Orientation, Program, and Transition. Orientation is the first phase lasting two weeks. In this phase, participants are introduced to the program and its rules and must report five days each week. The Program phase is six to eight weeks in duration and involves the main programming for treatment. Participants enter the Transition phase during their final two weeks in the center and complete successfully when they have served the equivalence of their original jail term. Participants who complete are then phased into an intensive supervision program.

Chicago's Safer Foundation, established in 1972, provides a variety of services related to employment for released inmates (Finn, 1998). In fact, it is the largest provider of employment services in the United States for exoffenders. The Safer Foundation is different from many day reporting programs in that its programming begins while inmates are still incarcerated. During that stage of programming, Safer Foundation Staff offers employment and educational readiness programming for inmates at the Cook County Jail. The program also relies on small group and peer-led programs designed to help released inmates overcome the barriers they face when making the transition back into community living. "Lifeguards," or case managers, help participants in their transition for up to one year after release.

Day Reporting Centers as Probation and Parole Enhancement Mechanisms

Day reporting centers are also used as a means to enhance the regular supervision of offenders on probation and parole. The 1994 national survey of day reporting centers found that 87% of centers enroll offenders sentenced to probation (Parent, Byrne, et al., 1995). When used in this way probation or parole is "enhanced" with the additional requirement of participation in a day reporting center. Enhancement models are used for (1) offenders newly placed on probation and parole who appear to need additional supervision, control, and treatment than regular supervision provides; and (2) offenders who violate the conditions of probation and parole and who do not require incarceration. In Virginia, for instance, the Fairfax Day Reporting Center is staffed by probation and parole officers and is used as a non-custodial punishment for probationers and parolees who have committed a technical violation (Orchowsky, Lucas, & Bogle, 1995).

The Utah Day Reporting Center serves male and female probationers and parolees who are in need of additional structure and assistance beyond routine probation and parole (Bureau of Justice Assistance, 2000). It is designed specifically for high-risk and high-need offenders who have drug and alcohol problems and who have either committed a new offense or who have a technical violation. The center offers probationers and parolees educational opportunities, means to develop employment skills, psycho-educational programming, substance abuse treatment, intensive mental health therapy, domestic violence groups, groups dealing with sexual orientation, increased contact with staff, and a daily structure. These services are crafted to the treatment needs of each participant. The center is accessible to participants six days a week and transportation is provided for those participants who reside in halfway houses.

PROGRAM CHARACTERISTICS

Day reporting centers are nonresidential programs where defendants, convicted offenders, jail or prison inmates, and probationers and parolees report on a prearranged basis, often daily or nightly for treatment and services. Depending on their legal status, when participants successfully complete the programs they may return to court for processing, be placed on probation or parole, or exit the criminal justice system. Day reporting centers differ from one another in ways such as size, participants, staff expertise, programming, target populations, and locations, but they share some common characteristics (Parent, Byrne, et al., 1995):

- The center offers a variety of treatments and services on-site and through referrals;
- Participants progress through the center in phases of supervision;
- Participants spend about five months in the centers;
- Participants usually must report to the center in person about five times per week;

- Centers are open and accessible to participants about 54 hours per week;
- Telephone, home visit, and other contacts are required;
- Participants must abide by a curfew and submit to drug testing;
- Most centers are run by public criminal justice agencies;
- The participant-to-staff ratio is 7:1;
- Centers admit slightly more than 200 participants annually and serve fewer than 85 participants at one time;
- Most centers recruit participants from more than one source (such as from jails and probation);
- Most participants come from probation and parole populations;
- Offenders with violent histories and weapons offenses are normally excluded from eligibility.

Specialized and Comprehensive Day Reporting Centers

The programming in day reporting centers can be specialized and comprehensive. Some centers offer programming carefully designed to meet the treatment needs of special populations, such as for substance abusers or for domestic violence offenders. Other centers offer general types of treatments thought to be appropriate for most offenders. The focus of the center depends on resources, staffing, treatment and service providers in the community, and the target population served.

Figure 5.3 describes three centers operated by a private agency in New York City (Freedom, Flametree, and DAMAS). Each differs in the target population served and the type of programming offered. Freedom is a comprehensive program. Its target population includes men and women charged with felony offenses. Freedom does not admit substance abusers and those with serious mental health issues, because it is designed as a general treatment program. Treatment includes group counseling, educational and vocational programming, and leisure activities. Flametree is a DRC targeting men and women who have substance abuse problems. It specializes in the treatment of substance abuse and recovery. In addition to substance abuse treatment, the program also offers a core set of services very similar to the services provided in the comprehensive type of day reporting centers. This is characteristic of many specialized programs. Specialized centers differ from the comprehensive centers in that the treatment environment is geared specifically toward a particular group (substance abusers in this case). The third center listed in the figure is a program designed for women who would otherwise be incarcerated for at least one year in prison. DAMAS (Daughters and Mothers Alternative to Incarceration Service) assists women in the transition from criminal activity to positive and productive lifestyles by addressing the physical, emotional, psychological, and psychosocial services specific to women involved in the criminal justice system. Participants are exposed to programming designed to help them develop practical life skills and strategies for healthy lifestyles, programming in education, HIV education and support groups, career development, and recreation.

A Focus on Treatments and Services

A distinguishing characteristic of day reporting centers is the variety of treatments and services provided to participants. One of the most common goals of day reporting centers is the rehabilitation of offenders. To that end, programs offer job training and placement services, group counseling, basic adult education and GED; drug treatment; life skills training; health skills training; anger and stress management; individual counseling; transitional housing; and recreation. Substance abuse counseling is considered a foundation of most programs (Roy, 2002). Depending on the type of center and its resources, treatments, services, and activities are located primarily in-house (e.g. at the center) or in-house and through referral to other community agencies. Some programs also offer monetary relief for participants for such necessities as housing, food, transportation, lunches, and money for emergencies, rent, and medication (Young, Porter, & Caputo, 1998).

Figure 5.4 illustrates treatments and services provided by day reporting centers and the location of the treatment and service. Nearly all of the 55 centers included in this 1994 national survey by the National Institute of Justice offer employment-related services, such as job-seeking skills and job placement. Drug abuse education and treatment are quite common. Most of the services are provided in-house by day reporting staff. Core services are often adjusted and individualized to meet the specific needs of participants. The programs typically incorporate group and individual counseling and this is characteristic of other programs. In New York City, most of the programming occurs in small groups, classes, and larger group meetings (Young, Porter, & Caputo, 1998).

Freedom	Flametree	DAMAS
A Front-End Prison Diversion for the General Population of Felony Offenders	A Front-End Prison Diversion for Felony Offenders who are Substance Users	A Front-End Prison Diversion for Women Felony Offenders
Program Description Freedom is a comprehensive day reporting program. Its target population includes men and women charged with felony offenses who are facing at least a year in prison. The program excludes those with significant drug treatment and mental health needs. Participants attend the program lieu of serving prison terms. Offenders who are selected receive a conditional discharge. A conditional discharge is a criminal sanction signifying conviction, and requires the offender to comply with conditions of the placement into the program. All Fortune staff interacting with participants are former offenders or in recovery from substance abuse.	**Program Description** Flametree targets men and women with substance abuse problems. Individuals who are facing sentences of a year or more are referred to Flametree by Fortune's court advocacy unit. The program is designed to promote substance abuse recovery. Eligible defendants are placed in Flametree for 6-12 months with a conditional discharge.	**Program Description** DAMAS – Daughters and Mothers ATI Service – is a female specific alternative to incarceration program for defendants who would be incarcerated for at least a year in prison. It addresses the needs of women and provides a supportive and relational context. The program aims to assist women in making the transition from criminal activity to positive and productive lifestyles by addressing the physical, emotional, psychological, and psychosocial services specific to women involved in the criminal justice system. Staff are former offenders or in recovery from substance abuse.
Three Phase Program Offenders usually spend 6-12 months in the program. The program is structured according to three phases in which restrictions and requirements are greatest at Phase One. At least 85% attendance is required to advance in each phase. Participants must develop a schedule and treatment plan at the start. Participants may be removed for a new arrest or a technical violation and be sent to prison or to a more restrictive placement.	**Core Services** The program offers a core of services, including drug treatment and counseling, life skills, education, job training, and job placement. Participants progress through three phases of treatment and supervision. Requirements are the most restrictive and demanding at Phase One and least restrictive and demanding at Phase Three. At least 85% attendance is required to advance in each phase. Participants develop a schedule that includes individual counseling, general activities such as house meetings and recreation, and group counseling and classes. Participants remain at the program or engage in neighborhood services during the day. The program aims to promote self recovery and emphasizes building a sense of self-worth. Personal responsibility and accountability are emphasized.	**Programming through Phases** This 6-12 month program involves three phases. Phase I is highly structured and involves orientation to the program. In Phase II, participants are trained to develop practical life skills and coping strategies for healthy lifestyles. Participants may become leaders during In Phase III, when they engage in additional community work. They become peer counselors, and help to orient new participants. Participants have access to programming in education, including Basic Adult Literacy, ESL, and GED, as well as HIV education and support groups, career development, and recreation.
Program Requirements In addition to reporting to the program, participants must abide by conditions including: ❑ Engage in 25 hours each week of program activity ❑ Attend on-site programming for 35 hours each week ❑ Engage in at least 10 hours each week of program activity if employed or involved in an educational or vocational program ❑ Participating in treatment to develop educational and vocational skills consistent with legitimate employment ❑ Participate in individual counseling, recreation activities, group counseling, house meetings. ❑ Submitting to random urinalysis	**Program Requirements** Participants must meet the following conditions: ❑ Attend individual counseling weekly and as needed ❑ Mandatory drug testing ❑ Maintain employment or school attendance ❑ Attend on-site programming for 35 hours each week ❑ Participate in treatment, particularly all substance abuse treatment and programming ❑ Attend groups two or three times daily and attend individual counseling weekly	**Program Requirements** In addition to having to report daily or as scheduled, participants must abide by the following conditions: ❑ Attend groups two or three times daily and attend individual counseling weekly and as needed ❑ Mandatory drug testing ❑ Take part in educational or vocational training ❑ Attend on-site programming for 35 hours each week ❑ Participate in treatment programming, particularly related to substance abuse, employment, and counseling

Sources: The Fortune Society, n.d.; Young et al., 1998

Figure 5.3. Fortune Society (NYC) Day Reporting Programs

Type of Treatment	Percent of DRCs Proving Treatment	Treatment is Delivered at DRC	Treatment is Delivered through Referral	Treatment is Delivered at DRC and through Referral
Job seeking skills	98%	79%	13%	8%
Drug abuse education	96%	69%	17%	14%
Group counseling	96%	80%	12%	8%
Job placement services	93%	62%	34%	4%
Education	93%	55%	31%	14%
Drug Treatment	92%	31%	54%	15%
Life skills training	92%	92%	6%	2%
Individual counseling	89%	72%	17%	11%
Transitional housing	63%	13%	81%	6%
Recreation and leisure	60%	74%	16%	19%

Source: Parent, Byrne, et al.,1995

Figure 5.4. Programming in 55 Day Reporting Centers

Phases of Supervision and Treatment

Phased treatment and supervision is a central component of most day reporting centers (Parent, Byrne, et al., 1995). The logic behind phased (or staged) programming is to provide a structure and flow to the day reporting experience. Most centers that incorporate phased treatment use a three-phase model. In the initial phase, participants are usually oriented to the program and assessed for treatment and services so that case managers may craft the variety of programming to meet the specific needs of each participant. Attendance and surveillance are most stringent at this phase. The next phase or set of phases is geared to the delivery of treatment and services for participants. The final phase is usually geared to the transition of participants out of the program and may include an aftercare component. Attendance and other reporting as well as surveillance and control should be less stringent at the final phase.

The duration of each phase depends on the design of the DRC. According to research by the Vera Institute of Justice (Young, Porter, & Caputo, 1998), participants of the felony front-end centers must spend between two to six months in the three phases of those centers; however, movement through the phases is marked by participant progress. This means that participants may be "held back" from moving into the next phase if they violate rules or if their treatment progress is not in line with staff expectations.

The total length of time a participant spends in a day reporting program also varies. Research by Parent (1990) found that duration can range from short stays of about 40 days to stays of six months or longer. Programs that incorporate phases of supervision and treatment are longer than single-phase programs. Single-phase centers are typically 154 days in duration, while programs with multiple phases are 173 days on average (Parent, Byrne, et al., 1995). Duration in a day reporting program is also influenced by a participant's progress through phases. When a participant is required to repeat a phase of the program, his or her total duration in the DRC is extended. Additionally, duration of participation also depends on the legal status of participants. The duration of participation for defendants diverted from detention into pretrial release centers depends on such factors as the ability of a defendant to post bond and the progress of a defendant's case through the courts. The duration of participation for an offender involved in a front-end, enhancement, or back-end program is more predictable and depends on sentencing and release conditions.

Regular Attendance is Required

Day reporting centers require participants to report in person and over the telephone regularly as a condition of supervision. The amount of contact between participants and staff in day reporting centers is greater than regular community supervision, such as probation and parole (Craddock, 2000). The attendance requirements for day reporting programs depend on such factors as the legal status of the offender and the length of his or her sentence (McEwen, 1995). The 1994 national survey found that on average, participants are required to be on-site 18 hours weekly during the most intensive phases. Participants who are employed or actively engaged in job searches may spend less time at the centers (Parent, Byrne, et al., 1995). Most of the privately operated programs for adult felony offenders in New York City require participants to attend the centers for up to 35 hours each week (Young, Porter, & Caputo, 1998). Some programs require daily daytime attendance, while others allow participants flexibility in determining a schedule and permit evening reporting. This is especially helpful to participants with employment, educational, and other responsibilities. Attendance requirements may be most intensive at the initial stages of participation in day reporting centers and become gradually less intensive.

In two Wisconsin centers, for example, participants must attend every weekday for five hours during the initial phase, three days weekly for five hours during the second phase, and then two days per week at the final phase (Craddock, 2000).

Various Surveillance and Control Mechanisms

Surveillance and control mechanisms are ways to protect the community from crimes that participants of day reporting centers may commit while they are engaged in center activities and also when they are not attending center programming and activities. These mechanisms restrict opportunities to commit new crimes and technical violations and increase the likelihood of detection when participants do not comply with program rules. Surveillance and control are achieved through various means. Every program uses a set of rules and regulations with which participants agree to comply upon entry into the program. These rules and regulations include requirements for attendance, submission of daily itineraries to staff, adherence to curfews, random drug tests, attending school or work, meeting with counselors or case workers, and participating in treatment (Roy, 2002). Participants may also be required to perform community service and make restitution to victims.

Daily Itineraries

The daily itineraries are schedules, outlining exactly where the participant will be during each hour and the activity in which he or she will be engaged. They are developed by the participant with the help of staff members and are organized around the treatment plan of the participant. Itineraries should help participants with planning and keeping to a schedule, assist in the treatment process by outlining the targeted treatments, services, and activities, and provide a mechanism for staff to keep track of participants and their compliance with the schedule. If staff want to check on the whereabouts of a participant, the itineraries indicate where a person is, whether at the center engaged in treatment or off-site at school or work, and how they can be contacted.

Curfews

Curfews limit opportunities for participants to commit technical violations and new crimes by restricting their movements while they are not directly engaged in center programming. The national survey of DRCs (Parent, Byrne, et al., 1995) found that just more than half of the 54 centers responding to the survey incorporate a curfew requirement. Staff of day reporting centers may use telephone contacts, electronic monitoring devises, and random home visits to ensure that participants are complying with curfew orders.

On-Site and Off-Site Surveillance

On-site surveillance and off-site surveillance are two main types of surveillance used for monitoring participants' compliance with attendance, itineraries, drug tests, curfews, and participation in treatment, education, and work (Parent & Corbett, 1996). Some day reporting centers monitor participants' whereabouts, activities, and compliance when they are on-site only or engaged in day reporting activities. This is the case in New York City. Other centers also monitor participants after program hours and even around the clock using electronic monitoring, home and field visits, and telephone calls to work locations and residences. The 1995 National Institute of Justice survey found that 60% of DRCs monitor participants in the community during the day, evenings, or both and that participants are subject to monitoring for about 67 hours per week (Parent, Byrne, et al., 1995).

Officials and agencies administering day reporting centers rely on an assortment of means to deal with noncompliance on the part of participants. Participants who fail to comply with rules and regulations (commit technical violations), who relapse, or who commit new crimes may be reprimanded when the infraction is minor and terminated from the program and returned to custody when the infraction is repeated or serious. Other means include: increasing controls over participants; requiring additional conditions, such as community service hours; moving a participant to an earlier phase of the program; and requiring a longer period of participation.

Administration and Location

Day reporting centers are operated by public and private agencies. The private centers usually contract with counties or states to provide services to offenders. Compared to publicly operated centers, privately run centers tend to offer more treatment and services and are open and accessible to participants for a greater number of days and hours per week (Parent, Byrne, et al., 1995).

The location of day reporting centers can vary. Some day reporting centers are stand-alone programs that operate out of a facility in the community while others operate on the grounds of existing correctional centers and in conjunction with other correctional programs, such as halfway houses and probation departments. Day reporting centers are non-residential programs, but in some cases participants are also participating in halfway houses, which are residential facilities. For example, the Orange County, Florida, day reporting center operates in a jail work release center and in conjunction with work release participants (Diggs & Pieper, 1994).

RESEARCH ON DAY REPORTING CENTERS

Program Completion

Program completion refers to the percentage of participants who successfully complete the day reporting center program. Participants may fail to complete when they commit a technical violation or a new crime. Research findings vary from 14% to 85% successful completion (Roy, 2002). The participant population appears to be a key factor in completion rates. For example, research on the Hampden County, Massachusetts, pretrial release center, a program probably serving relatively low-risk offenders, showed a 79% completion rate, whereas a North Carolina program, which serves a more serious and prison bound population, showed a 14% rate (Craddock, 2000). Similarly, the Cook County day reporting program designed as a pretrial release mechanism reported a 63% successful completion rate (Martin, Olson, & Lurigio, 2000) and the center was quite effective at preventing the commission of new crimes during participation (McBride & VanderWaal, 1997). New York City programs geared to felons as an alternative to incarceration show a recent completion rate of 55% (Kramer & Porter, 2000). It is difficult, therefore, to make general statements as to the effectiveness of day reporting centers in this way given the diversity in programming and the different target populations. To the benefit of programs, it does appear that most of the violations and terminations appear to be technical rather than a result of the commission of new crimes.

Research has also identified participant and program factors associated with successful completion of day reporting centers. As to participant characteristics, research of a pretrial day reporting program in Vigo County, Indiana, showed felons, participants 40 years of age or younger, unmarried participants, and those with long histories of substance abuse were least likely to complete (Roy, 2002). The Vera Institute also reports that substance abusers failed more frequently (Kramer & Porter, 2000). Recent research of a North Carolina program for prison-bound offenders found that employment and higher education are associated with successful completion (Marciniak, 1999). As to program factors associated with completion, Parent and colleagues (1995) identified four factors correlated with increased technical violations from a study of 114 programs: (1) privately run programs; (2) a higher level of services provided; (3) a high level of staff turnover; and (4) no curfew policy.

Recidivism

In the absence of long-term and comprehensive research of day reporting centers, it is unclear as to the impact of participation in day reporting centers on reoffending. Albeit limited, several studies have been conducted with promising results. A National Institute of Justice study compared the rearrest rates of offenders who completed day reporting centers with the rates for those who were terminated. It found that participants who completed were rearrested at low rates (less than 20%) and at significantly lower rates compared to those who failed to complete (Craddock, 2000). The same research compared participants in the day reporting centersm that were designed as probation enhancements, with offenders on regular probation and found no difference in rates. Research of the Cook County Day Reporting Center program found that participation in the program reduced the likelihood of rearrest (Martin, Olson, & Lurigio, 2000). And a study of Utah's program showed a recidivism rate of 33% (Bureau of Justice Assistance, 2000). Recent research by the Vera Institute on New York City's network of day reporting programs found no difference in rates of reoffending between participants and a comparison group (Porter, Lee, & Lutz, 2002). As discussed in earlier sections of this book, research on treatment programs generally has found that providing treatment and services to offenders (which is the hallmark of day reporting centers) is more effective at reducing reoffending than providing supervision without treatment.

Net Widening

Day reporting centers that draw participants from inmates have the greatest potential for relieving crowding in jails and prisons, since inmates are released from confinement. This is especially the case when participants complete programs and are moved to less restrictive correctional options, such as parole, or diverted out of the criminal justice system completely. The front-end programs, pretrial release programs, and probation and parole enhancement models are the most subject to net widening. Net widening may result when:

- The day reporting center designed as a front-end diversion from incarceration is comprised of offenders who are not likely to receive more restrictive sanctions, usually jail and prison;
- The day reporting center designed as a diversion from pretrial detention is comprised of defendants who are not likely to be placed in jail while their cases are being processed through the courts;
- The day reporting center designed as a probation and parole enhancement mechanism is comprised of probationers and parolees who do not pose significant risks to the community and who would otherwise be adequately supervised on regular probation and parole;
- The day reporting center designed as an early release mechanism is comprised of inmates who would otherwise be placed in a less restrictive program, such as regular parole.
- Participants of day reporting centers fail to complete programs and are placed into more restrictive alternatives, such as jail and prison.

As to evidence of net widening, the 1994 national study of day reporting programs (Parent, Byrne, et al., 1995) estimated that less than half of the offenders in the 54 programs studied were jail-bound or released early from jail. More recent research of North Carolina's program found similarly that judges sentenced some offenders to the center who were not likely to receive prison terms (Marciniak, 1999). A key to minimizing net widening is in the proper selection of participants. New York City has incorporated stringent case screening when selecting participants. The selection criteria are the product of sophisticated statistical analyses and research on jail and prison displacement (CASES, 1994a; 1994b). In that research, the Criminal Justice Agency and the Vera Institute of New York City developed statistical models to estimate the jail and prison displacement effects of hypothetical day reporting programs. The research was used to identify background factors (mostly criminal history and offense information) that predicted different jail and prison sentences. Researchers then matched these factors to criteria used by programs to estimate the average custodial "bed years" saved. According to the research, day reporting centers were estimated to save 1.3 years of prison bed space for each participant correctly selected into the program (Belenko, Winterfield, et al., 1995). Recent research of existing centers suggests the city's screening system is targeting defendants who are likely to serve jail or prison terms, since the majority of participants were detained during court processing and charged with serious crimes for which incarceration is appropriate (Young, Porter, & Caputo, 1998).

Cost Effectiveness

According to Parent and colleagues (1995), the daily cost of the day reporting centers included in the national survey averaged $35.04 per participant, while some centers cost less than $10 and others cost more than $100. Costs depend on staffing levels, services provided, and the types of surveillance used. Agencies may reduce costs by requiring participants to pay a fee for participation much like the monthly supervision fees paid by probationers and parolees. In Nashville, for example, participants of the jail diversion DRC pay $40 monthly (Crocker, 2003). Evidence of the cost effectiveness of day reporting centers is uncertain as a result of the limited empirical research on the issue. However, research comparing the cost of day reporting centers with that of confinement has shown that day reporting centers are less costly to administer. For example, the Maricopa County Day Reporting Center, which diverts offenders from jail, cost about $20 per participant compared to $37 for confinement and resulted in savings of about $17 for each offender diverted to the center (Jones & Lacey, 1999). Even though day reporting centers are less costly to operate, there is always the danger that large numbers of participants may be terminated and reprocessed through the criminal justice system, which of course would increase costs. This was the case in North Carolina where the rate of termination was high (66%) and most participants who were terminated returned to prison (Marciniak, 1999).

Behavioral Change/Treatment Effectiveness

Research has not addressed the impact of participation in day reporting centers with long-term changes in behavior and treatment effectiveness. The Vera Institute did report that participants of the day reporting programs in New York City were satisfied with the treatment and services they received and that most did reduce their drug use while they were participating (Porter, Lee, & Lutz, 2002). Research of Cook County's program also found that participants reduced their use of drugs during program participation. The Cook County center, which is a pretrial release program, has also reported improvement in court appearance rates for those who have participated in that program (Martin, Olson, & Lurigio, 2000). Especially since day reporting programs are crafted to meet the diverse needs of many different types of offenders, new research should focus on the extent to which the programming has a positive impact on the lives of participants.

SUMMARY

Day reporting centers have been referred to as more of a concept than an actual program because of the diversity in programming and the types of offenders who participate. Day reporting centers are used for defendants who cannot afford bail as an alternative to pretrial detention, for first time offenders and serious offenders as an alternative to jail and prison, for inmates as an early release program, and for higher risk probationers and parolees who require more stringent supervision. Depending on the needs of participants and their legal status, some programs stress strict supervision and include 24-hour electronic monitoring, while other programs supervise participants while they are engaged in center activities. Unique to day reporting centers is a special focus on the provision of core services on-site and through community resources, phased programming, and stringent attendance and supervision requirements. Thus day reporting centers can be crafted to provide services to a broad range of offenders and can be a quite restrictive intermediate sanction.

 **CHAPTER 6**

Home Confinement with Electronic Monitoring

Jon'a F. Meyer

BACKGROUND

Spiderman had possibly met his match; the poor super hero had no idea what his nemesis, the Jackal, had in store for him. Like a number of villains in the popular Spiderman comic series, the Jackal was a professor and an evil one at that. In a fit of sheer brilliance, the Jackal had developed a tracking device and fitted a sedated Spiderman with it (Lee, 1974). Spidey awoke to find his lower forearm encased in the fiendish bracelet. If removed, the device would explode and render Spiderman's arm useless for life. If left in place, however, it allowed the Jackal to know Spidey's whereabouts. Spiderman finally defeated the nefarious device and many scholars now attribute the birth of electronic monitoring of criminal offenders to the January 1974 issue of the comic in which Spidey and the Jackal engaged in their technologically enhanced battle.

Albuquerque-based judge Jack Love read the comic in 1977 and became convinced that the premise behind the Jackal's tracking device could work in the corrections field, enabling better monitoring of those ordered into home detention. Satisfied that the idea merited consideration, he sent a memo, a copy of the comic, and a news article about devices used to track cargo and animals to the New Mexico Department of Corrections (U.S. Congress, 1988, p. 34). Possibly because the idea of basing correctional approaches on the adventures of comic book super heroes was somehow unthinkable, the memo had no effect. When America moved ahead in the international prisons race in the early 1980s, due in part to the War on Drugs, Judge Love thought back to the Spiderman comic and the curious contraption manufactured by the Jackal (U.S. Congress, 1988, p. 34). He was also affected by the bloody Santa Fe prison riot in 1980, to which overcrowding had unfortunately contributed (Renzema, 1992, p. 44). He then asked Michael Goss, an engineer, if he could manufacture such a device and the GOSSlink electronic monitoring device was created. The GOSSlink device shared only cursory similarities to the one created by the Jackal; instead of actually tracking an offender, it could only serve as a mechanical supermonitor to ensure that the wearer stayed within a certain number of feet from a base unit that was installed in the offender's residence. Instead of blowing up if an offender attempted to remove it, the GOSSlink device, like all of its contemporary cousins, alerted authorities that the wearer had departed from the area to which he was confined. Judge Love was pleased with the device and sentenced the first offender to electronic monitoring in 1983 (Beck & Klein-Saffran, 1990; Berry, 1985, p. 3).

Though many credit Stan Lee with the invention of electronic monitoring, a similar device had actually been developed in the early 1960s and patented in 1969 by Harvard psychologist Dr. Ralph Schwitzgebel (Schwitzgebel et al., 1964; Nellis, 1991).[1] That mechanism was ahead of its time, however, and does not appear to have ever been used except in academic testing and research. Schwitzgebel's device was a behavioralist's dream as it tracked an offender's travels within certain areas, monitored body functions such as heart rate, and allowed for communication between client and human supervisor, automatically providing many reinforcements to behavior modification. The device was tested on volunteer parolees, mental health patients, and researchers before it was patented (U.S. Congress, 1988, p. 34). Despite Schwitzgebel's pioneering efforts, however, it appears that electronic monitoring became a viable corrections tool through the Spiderman-inspired efforts of Judge Love and his engineer acquaintance, in response to a significant jail overcrowding problem.

Home confinement, also called house arrest and home detention, had been in use for some time. It was used internationally, especially in South Africa during the apartheid regime (e.g., Hinds, 1999, p. 268), but it was not implemented in the United States until a 1971 program aimed to reduce the negative effects of incarceration on juveniles by sentencing them to home confinement (Renzema, 1992, p. 46). Due in part to the high staff demands to properly supervise at-home prisoners, home confinement was limited to a few small projects, serving juveniles and other special populations. Ensuring that detainees actually adhered to the conditions of their sentences meant that probation officers had to spend inordinate amounts of time checking up on their clients through random home visits or telephone calls. Since some clients refused to abide by the terms of their sentences, coming and going as they pleased or simply absconding totally, home confinement was not a practical sanction except in a few carefully selected cases.

The advent of electronic monitoring (EM), however, changed the feasibility of home confinement, making the sanction "practical and affordable" (Gowdy, 1993, p. 5). Correctional authorities could rely on electronic monitoring devices to help ensure that offenders remained in their homes when they were ordered to do so, creating what Bonnie Berry (1985) appropriately called "electronic jails."

With EM, the use of home confinement began to increase rapidly. By 1985, there were two electronic monitoring systems, the GOSSlink system and the Supervisor, a system implemented in Florida; together, the systems monitored 17 offenders (Beck & Klein-Saffran, 1990; Berry, 1985). One year later, 95 offenders were counted on EM during a survey, so one could expect 95 offenders to be on EM on a typical 1986 day; the figure increased by nearly 900% to 826 offenders a day on EM in 1987, then to 2,277 in 1988 and 6,490 in 1989 (Renzema & Skelton, 1990). The rates then hit a bit of a plateau, staying around the 6,500 mark until 1996, when the daily client count rose to 7,480; by 1998, the daily rate had risen to 10,827 (Gilliard, 1999). By 2002, 13% of offenders in community corrections programs were on electronic monitoring, an estimated 9,706 per day (Harrison & Karberg, 2003). At the same time, the use of home confinement without electronic monitoring was on a general incline. See Figure 6.1 for a graph charting the rapid growth, then stabilization in the use of electronic monitoring.

Electronic monitoring programs appear around the world, including in Australia, Canada, England and Wales, the Netherlands, New Zealand, Singapore, South Africa, Sweden, and other countries (National Law Enforcement Corrections Technology Center, 1999, p. 1; Nellis, 1991; Whitfield, 2001, pp. 74–78).

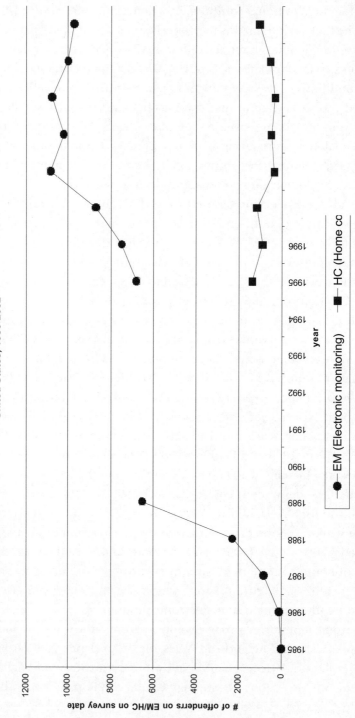

Figure 6.1: Estimated daily offenders on electronic monitoring and home confinement in the United States, 1985-2002

Source: 1985 data were obtained from Beck and Klein-Saffran (1990) and Berry (1985). 1986–1989 data were obtained from Renzema and Skelton (1990). 1995 and 2000–2002 data were obtained from Harrison and Karberg (2003). 1996–98 data were obtained from Gilliard (1999). 1999 data were obtained from Beck (2000).

THE PURPOSE OF ELECTRONIC MONITORING

Unlike the other approaches discussed in this book, electronic monitoring itself is not a sanction per se. Instead, it is a method of enforcing home confinement, curfew, or boundary avoidance. It has also been recently used in behavior modification by probation officers.

Home confinement on EM was born from the need to alleviate prison and jail overcrowding in the early 1980s. America's get-tough policies rapidly filled existing detention facilities and mandated the building of new ones. As prison and jail populations continued to soar, criminal justice decision-makers were desperate to find cheaper ways to protect communities and victims. EM allowed criminal justice policy makers to incapacitate individuals so they could not commit new predatory offenses, while avoiding the expenses and negative effects on prisoners of incarceration.

EM differs from other forms of community corrections because it is not primarily rehabilitation-oriented. Most other community corrections approaches attempt to reform or rehabilitate offenders, but EM has only recently been used for these purposes as probation officials have discovered new ways to use the surveillance technology provided by their corrections departments. Even with the new advances, the principal goal of EM is to provide a cheaper way to punish and protect the public:

> However, unlike the community corrections programs of the past, which had rehabilitation as a main goal, the primary goal of current community corrections programs is to provide punishment in a less expensive manner while, at the same time, emphasize public protection. (Beck & Klein-Saffran, 1990, p. 22)

When properly implemented, electronic monitoring programs are able to save jurisdictions significant sums of money. Although EM is the most expensive form of probation/parole when compared to regular, special (e.g., boot camp or substance abuse treatment programming), and intensive supervision (Camp & Camp, 2000, p. 189), it can save jurisdictions money when compared to the costs of incarceration. The Bureau of Prisons, in an evaluation of its Curfew Parole Program for federal parolees, reported a savings of $4 million in four years through substitution of home confinement on EM in place of residence at a community correction center for 60 days (Beck & Klein-Saffran, 1990). In addition to the monetary savings, the program also enjoys a low violation rate (less than five percent). One county in western Pennsylvania saved $74,722 by sentencing 57 drunk drivers to home confinement on EM rather than mandatory jail terms; the calculations included acquisition of the EM devices and salaries for the staff to oversee the EM program (Courtright, Berg & Mutchnick, 1997). Even the more expensive GPS programs (discussed later in this chapter) are capable of saving money. The state of Florida routinely implements home confinement on EM in place of jail at a savings of more than $40 per prisoner per day (Ko, 2002).

Of course, mere financial savings should not drive correctional policy. Predicting a savings of seven to ten million Canadian dollars, officials in Ontario closed all of the regional halfway houses in 1996 to fund its new EM program (Evans, 1996). Since home confinement on EM is not appropriate for everyone, the Ontario officials acted a bit hastily. Instead, candidates for EM should be carefully screened to ensure that they will fit an individual program's ability to supervise clients. One writer claims that carefully transferring 10% of America's prisoners (including only non-violent offenders) from detention facilities to home confinement with EM could save nearly four billion dollars without compromising community safety (Bowers, 2000).

Because the systems may be leased and jurisdictions often require offenders to pay a fee for being on EM, some EM systems do not require substantial financial outlays to operate. The EM program in West Palm Beach, Florida, for example, "cost the county virtually nothing," averted the need to build a new jail, and saved the county at least $320,000 over five years (Lilly & Ball, 1992). Offenders who are not incarcerated are also better able to work to support their families (thus avoiding the necessity for the families to rely on assistance programs) and pay taxes (National Law Enforcement Corrections Technology Center, 1999, p. 1).

Of interest, EM can only save money if it is used regularly. If a jurisdiction sets up a program that only sporadically serves offenders, it may cost more than jailing the offenders, especially if the monitoring devices are purchased rather than leased. One Kentucky county, for example, purchased 12 EM devices but found that it cost the county $10,000–$20,000 more to supervise the 23 offenders who used the devices than it would have cost to jail them; if the devices were in constant use over a one-year period, however, the county would have experienced savings of about $65,000 (Rackmill, 1994) and would have saved even more in future years of the program. This makes sense; the purchase of a new car to make Sunday trips to church would certainly cost much more than taking a taxi for those relatively isolated trips. It is only as more and more trips are made that the car becomes a cost-effective investment. To save money, EM programs must recycle the monitoring devices rapidly after the expiration of sentences, keeping them in regular use.

If an EM program is operated in a jurisdiction that does not have a jail overcrowding problem, the EM program will save less money because diverting offenders from jails with empty cells does not reduce the costs of operating those facilities by much (Lilly & Ball, 1992). At most, the jurisdiction might eliminate some minor expenses, such as costs for meals and medical attention (e.g., Renzema, 1992, p. 48). Electronic monitoring programs, then, are best able to save funds in jurisdictions where they are used to prevent expansion of current jail facilities.

One reason the cost for EM programs can spiral out of control is the need for staff salaries. An EM program is not like a Ronco Rotisserie Oven, the darling of the infomercial circuit—you cannot just "set it and forget it." Staffers must be hired to supervise the clients, and most scholars and administrators recommend a relatively low client to staff ratio—25 or fewer clients per staff member (Beck & Klein-Saffran, 1990; Klein-Saffran, 1995). Since most violations happen at night or on weekends (Rackmill, 1994), programs must have at least some staffers available twenty-four hours a day.

SOME DEFINITIONS

There are several forms of home confinement that need clarification. Curfew means that a client must be home by a certain time (Rackmill, 1994). Individuals sentenced to curfew are allowed to leave their homes during the day, but must return before their established curfews, which may be tailored to their individual cases. Some agencies use electronic monitoring simply to verify that a client is at home by his/her curfew (e.g., Renzema, 1992, p. 42).

Home confinement is more stringent than curfew and means that an individual must remain at home at all times, unless granted permission to leave (Rackmill, 1994). Typically, individuals on home confinement are allowed to leave for work, school, religious, medical, and treatment-related (e.g., to attend AA meetings) reasons, but some individuals are limited in their out-of-home activities. If necessary, individuals on home confinement may be allowed to leave their homes to shop for food or other necessities. Offenders under home confinement sanctions tend to spend an average of fifty hours a week outside their homes working, attending treatment sessions, completing community service, or other tasks permitted by their correctional supervisors (Renzema, 1992, p. 41). Because home confinement is a form of punishment, even visitors may be limited or forbidden (Rackmill, 1994). Since incarcerated individuals cannot consume alcohol, some home confinement programs forbid participants from drinking, even in their own homes (National Law Enforcement Corrections Technology Center, 1999, p. 3).

Electronic monitoring is merely a method of monitoring individuals on curfew or sentenced to home confinement. Electronic monitoring devices, for example, can be used to help ensure that individuals are where they need to be at their curfew time. The devices can be used with home confinement to verify that an individual has not left his/ her house and some EM devices can collect random breathalyzer information (by having the client blow into a straw-like device connected to the monitoring device) to help ensure that clients do not consume alcohol.

It is important to note that not all individuals on home confinement are on electronic monitoring. In some jurisdictions, especially historically, the number of individuals on home confinement without EM exceeds the number who are on EM (e.g., Renzema, 1992, p. 42). Home confinement can be monitored without the use of EM devices. In some programs, clients are telephoned at random times to ensure that they are home. Some of these systems are automated so that a computer calls the client's home and records the client's voice for later review by correctional staff (Schmidt, 1991). A rather time-consuming but effective approach involves correctional staff visiting clients at their homes.

HOW ELECTRONIC MONITORING WORKS

Due to its highly technical nature, electronic monitoring is difficult to stereotype. The only similarity between all of the devices is that they serve to electronically monitor the presence (or absence) of a client in a particular area, typically the client's home. There are two main classifications of EM: radio-frequency (the traditional form of EM) and newer systems that rely on GPS (Global Positioning System).

Radio frequency (RF) form of electronic monitoring

Electronic monitoring that relies on radio frequencies is the first form of EM. The GOSSlink system and all of its contemporaries, in addition to many modern systems, rely on radio frequencies. Radio frequency (RF) systems involve two components: a transmitter device that is typically worn around the ankle or wrist and a base unit (though some are worn around the neck, del Carmen & Vaughn, 1986). The transmitter anklet/bracelet emits a digital code unique to each client that verifies the client's presence or absence within a certain radius, 150–200 feet from the base unit in the early EM systems (Berry, 1985, p. 2), but now typically 800 feet from the base unit (Bowers, 2000). The base unit communicates with the transmitter anklet/bracelet via radio frequency signals. Whenever a client leaves the pre-defined radius, the base unit can no longer detect the transmitter and issues an alert to authorities that the client is no longer in his/her prescribed detention area. A central computer keeps records for all individuals being monitored, tracking when they come into and leave the pre-defined radius.

There are two types of radio frequency EM systems: passive and active. Passive systems require some client interaction in order to function. The central computer places pre-programmed telephone calls to the client's home, after which s/he is expected to insert his/her transmitter into the home base for verification (Gowdy, 1993, p. 5). Because those systems were fooled by some deceptive clients who had others insert the transmitters into their home bases, many newer systems also require the client to verbally repeat a random sentence that is compared to a voice sample stored in the central computer or to perform some task in front of a camera unit such as holding up a certain number of fingers. Even if a client leaves his/her home, the appropriate authorities are not alerted until a call goes unanswered.

Active systems are the most "popular and reliable of the two" types of EM (National Law Enforcement Corrections Technology Center, 1999, p. 1). Active systems continuously emit a signal that is monitored by the base unit whenever the client is expected to stay within the confines of the pre-determined radius (the client is typically allowed to leave the radius to work, attend school or religious services, and for medical/treatment appointments). In active systems, a security breach is immediately detected when a client leaves the predetermined radius.

In both forms of radio frequency EM systems, the transmitter anklet/bracelet and the base unit are tamper-proof. In the initial stages of EM, some crafty individuals were able to outsmart their sentinels by carefully stretching the straps used to fasten the transmitter anklet/bracelet to the client (e.g., Beck & Klein-Saffran, 1990), allowing them to leave the transmitter near the base unit while they left the premises, or by using call forwarding or cell phones to allow them to move about and still receive signals and/or calls from correctional staff or computers (e.g., Schmidt, 1991). It also took some time for technical issues to be ironed out such as preventing the transmitters from shorting out, preventing water from leaking into the devices (important since they cannot be removed, even when bathing), finding a battery type that would hold an adequate charge, making the straps and devices more tamper-resistant, and ensuring that everyday furniture does not prevent or block the home base from receiving the signals emitted by the transmitter anklet/bracelet (e.g., Beck & Klein-Saffran, 1990).

Some of the newer radio frequency EM systems also have portable receiver units that can be carried by correctional authorities to ascertain, without leaving their vehicles, whether a client is somewhere s/he should or should not be. For example, probation officers could drive by their clients' worksites with a portable unit that would read the unique signals emitted by the clients' transmitters to verify each client's presence at work without interrupting the workday of the clients or their employers. Alternatively, a probation officer could drive by notorious liquor establishments to determine whether any of his/her monitored clients were inside.

In 1998, a unique form of radio frequency EM system was developed for use in stalking and domestic violence cases. JurisMonitor works in reverse of the traditional EM system; rather than having to stay within a certain radius of a home unit, the client is ordered to stay away from another location, typically a victim's home. If the client enters the forbidden radius, thus coming within proximity to the home base at the victim's home, the victim and appropriate authorities are notified.

Global Positioning System (GPS) form of electronic monitoring

In 1997, a new form of electronic monitoring was developed and tested that relied on the Global Positioning System (McGarigle, 1997). The Global Positioning System (GPS) is formed by 24 military satellites in orbit around the planet; data from three to five of the satellites can provide the coordinates of a GPS receiver anywhere in the world (Greek, 2002).[2] The GPS system may be best known for its civilian uses by travelers, hikers, and sportsmen. Using the GPS system, the whereabouts of EM clients can also be ascertained and logged into central computers.

Under this form of EM, the client must wear or carry two components: a small anklet or bracelet that must be kept within a certain number of feet of a GPS receiver that may be carried in a fanny pack, handbag, or other container (McGarigle, 1997). If the anklet/bracelet and GPS receiver are separated, the appropriate authorities are notified.

Data provided by the anklet/bracelet and GPS receiver can be used to track, in realtime, the individual wearing the device. In 2000, the jury was still out on GPS systems, with most scholars labeling them as "experimental" (e.g., Bowers, 2000). At that time, GPS systems were still rather bulky and the costs were much higher than radio frequency EM systems (McGarigle, 1997; Greek, 2002), making them less feasible for field use.[3] The data were also much more difficult to maintain and interpret. GPS systems are now much more streamlined and popular, though only 1,200 units were in operation in 2002 (Greek, 2002). One study of probation officers who used both radio frequency and GPS units found a clear preference for the GPS units among the professionals (Mercer, Brooks, & Bryant, 2000).

The most significant difference between GPS and radio frequency EM systems is the ability to actually track clients' travels. Through the GPS, correctional authorities can determine when clients leave and enter their homes, go to and leave work, and attend mandatory treatment sessions. They can also determine if their clients have been going to forbidden areas, such as a victim's home or workplace or to taverns or other establishments that serve alcohol.

Another key difference between radio frequency EM systems and their newer GPS counterparts is the ability to program exclusion or hot zones into which clients are not allowed to travel. These zones are unique to each client and can be established around victims' homes or worksites, schools or other sites frequented by children (especially for monitored pedophiles), or other locations. The size of the zones can be customized to individual cases or made large enough (e.g., five miles) to allow for response by appropriate authorities (Renzema, 2000). If the client enters into one of these forbidden zones, the anklet/bracelet emits an alarm and displays a message to the client to leave the area immediately. At the same time, correctional authorities are alerted. In one test of a GPS system, authorities arrived at the violation scene within four minutes (Merce, Brooks, & Bryant, 2000) and response times typically average 20 minutes or less (National Law Enforcement Corrections Technology Center, 1999, p. 1). The zones can even vary by time of day for cases in which timing is important; for example, to allow a client to enter a building for treatment that is generally in an off-limits area (Miller, 2000). Under GPS EM systems, the victim can also be provided with a tracking device that alerts him/her whenever the client is nearby, even when they are both traveling (McGarigle, 1997).

As an added feature, correctional authorities can share the data generated by GPS EM systems with law enforcement agencies for use in linking EM clients to crimes, by generating "hit reports" when EM clients were at or near the scene of a crime during the past day (Greek, 2002). While this feature is ominously reminiscent of George Orwell's "Big Brother," GPS systems are similar in some ways to advances in DNA analysis. Like DNA evidence found at crime scenes, GPS data may link some clients to crimes, but it has also cleared some from official scrutiny (Miller, 2000; Renzema, 2000). In one jurisdiction, "most" complaints by victims of stalking were unfounded based on GPS-generated data that showed the accused client was nowhere near the victim. Individual cases like the released sex-offender in Texas who was cleared when his GPS unit showed that he was not nearby when a local child disappeared, are not uncommon (Renzema, 2000, p. 7).

Like radio frequency EM systems, GPS programs can be outsmarted by the occasional client who works at beating the system. One GPS dealer noted that clients could impair the tracking ability by simply covering the device's antenna (Ko, 2002, p. 27). The receiver devices can also be disposed of, thus destroying the tracking ability of the device, but alerts are immediately issued when this happens (McGarigle, 1997).

Unfortunately, neither GPS nor radio frequency EM systems can prevent a client from leaving his/her prescribed area, and radio frequency

EM cannot track the client after s/he has left the area. Both types of systems can be cut off and disposed of by clients, but both also alert appropriate authorities immediately. One scholar feels that the next generation of electronic monitoring devices will shock clients who attempt to remove them (Coyne, 1996), but this feature is not reality at this time.

The primary value of EM systems is that they act to increase the certainty that a violation will be detected. Clients who freely left their residences under home confinement were suddenly faced with a system that alerted the appropriate authorities that they were no longer in their homes or had gone too close to a victim. Cesare Beccaria (1775/1983), the father of Classical theory (on which deterrence doctrine is based), would likely have appreciated EM systems as they increased certainty of detection (and punishment) of violations, thus making it easier for would-be offenders to decide that a planned deviant act was not worth the risk. Faced with the knowledge that his/her violation will definitely be discovered and acted upon leads most EM clients to observe their curfews and boundaries.

TARGET POPULATIONS

The target population for EM has changed over the years and also varies by EM form. In the earliest stages of EM, criminal justice decision-makers were careful to select only the "*crème de la crim*," the lowest-risk offenders who were perceived as surely able to succeed on EM. Some programs deliberately included only certain types of offenders, such as drunk drivers. Others were careful not to select as candidates clients who might make their program look bad through their recidivism or continued criminality.

Law in some jurisdictions excludes certain types of offenders from EM (e.g., those with a history of violence or who have prior convictions) and sometimes enumerates a short laundry list of offenders who may be included in the programs. Pennsylvania's 1990 County Intermediate Punishment Act, for example, limits EM to only non-violent offenders convicted of drunk driving, writing bad checks, or committing retail theft, simple assault, or second-degree burglary (Courtright, Berg, & Mutchnick, 1997).

The first offenders sentenced to EM were literally a hand-selected bunch; decision-makers felt it would be foolish to foray into uncharted waters and risk failure by sentencing difficult offenders to EM. In 1987, the typical EM client was a male drunk driver; the list expanded by 1989 to include burglars and minor drug offenders (Renzema & Skelton, 1990). Once the sanction achieved some popularity in the early 1990s, the typical offenders who were sentenced to home confinement on EM included those convicted of burglary, disorderly conduct, drug offenses, forgery, theft, habitual traffic offenses, and major traffic violations such as drunk driving and driving on a suspended license (Gowdy, 1993; Rackmill, 1994). One 1992 evaluation found that less than two percent of the largest EM program's caseload were violent offenders (Lilly & Ball, 1992).

Modern EM caseloads are quite different, however, and are much more likely to include serious or violent offenders, including sex offenders (e.g., Finn & Muirhead-Steves, 2002), domestic abusers (e.g., Bowers, 2000), and other offenders who would have been considered taboo just a decade ago.

One can see a changing caseload even within individual EM programs. During piloting, criminal justice decision-makers may test the devices on themselves before using them on offenders. Several judges, for example, have tested the devices, trying to outsmart them before agreeing that they were suitable for use (e.g., U.S. Congress, 1988, p. 34; Mercer & Brooks, 1999). After piloting the devices, the selection criteria might be quite exclusive. As program staff become accustomed to and learn to trust the EM systems in their jurisdictions, they begin to see EM as appropriate for more and more types of offenders. One probation officer wrote about his department's gradual loosening of the criteria for inclusion in their EM program:

> Initially, our selection criteria restricted participation in home confinement to a very select group of offenders (i.e., those with no violent, mental illness, or severe substance abuse history). With many new home confinement programs, as confidence with electronic monitoring technology grows, so does the acceptance of more high risk offenders. (Gowen, 1995)

Some EM program staff feel that EM should be used with serious offenders and those who need the most direct surveillance. One program strives to include nuisance probationers who fail to comply with the terms of their probation such as those who lie to probation staff, fail to report for meetings, or do not complete their community service orders

(Gowen, 1995). The Florida Department of Corrections Bureau Chief explained his state's efforts to use EM on difficult offenders who need more supervision:

> We want electronic monitoring on the worst of the worst, because they are going to cause the most problems. For example, we haven't used electronic monitoring on nonviolent drug offenders. We've used it on sex offenders and pedophiles because we believe they pose a greater threat to the community. (quoted in McGarigle, 1997)

There are also differences between caseloads for GPS versus radio frequency EM systems. Because radio frequency EM systems are best for curfew enforcement or for ensuring that clients remain in their homes, it is best for offenders who pose less of a risk to the community or to a specific victim. GPS, on the other hand, allows for true surveillance and tracking of a client's whereabouts and his/her travels into forbidden zones. One research team queried probation staff who use both GPS and radio frequency EM systems in Florida to learn about their experiences with and preferences for the two systems. They found that radio frequency EM was perceived to be best for non-violent offenders while GPS was believed to be best for violent offenders (Mercer, Brooks & Bryant, 2000). In fact, some of the probation staff complained about misguided judges who mistakenly assigned routine cases such as habitual traffic offenders, bad check writers, and drug addicts to GPS monitoring; doing so wasted time and money (because GPS systems cost more to run and are more time consuming to use) and added nothing to public safety. GPS monitoring, the probation staff felt, should be limited to those whose whereabouts need to be known in order to protect the public or a specific victim.

While not everyone feels electronic monitoring is a panacea, they still see it as appropriate for certain offenders. The most conservative individuals may wish to limit its use to those who are severely ill or disabled, or whose presence in their home is essential to others (e.g., caregivers to young children or the aged). Others may feel that it is suitable for non-violent offenders who pose little risk to others or who are the best candidates for successful completion. Yet a third group feels that EM should be used more often as a way to divert offenders from incarceration for financial or humanitarian reasons, but also believes that violent offenders should be carefully screened before inclusion in

EM programs. The final group includes those who believe that EM is appropriate for most offenders, including those convicted of manslaughter.

EM PROGRAM MODELS

Because it is not a sanction, electronic monitoring has popped up in some interesting places. Designed for use as a post-trial add-on to home confinement (to make that sanction more practical), it was quickly adapted for pre-trial use, as a way of releasing defendants on bail who might otherwise be considered too risky. It is useful in enforcing conditions of bail such as avoiding victims or certain locations (such as those frequented by children). It is commonly used as a community corrections alternative to jail or federal prison and as a way of increasing surveillance of parolees. It has been used as a graduated sanction between increasing the number of contact meetings and revocation of probation or parole. It is ideally suited to work-release or temporary release (Berry, 1985, pp. 11–12). It has even been used during the appeal of bonds and in non-support cases (e.g., Texas Department of Criminal Justice, 1999). One scholar notes that some correctional institutions have expressed an interest in acquiring EM anklets/bracelets for their staff as a security measure; staff members who are attacked or injured while wearing the devices are easier to locate (Berry, 1985, p. 12). In the future, new uses will undoubtedly be discovered for electronic monitoring.

Electronic monitoring programs are typically operated at the county level, though they may be statewide in operation. The federal government operates pre- and post-trial EM programs and positive evaluations have been conducted for federal parole programs that rely on electronic monitoring.

Most EM programs require participants to pay a fee, ranging from five to fifteen dollars per day (Bowers, 2000; Courtright, Berg & Mutchnick, 2000; Lilly & Ball, 1992; Payne & Gainey, 2000; Rackmill, 1994; Renzema, 1992, p. 51). These fees may be used to pay the leasing fee for the EM devices or to offset the costs of supervision. Many programs charge a sliding fee so they can include low-income clients in the programs (e.g., Berry, 1985, p. 19; Lilly & Ball, 1992; Rackmill, 1994; Renzema & Skelton, 1990), meaning that higher-income clients pay more to avoid jail.

When home confinement with electronic monitoring is used as a sanction, most jurisdictions offer offenders a choice between EM and jail. In post-sentence cases, parolees may be given the option of EM instead of a halfway house or community correction center. In such cases, some offenders will choose incarceration. Some feel that jail is easier to complete due to the high level of surveillance and supervision associated with EM (e.g., Hinzan, 2000). Individuals with families tend to prefer EM because it allows them to live at home (Beck & Klein-Saffran, 1990).

Some administrators feel that charging a fee may lead clients to opt for jail instead, thus reducing the cost savings associated with diverting individuals from jail (Payne & Gainey, 2000). This is true, so programs that need participants to realize higher financial savings might consider charging more modest fees. Another issue that sometimes leads clients to choose jail is the inability to generate good-time, meaning that those who choose jail will complete their terms sooner (Payne & Gainey, 2000, p. 504).

PROS AND CONS OF HOME CONFINEMENT WITH ELECTRONIC MONITORING

Possibly because it is so technologically-oriented, home confinement with electronic monitoring is well enmeshed in controversy. Advocates of EM claim that it can help supervise clients and protect the public, while additionally saving significant sums of money. Opponents of the approach, however, claim it is unusually intrusive and has been one of the greatest sources of net-widening, thus making it more expensive than more appropriate alternatives.

One of the benefits of EM is that it has allowed the use of home confinement to expand. Had EM not been developed, far more individuals would be in jail or prison, rather than completing their terms at home. On any given day, somewhere around 10,000 individuals under jail supervision are on EM, the vast majority of whom would otherwise be incarcerated (Harrison & Karberg, 2003). To that number we must add the number of clients assigned to EM as a condition of pretrial release, probation, parole from prison, prison furlough, or other programs unaffiliated with jails. Permitting individuals to serve out their terms at home allows criminal justice decision-makers to conserve precious jail and prison space for more deserving offenders. It also reduces legal liability resulting from incarceration, such as inmate lawsuits for abuses ranging from obnoxious claims of being served broken cookies at lunch to more substantial and legally thorny issues such as tolerating or encouraging physical or sexual assaults.

That overcrowding is the primary impetus for the development of EM systems is revealed by a survey of programs that utilize EM. In 1990, "virtually all" of 335 EM-using agencies noted that one of their primary goals in developing and operating an EM program was to reduce jail populations (Renzema, 1992, p. 46). When used appropriately, EM can help jurisdictions achieve this goal. It is important that EM programs in areas characterized by overcrowding select as clients only those individuals who would otherwise be incarcerated. Otherwise, the EM program is merely widening the net of social control to include those who would otherwise be put on probation or under other less intrusive means of control. And, in so widening the net, the programs will have little, if any, overall effects on jail populations (or budgets).

A side effect of reducing our reliance on incarceration is the financial savings that EM programs can generate. Programs in jurisdictions facing financial difficulties can save significant sums of money by diverting some offenders from jail to home confinement on EM. Improper selection of clients, failure to keep monitoring devices in constant or near constant use, or other problems can increase a program's costs and reduce its capacity to save money. It is important, then, that programs seeking to generate financial savings are carefully designed and have clear goals and objectives that permeate their daily functioning.

Community corrections options such as EM also have fewer "social costs" than detention facilities. There is reduced stigma associated with community corrections, and community corrections participants are better able to retain their valuable family and community ties. In addition, community corrections are believed to be less criminogenic than incarceration; keeping first-time and youthful offenders out of "crime schools" has long been a goal of corrections experts. EM fits neatly into this framework and can be a more humane and safe form of social control when compared to incarceration.

As a component of community corrections, EM programs have augmented the toolbox of judicial options. As an add-on to home confinement or a way to extend bail to an otherwise risky candidate, EM affords judges the opportunity to customize justice in ways that could not be achieved when the only alternative was home confinement without EM. With the advent of EM, intensive supervision probation (ISP) programs have been able to evolve into programs that are better able to monitor their clients and protect society.

Another benefit is that home confinement on EM serves multiple sentencing philosophies, including incapacitation, retribution, deterrence, and rehabilitation. The incapacitation-related elements of EM are clear-cut; as long as clients' devices are adequately monitored by appropriate authorities, thus ensuring that they are at home when they should be, incapacitation may be achieved (under certain circumstances). If the systems' alerts are ignored or repeated curfew violations are not responded to in a suitable fashion, however, then the program will lose credibility and any potential incapacitation effects will disappear. It is important to note that EM does not fully incapacitate any would-be criminal. While it may help keep him/her off the streets, crimes may still be committed in or sufficiently near one's home. And, offenders can easily break through the electronic bonds that attempt to confine them by snipping off the devices and fleeing as did former prosecutor Nicholas Bissell, who was awaiting an expected sentence of eight to ten years in federal prison for mail fraud and other charges (Hanley, 1996). EM and its accompanying sanctions for violating conditions are only effective if clients are able or willing to make it successful. Clients who cannot or who refuse to comply with the conditions of their electronic monitoring will not be incapacitated and will contribute to the declining dignity of the criminal justice system.

Retribution can also be achieved through EM. As luxurious as home detention may sound, it is a significant punishment to be confined to one's home. In one classroom experiment, college students were asked to restrict themselves to their homes for just forty-eight hours; many reported that the experience was punishing due to the boredom and restricted freedom for those two days (Stinchcomb, 2002). In addition, there are punishing aspects of the EM devices. EM clients often report being embarrassed or bothered by the transmitter anklets/bracelets they must wear; some tell others the devices are heart monitors or other medical devices, pagers, battery chargers, or even electronic fish callers (Beck & Klein-Saffran, 1990; Gainey & Payne, 2000; Lilly & Ball, 1992). EM programs that emphasize punishment tend to use bulkier devices that are harder to conceal and make many calls to offenders, sometimes at annoying times (Renzema, 1992, p. 46). One pair of scholars (von Hirsch , Wasik, & Greene, 1989, p. 607) note that a variety of factors could increase the "discomfort" of certain community sanctions, thus making them more severe in a retributive scale of community-based punishments; increased levels of embarrasment or perceptions by offenders of EM as more onerous than other non-custodial sentences would certainly be valid in this schema, making EM a relatively severe and retributive sanction.

The experience of home confinement on EM is sufficiently painful (to borrow a term from Classical theory) to deter clients from future actions. While some individuals deride EM as "being grounded" (e.g., Ko, 2001, p. 32; Rackmill, 1994, p. 45) or as "Commit-a-crime-go-to-your-room" (Meyer & Grant, 2003, p. 408), those on EM report that the restrictive conditions are actually quite punitive and a sanction that offenders do not want to repeat (Gainey & Payne, 2000). Half of EM clients in one study felt it was as punitive as being incarcerated in a halfway house (Lilly, Ball, Curry, & McMullen, 1993). In fact, one EM participant asked to be sent to jail instead of continuing on EM, because he felt the "'pressure' for self-control was too great" (Lilly & Ball, 1992). Deterrence should occur in such programs.

The rehabilitative aspects of EM are both indirect and direct. The indirect aspects include the fact that clients are able to remain in the community, where corrections experts feel rehabilitation is most likely to occur. For example, they are able to retain their family ties and to work. EM also has direct rehabilitation-oriented features. Some probation officers, for example, are using EM to provide a stick and carrot approach to corrections. One Michigan probation officer extends curfews to reward good behavior such as catching up on restitution payments or not having any positive drug tests, while making his clients' schedules more oppressive if they engage in any prohibited behavior, such as using drugs (Renzema, 1992, p. 50). By doing so, this official seeks to engender within his clients a sense of personal accountability that may continue after they are no longer monitored electronically. Using EM to instill a sense of responsibility to a curfew or avoiding forbidden areas is another direct use of the technology (e.g., del Carmen & Vaughn, 1986). When used in these ways, EM is unique among community corrections in its ability to help offenders change themselves. Some EM clients, for example, have reported that they have been better able to avoid high-risk situations (such as hanging out with drug-using friends) and have been less likely to skip work due to their knowing that probation officers will immediately know about their absences (Gainey & Payne, 2000, pp. 88, 92–93). If these types of skills continue when clients are no longer monitored electronically, then rehabilitation is a more realistic goal.

Home confinement on EM is not without its drawbacks. Due to the attractiveness of technological gadgets and gizmos, some agencies may acquire them without considering how their program will operate or what its goals will be. This is dangerous policy and can lead to disjointed programs that contribute to a lack of community safety and deleteriously affect the credibility of other criminal justice programs. One of the leading experts on EM cautions that the devices should not become "equipment in search of a program" (Schmidt, 1991, p. 52). Fancy trinkets that emit beeps and feature flashing lights will not make an EM program successful. It is the staff who supervise the EM clients that can make a program work; EM devices are merely a way to enhance supervision of program clients.

Another drawback to EM programs is that they may be oversold, by emphasizing both real and imagined benefits while minimizing discussion of pitfalls. Claims that EM will protect the public without a significant investment in resources, for example, would be untrue. Downplaying the potential for equipment malfunctions would exaggerate the effectiveness of EM. Papy and Nimer (1991, p. 33) note that EM program advocates should avoid "overselling" programs to criminal justice officials, the public, or the media: "a balanced presentation that states the assets and liabilities . . . is a more prudent course."

As discussed above, EM can actually cost more than incarcerating offenders if it is used improperly. Programs that operate in jurisdictions that have adequate jail space may find that launching an EM initiative will not save great amounts of money. Of course, such programs may be profitable in terms of social or humanitarian costs, but they may not benefit financially like their cousins in jail-space-strapped communities.

Though equipment malfunctions are being addressed by manufacturers, they are still a source of aggravation for EM program staff. Responding to false alarms in the middle of the night is necessary to ensure that the client has not violated the terms of his/her electronic monitoring, but can take a toll on the morale and fortitude of corrections officials. Gone are the days when clients could easily slip out of transmitter devices and slip away into the night undetected by anyone, but escapes do occasionally happen and embarrass criminal justice officials. In order to reduce the likelihood of annoying equipment malfunctions, program staff should be careful to select well-tested equipment that has a reputation for integrity and hardiness.

Due to their relative newness, one of the drawbacks of EM programs is that we are not yet certain if EM "works" to help reduce recidivism. Most of the studies of effectiveness have been on small samples or with inappropriate control groups, if any. One of the few adequate experiments found no real differences between jailed individuals and those sentenced to home confinement on EM for likelihood of future arrest, revocations of parole after completing the sanction, or drug/alcohol use while on parole; the evaluation did find that employed parolees on EM were more likely to succeed than their counterparts who were not monitored electronically (Courtright, Berg, & Mutchnick, 2000). What is needed are more studies that examine the effectiveness of home confinement on EM versus other sanction approaches. We need some high-quality experiments replicated in a variety of contexts and situations (since EM is used in so many ways). The lack of research evaluations should not be disturbing since EM is a relatively new addition to the community corrections toolbox, but the time has now come for sound research and evaluations. Lackluster research that has no control groups, occurs on small samples, and involves significant selection bias can no longer be tolerated (Vollum & Hale, 2002).

While most scholars and EM clients consider the proximity to family to be a positive element of home confinement on EM (e.g., Beck & Klein-Saffran, 1990), the reality that family members and other household guests must share some of the conditions of confinement can be a negative outcome of the sanction. Repeated phone calls or visits to the home to verify the client's presence or to collect information annoy not only the client but his/her housemates. In homes in which telephones are used a lot, reduced access to use of the phones and the inability to have certain features such as call forwarding or three-way calling installed can be irritating, especially to teen members of the household. For some families, presence of the equipment is a bother. And, possibly most importantly, the inability of the client to leave the home means that others must either cope with his/her constant presence or leave the home themselves to gain a respite from being around him/her. For some families, especially if the EM client is surly or otherwise emotionally challenging, this could be a looming issue that makes their lives more difficult. In some cases, EM may actually lead to domestic violence.

A final drawback to EM systems can be that they are mechanical, and as such, represent the dehumanization of society. "Big Brother"-like in their operation, EM devices, in many ways, reduce individuals to wards of machines. This may make some clients petulant or less amenable to rehabilitation. Due to their mechanical nature, some clients may view them as challenging adversaries and be induced to try to "outsmart" the devices or test their limitations, leading to increased rates of revocation and return to incarceration.

ETHICAL IMPLICATIONS

Although some of the ethical implications were discussed above, a few others should be mentioned. The first ethical consideration is that of net widening. EM was designed as a true diversion from jail, and "at least half" of EM clients are diverted from incarceration (Renzema, 1992, p. 47). Some clients, however, pose little risk to the community and appear to be put on home confinement with EM rather than on less restrictive (and more appropriate) means of social control (Vollum & Hale, 2002). Net widening is a risk with all community corrections, but this issue may be more troublesome and likely when clients are sentenced to home confinement on EM due to the ease with which clients may be outfitted with transmitting devices and the potential for collecting fees from clients.

Some individuals worry about the effect of charging fees to participate in EM programs. If the fees are too high, some clients will be unable to participate, meaning they may be incarcerated instead (del Carmen & Vaughn, 1986). Allowing wealthier offenders to buy themselves out of jail sentences is inappropriate. To address this problem, most EM programs charge sliding scale fees so they can serve low-income individuals, but some programs exclude those who cannot pay (National Law Enforcement Corrections Technology Center, 1999, p. 6). This issue represents a possible constitutional challenge.

Due to the mechanical nature of EM monitoring devices and systems, ethics requires that we examine the type of "proof" that is sufficient to revoke an individual's probation or parole on EM and return that individual to incarceration. What documentation or evidence will be required by authorities such as judges who are responsible for implementing official sanctions against those who are accused of violating the terms of their electronic monitoring (Schmidt, 1991)? Will printouts generated by a computer be acceptable as evidence or must the alleged activities be supported by verification of the violations by staff (Berry, 1985, p. 5)? Can clients challenge the introduction or accuracy of printouts or computerized data at criminal justice hearings to determine whether and how they will be sanctioned for violating the terms of their home confinement on EM? These are important considerations with ethical dimensions. Are we ready as a society to trust someone's fate to an imperfect machine that may malfunction or be improperly programmed by an anonymous technician?

A related ethical consideration centers on how the criminal justice system should react to tampering and security breaches reported by EM devices. What seems like a relatively straightforward issue is actually a difficult quandary because the devices are not fool-proof and sometimes emit false alerts. Devices that are handled roughly, such as during sporting events, will sometimes falsely signal authorities that tampering has taken place (Schmidt, 1991). The devices are also well-known for false alerts that the client has left his/her home, due to household furniture blocking the transmitter's ability to communicate with the base unit or a host of other possible issues. Due to the number of false alerts, one writer stressed the importance of having a staffer call or visit a client to verify his/her absence (Rackmill, 1994). One program reported that a zero tolerance policy for EM violations in one jurisdiction greatly reduced the need for probation staffers to check up on EM clients (Renzema, 2000, p. 8), but some may wonder how many clients who had not tampered with their systems or violated the terms of their electronic monitoring were jailed due to the policy.

Some scholars worry that clients are "coerced" into EM (e.g., Berry, 1985, p. 15). These writers note that being offered a choice between jail and home confinement on EM somehow naturally lacks the elements of a true choice and may be forceful. If the goal of an EM program is to save funds, additional pressure might be put on defendants and offenders to consent to home confinement on EM, though the chances of their violation and return to incarceration might be high. When the alternative is incarceration, it is acceptable to offer individuals the choice to participate in home confinement on EM programs. Such a decision would not be significantly more coercive than a choice between intensive supervision probation and jail. If the individual would likely be released on a less restrictive form of community corrections such as probation, however, then it is unfair to offer a forced-choice option limited to incarceration or home confinement on EM. To combat this possibility, EM program staff should be certain that possible candidates for their programs are adequately screened.

CONCLUSION

A newcomer to the corrections field, home confinement on EM is rapidly becoming more and more popular. With new advances using GPS technology, it appears that EM programs may soon satisfy the goal of diverting individuals from incarceration while saving money and protecting the public. Due to its technological basis, few can predict what the future holds for this innovative addition to the community corrections toolbox. See figure 6.2 for a description of the Suffolk County Women's Resource Center, a treatment program that utilizes electronic monitoring.

Is EM effective? Does it reduce recidivism or at least compare favorably with incarceration? Due to the lack of adequate research, all that can be said at this point is that it is one of many options in the community corrections diorama, albeit an option that has a lot of promise.

[1] In fact, the idea dates back to 1919, when the Army Signal Corps developed a system to track ships and aircraft through the use of radio signals; by the late 1960s, electronic monitoring was being used by researchers to track and study animal life (Klein-Saffran, 1995).

[2] Under current government guidelines imposed by the Department of Defense, GPS data are "dampened" or made less accurate for non-military uses; this dampening feature is scheduled to be removed by 2007 (McGarigle, 1997).

[3] In 1999, the typical GPS battery for EM systems weighed a minimum of five pounds and needed to be recharged daily (National Law Enforcement Corrections Technology Center, 1999, p. 5).

Figure 6.2:
The Suffolk County Women's Resource Center:
A treatment program that utilizes electronic monitoring

Program Characteristics:

In order to address the unique needs of female offenders, the Suffolk County (Massachusetts) Women's Resource Center opened in January 2001. This program seeks to provide at-risk female offenders with substance abuse treatment and life skills training while simultaneously protecting the community. The program attempts to utilize a female-centered treatment approach that takes into account the particular needs and characteristics of women offenders, such as their tendency to commit crimes to support their families, use drugs to self-medicate, and be victims of prior sexual abuse.

The Suffolk County Women's Resource Center is run at the county level with state support and is operated jointly by the Suffolk County Sheriff's Department, the state Office of Community Corrections, and the Office of the Commissioner of Probation. The program utilizes a team approach with representatives from the three supporting agencies contributing to the treatment of the clients.

Selection of participants:

Unlike most programs that involve electronic monitoring, the Suffolk County Women's Resource Center serves only women. Due to its emphasis on drug and alcohol treatment, only substance abusing women may enter the program. Women convicted of crimes resulting in death or serious bodily injury (unless negligence led to the outcome) are ineligible for participation as are those convicted of sexual assault or any crime involving the use of a firearm.

Though many types of offenders form the program's client pool, the "primary basis" of their offenses is drug or alcohol abuse. Some clients were convicted of possession or distribution of drugs or were under the influence at the time of their offenses.

Program Levels:

New admittees to the Suffolk County Women's Resource Center progress through four levels of treatment. The first level involves 24 hour restriction on electronic monitoring accompanied by random drug/alcohol testing and community service.

(continued)...

Figure 6.2 (continued):

Program Levels (continued):

Women who complete the first level may progress to the second level, "Daily Accountability," which features less restriction, a possible reduction in the use of electronic monitoring, and the ability to seek employment (women on the first level are restricted 24 hours a day, so they cannot work). After three months at the second level, each client is assessed to determine whether she is ready to move to the third level or must remain in the second level.

The third level, "Standard Supervision," involves community service, random drug/alcohol testing and the possibility of electronic monitoring. By the time the clients reach the final level, "Financial Accountability," they are no longer monitored through EM and have completed many classes and treatment options.

The four levels of the program rely on a combination of restrictions on personal freedom, community service, education, and restitution. The goal of the program is to "foster change" through the use of these program elements. At the end of the program, it is hoped that the clients will have built "new and healthier lives."

Program Performance:

The program at the Suffolk County Women's Resource Center is currently being evaluated by the Office of Community Corrections and the Office of the Commissioner of Probation. Though the program is too new for the evaluation to have been completed, the program staff hope that their approach will reduce the likelihood of recidivism among their clients as well as provide their clients with the life skills to rebuild their lives in a positive way.

The role of electronic monitoring in the program:

Electronic monitoring is used to protect the community. In doing so, it allows women who might not otherwise be given the opportunity to participate in such a program to take advantage of the innovative treatment options offered at the Center. EM helps the women develop personal accountability as they know they will be sanctioned if they violate the terms of their monitoring. Electronic monitoring also satisfies the public's desire for retribution as clients must spend at least three months at the first level, meaning they are restricted 24 hours a day. EM is used appropriately by the Center, as part of a larger treatment program, rather than as the sole foundation of their approach.

Source: Johnston (2001).

 **CHAPTER 7**

Monetary Penalties: Fines and Restitution

FINES

BACKGROUND

Fines are monetary penalties requiring the offender to pay money to the court as full or partial punishment for criminal offending. Other financial penalties, such as court costs and supervision fees, are not intermediate sanctions. Court costs offset the costs incurred by the court in the processing of a criminal case. Supervision fees are monies by a person under supervision and are commonly applied to offenders in an effort to offset the cost of corrections, such as probation supervision.

The fine is one of the oldest known penalties, dating back to before Biblical times when it was used for punishment of criminal and moral offenses (Mullaney, 1988). In the 10th century, kings and other royal officials imposed fines for criminal punishments and by the 13th and 14th centuries, fines became one of the most frequently used punishments in Europe when criminal justice systems began to develop. Then it was commonly used in combination with capital punishment, exile, and public shaming (Peters, 1995). The fine remained a viable penalty in England as the criminal justice system there became more fully developed in the 18th century. In addition to whippings, shaming, banishment, and hanging, the fine was among the most popular criminal sanctions in colonial America (Rothman, 1995).

Today the fine is widely used in many countries. European countries, such as Germany and Sweden, use fines as punishments for a wide array of crimes, including serious offenses (Bureau of Justice Assistance, 1996). In those countries fines are used as sole punishments as well as supplementary sanctions, such as with probation. In Asia and the Pacific region, which comprises countries such as China, India, Indonesia, Japan, the Philippines, and Singapore, the fine is the traditional alternative to imprisonment (Sugihara et al., 1994). Fines are the most frequently used noncustodial options in Australia and New Zealand (Challinger, 1994) and one of the three major criminal sanctions commonly used in Arab countries (imprisonment and capital punishment are the others). (Mezghani, 1994). In Canada, fines are used as dispositions in about 15% of all offenses, including serious offenses (Department of Justice, 1994).

Fines are very frequently used as criminal penalties in the United States (Hillsman, 1990; Hillsman, Sichel, & Mahoney, 1984; Vigorita, 2002). The use of fines (and restitution) has grown more dramatically than many other sanction in the 1980s (Mullaney, 1998). However the United States makes limited use of fines as an alternative to incarceration and as a sole punishment. Today in the United States, fines are used mainly for traffic offenders and as a condition of probation. It is estimated that more than $1 billion in fines is collected annually. According to data from the U.S. Sentencing Commission (2000), 58,742 offenders who were sentenced under the U.S. sentencing guidelines in 2000 were ordered to pay more than four billion dollars in fines and restitution (Figure 7.1). An offender receiving a fine may be required to make a lump sum payment or be permitted to make installment payments over time. In California, for instance, federal courts rely mainly on the installment method (U.S. General Accounting Office, 1998).

TARGET POPULATIONS

Fines can be applied to virtually all types of offenders. Persons guilty of traffic violations as well as persons guilty of assaultive offenses are imposed fines. Research by Michael Vigorita (2002) on fine practices of New Jersey judges found that the probability of being fined rests mainly with offender and offense factors. According to the research, the most-often-fined offenders are those who pose little risk to society and who commit minor crimes. Older offenders, those employed, offenders with little or no prior

Primary Offense	Total	No Fine or Restitution Ordered		Restitution Ordered/No Fine		Fine Ordered/No Restitution		Both Fine and Restitution Ordered		Amount of Payment Ordered			
		Number	Percent	Number	Percent	Number	Percent	Number	Percent	Total	Mean	Median	Sum
Total	58,742	41,647	70.9	8,380	14.3	7,763	13.2	952	1.6	17,094	245,399	4,723	4,194,848,713
Murder	77	35	45.5	22	28.6	17	22.1	3	3.9	42	27,044	5,160	1,135,841
Manslaughter	49	18	36.7	26	53.1	3	6.1	2	4.1	31	6,626	3,889	205,408
Kidnapping/Hostage Taking	73	53	72.6	14	19.2	4	5.5	2	2.7	20	59,837	5,625	1,196,749
Sexual Abuse	241	141	58.5	53	22.0	43	17.8	4	1.7	100	4,340	2,000	433,971
Assault	463	304	65.7	89	19.2	64	13.8	6	1.3	159	14,508	1,170	2,306,839
Robbery	1,658	453	27.3	1,092	65.9	55	3.3	58	3.5	1,205	37,167	5,130	44,786,762
Arson	66	15	22.7	49	74.2	2	3.0	0	0.0	51	426,093	60,489	21,730,761
Drugs – Trafficking	23,082	19,996	86.6	156	0.7	2,866	12.4	64	0.3	3,086	11,089	1,500	34,219,965
Drugs – Communication Facility	410	328	80.0	0	0.0	80	19.5	2	0.5	82	3,925	2,000	321,846
Drugs – Simple Possession	530	283	53.4	4	0.8	238	44.9	5	0.9	247	1,373	1,000	339,161
Firearms	3,491	2,646	75.8	159	4.6	669	19.2	17	0.5	845	19,000	1,286	16,055,362
Burglary/ Breaking and Entering	47	13	27.7	32	68.1	1	2.1	1	2.1	34	15,682	2,817	533,188
Auto Theft	212	91	42.9	85	40.1	27	12.7	9	4.2	121	40,687	10,000	4,923,094
Larceny	2,366	593	25.1	1,164	49.2	456	19.3	153	6.5	1,773	79,666	4,576	141,248,683
Fraud	6,060	1,585	26.2	3,464	57.2	715	11.8	296	4.9	4,474	627,326	27,278	2,806,656,656
Embezzlement	922	191	20.7	573	62.1	105	11.4	53	5.7	731	78,271	10,245	57,216,272
Forgery/Counterfeiting	1,270	517	40.7	548	43.1	128	10.1	77	6.1	753	34,737	1,806	26,156,630
Bribery	251	108	43.0	39	15.5	84	33.5	20	8.0	143	33,768	7,500	4,828,830
Tax	755	314	41.6	119	15.8	280	37.1	42	5.6	441	106,408	10,000	46,926,143
Money Laundering	962	579	60.2	141	14.7	226	23.5	16	1.7	383	1,102,251	10,000	422,162,035
Racketeering/Extortion	808	473	58.5	194	24.0	127	15.7	14	1.7	335	1,179,593	6,000	395,163,646
Gambling/Lottery	98	38	38.8	4	4.1	56	57.1	0	0.0	60	11,136	3,000	668,142
Civil Rights	86	43	50.0	13	15.1	29	33.7	1	1.2	43	13,601	2,000	584,827
Immigration	11,571	11,106	96.0	25	0.2	437	3.8	3	0.0	465	6,827	1,000	3,174,395
Pornography/Prostitution	513	327	63.7	13	2.5	172	33.5	1	0.2	186	6,763	3,000	1,257,953
Prison Offenses	295	261	88.5	7	2.4	27	9.2	0	0.0	34	2,051	500	69,741
Administration of Justice Offenses	1,014	682	67.3	90	8.9	221	21.8	21	2.1	332	284,465	3,000	94,442,379
Environmental/Wildlife	205	65	31.7	28	13.7	82	40.0	30	14.6	140	63,025	4,000	8,823,458
National Defense	17	11	64.7	0	0.0	6	35.3	0	0.0	6	129,583	6,500	777,500
Antitrust	40	2	5.0	5	12.5	23	57.5	10	25.0	38	891,550	34,827	33,878,894
Food and Drug	82	30	36.6	8	9.8	40	48.8	4	4.9	52	59,020	3,000	3,069,027
Other Offenses	1,028	346	33.7	164	16.0	480	46.7	38	3.7	682	28,672	750	19,554,555

Note: Of the 59,846 cases, 1,104 were excluded due to one or both of the following reasons: missing primary offense category (257) or missing information on type of economic sanction for cases in which orders were made (860). The total number of cases (17,094) used to calculate amounts of payment ordered is less than the total number of cases receiving fines and/or restitution (17,095) due to the exclusion of one case for which a fine and/or restitution was ordered, but the amount was not specified. Fine information includes either fines and/or the cost of supervision.

Source: U.S. Sentencing Commission, 2000.

Figure 7.1. Fines and Restitution for U.S. Sentencing
Guideline Cases, Fiscal Year 2000

record, and those who have committed minor offenses are most likely to be fined. Unlike many other criminal punishments, fines can also be used as a criminal penalty for businesses and individuals in organizations who violate laws and commit corporate crime (Canning & Harrigan, 2002). Figure 7.3 illustrates three models for the use of fines in the United States for criminal offenders.

Fines as Sole Penalties for Minor Offenders

The most frequent application of fines is for low-level misdemeanor and traffic offenders who are ordered by a judge to pay a specified amount within a certain time frame. For instance, a judge may decide to impose a fine upon an adult driver cited for reckless driving or a college student convicted of public intoxication. As a criminal punishment, the offenders agree to payment of a certain fine amount, usually to an office within the court. In these and similar cases, fines are used as sole punishments but they are not alternatives to incarceration. A study of municipal court judges in California by Meyer and Jesilow (1997) found that fines are used extensively in lower courts, particularly for shoplifters and traffic offenders.

Fines are rarely used as sole punishments for more serious crimes (Mackenzie, 1997), such as possession of a controlled substance, assault, or burglary, or for repeat offenders. According to the Bureau of Justice Statistics (2001) of the 68,156 federal offenders sentenced in U.S. district courts between October 1, 1999, and September 30, 2000, less than 4% were given fines as a sole punishment. Nearly all who received a fine (99%) were misdemeanor offenders. Violent offenders and drug offenders are the least likely to be assessed a fine as a sole sanction.

Fines as Supplemental Punishments

For most crimes, fines are used to supplement other penalties, such as probation (Hillsman, Sichel, & Mahoney, 1984; Vigorita, 2002). As Figures 7.1 and 7.3 indicate, fines are added as supplemental penalties

FINE MODEL 1	FINE MODEL 2	FINE MODEL 3
Fine is a sole punishment for very minor offenders	Fine is a front-end diversion from incarceration	Fine is a probation enhancement tool

Figure 7.2. Three Models for the Use of Fines

in roughly 15%-21% of felony convictions. Nearly 200,000 felons convicted in state courts in 1998 and nearly 9,000 felons sentenced under federal sentencing guidelines in fiscal year 2000 were given fines in additional to imprisonment or probation. For example, in Nueces County, Texas, nearly all adults serving probation terms for shoplifting have also been assessed fines of up to $500. Typically, each shoplifter is ordered to pay a fine of $200 or $250 (Caputo, 2004).

Fines as Alternatives to Incarceration

The third and least common use of fines in the United States is as an alternative to incarceration. Fines have been and still are used much more extensively outside of the United States for all types of criminal offenders and as an alternative to incarceration (Hillsman, 1990). This is particularly true in Europe (Wheeler et al., 1990). In 1979 for instance, 82% of all offenders in West Germany, including 66% of violent offenders, were assessed fines, more than 90% of all sentences handed down in Sweden were fines and in 1980 nearly half of all offenses in

Most Serious Conviction Offense	Fine	Restitution	Community Service	Treatment
All Offenses	21%	13%	6%	6%
Violent Offenses	18%	13%	5%	5%
Murder/Nonnegligent Manslaughter	9%	10%	3%	1%
Sexual Assault[a]	16%	11%	4%	8%
Rape	12%	10%	3%	9%
Other Sexual Assault	18%	12%	4%	8%
Robbery	12%	13%	3%	3%
Aggravated Assault	21%	14%	7%	6%
Other Violent[b]	22%	15%	6%	5%
Property Offenses	21%	24%	8%	5%
Burglary	19%	23%	6%	5%
Larceny[c]	21%	21%	7%	4%
Motor Vehicle Theft	12%	21%	5%	5%
Fraud[d]	24%	29%	11%	5%
Drug Offenses	22%	6%	6%	6%
Possession	19%	5%	8%	10%
Trafficking	24%	7%	5%	4%
Weapon Offenses	18%	5%	6%	4%
Other Offenses[e]	24%	9%	6%	6%

Note: Where the data indicated affirmatively that a particular additional penalty was imposed, the case was coded accordingly. Where the data did not indicate affirmatively or negatively, the case was treated as not having an additional penalty. These procedures provide a conservative estimate of the prevalence of additional penalties. A felon receiving more than one kind of additional penalty appears under more than one table heading. This table is based on estimated 927,717 cases. [a] Includes rape. [b] Includes offenses such as negligent manslaughter and kidnapping. [c] Includes motor vehicle theft [d] Includes forgery and embezzlement [e] Composed of nonviolent offenses such as receiving stolen property and vandalism.

Source: Durose and Langan, 2001.

Figure 7.3. Penalties Added to Incarceration and/or Probation State Felons, 1998

England in 1980 resulted in fines (Morris & Tonry, 1990). In England, fines are routinely imposed for serious crimes, including assault and sex offenses and in the Netherlands where the fine is the presumed penalty for all crimes judges must justify cases in which a fine is not imposed (Tonry & Lynch, 1996).

PROGRAM CHARACTERISTICS
Fixed Fines and Day Fines
Fixed Fines
Fines can be classified into two types: fixed fines and day fines. The tradition is the fixed fine where fine amounts are based on the relative severity of an offense. Fixed fines are often referred to as "tariff fines" (Winterfield & Hillsman, 1995). State and federal statutes set an upper fine limit for a certain offense level thereby allowing significant judicial discretion in setting the actual fine amount. Fines for misdemeanor offenses are typically lower than the fines for felonies. According to the Texas Penal Code for example, a person found guilty of a felony in the first degree in Texas, such as aggravated assault, would be subject to imprisonment and a fine of up to $10,000. A person guilty of the least severe type of crime in Texas, a class D misdemeanor such as driving while intoxicated, would be subject to a fine of up to $2,000 (See Figure 7.4). Fine amounts vary across states, even for the same offenses. For instance, in Virginia an offender convicted of a high level felony, such as burglary of a home, would be subject to a fine up to $100,000, or ten times the fine amount for the same offense in Texas. Similarly, conviction for disorderly conduct in Virginia ($2,500) is more costly than the same offense in Texas ($500) (Gould Publications of Texas, Inc., 2002).

Classification of Offenses	Fine Amount	Example Offense
Capital Felony	No fine	Capital Murder
First Degree Felony	Fine up to $10,000	Aggravated Assault
Second Degree Felony	Fine up to $10,000	Burglary of a Home
Third Degree Felony	Fine up to $10,000	Possession of Controlled Substance between 1 and 4 grams
State Jail Felony	Fine up to $10,000	Check Forgery
Class A Misdemeanor	Fine up to $4,000	Theft of Merchandise between $500 & $1,500
Class B Misdemeanor	Fine up to $2,000	Driving While Intoxicated
Class C Misdemeanor	Fine up to $500	Disorderly Conduct

Source: Gould Publications of Texas, Inc., 2002.

Figure 7.4. Fine Amounts in Texas

The fixed fine system has been criticized as inequitable and unfair to some offenders, since amounts are based upon the severity of the offense and not the financial resources of the offender (Bennett, 1995). A very poor and a wealthy offender convicted of reckless driving would be subject to the same fine amount. Critics argue that the punishment is unfairly burdensome to poor offenders and too lenient and of little deterrent value for the wealthy. And, when fines are set too high, poor offenders are subject to additional punishments when they fail to pay (Bureau of Justice Assistance, 1996).

Day Fines

A promising alternative to the fixed fine is the day fine system (often called the "structured fine"). Day fines have a logical appeal and they are said to address the inequities associated with the fixed fine (Bennett, 1995). Day fines are so called because the fine amount is tied to the daily earnings of an offender (Winterfield & Hillsman, 1995). With day fines, fine amounts are based upon both the financial resources of the offender and the seriousness of the crime. The day fine is a European innovation, introduced in Sweden in the 1920s (Bureau of Justice Assistance, 1996). Day fines have been used in Scandinavian countries since the early 1900s and in Germany since the 1970s, although they have yet to catch on in the United States (Tonry, 1997).

The most famous day fine project was set in Staten Island, New York (detailed below). The objective was to test the European day fine concept in a criminal court in the United States. Several other day fine programs were started in the 1990s, including programs in Wisconsin, Arizona, Connecticut, Iowa, and Oregon. Although the day fine model has been quite successful in Europe at generating revenue for courts and limiting the number of offenders sent to prison, it has not yet to be widely implemented across this country.

Calculating Day Fines

Day fines are considered more equitable than the fixed fine system, since the amount is suited to poor offenders and affluent offenders using standardized calculations (Figure 7.5). First, a judge determines an appropriate fine unit for a specific offense or offender (say five units for shoplifting). This may be a very structured system where judges have little or no discretion or a more flexible structure within which judges can increase or decrease fine units depending on aggravating, mitigating, and situational factors. Second, a judge determines the value of each fine unit based on the offender's income. This is done in different ways. Generally, the offender's net income is adjusted for subsistence needs, taxes, and so on. Third, the fine unit is multiplied by the value of the unit to determine the total amount of the day fine. Fines can be paid in full, but they are more often distributed over a specified period, where the total fine amount is divided according to the payment schedule. Collection methods are varied and allow for different payment locations and types (cash, credit card, cashiers check). Incentives (in reduction of fine amounts) may also be offered for early payment.

---

1. **Judge determines fair number of day fine units for a particular offense**
   Ex. 50 units for driving while intoxicated

2. **Judge determines the vale of each unit based on the offender's income**
   Joe earns $25,000 per year and therefore pays $10 per unit
   Jill earns $40,000 per year and therefore pays $15 per unit

3. **Judge determines the day fine by multiplying the value of the unit by the number of units**
   Joe is fined $500
   Jill is fined $750

Figure 7.5: Day Fine Systems Use Standard Calculations

The Staten Island Day Fine Project

As mentioned previously, the most famous day fine program in the United States was developed by the Vera Institute of Justice as a demonstration project in the late 1980s and carried out in Staten Island, New York. (See Greene, 1990, 1993; Hillsman & Greene, 1987, 1992; Winterfield & Hillsman, 1991, 1993, 1995.) The idea for the project was to replace the fixed fine system with day fines for misdemeanor offenses. With the assistance of judges and prosecutors, Vera planners developed guidelines for determining fine units according to offense severity and procedures for calculation (Figure 7.5). Rather than identifying specific fine units for different offenses, they introduced a range and a presumptive fine unit, which facilitated judicial discretion. For instance, judges could use their discretion when imposing day fine units for prostitution and thereby impose 13, 15, or 17 units depending on contextual characteristics of the particular offense situation. For each offender, the value of the fine unit was calculated as one-third of an offender's daily income minus the number of his or her financial dependents. Planners created an elaborate valuation table specifying the exact dollar value of one fine unit based on net daily income and number of dependents (Figure 7.6). Using the day fine unit scale and the valuation table, judges determined the appropriate fine for different criminal offenders. For example, according to the system an offender convicted of prostitution would be fined a minimum of 13 fine units. If the offender has three dependents and earns $50 per day, the offender would pay $18.15 for each fine unit assessed, or a total of $240.50. If the offender has no dependents and earns $80 per day, the offender would pay $44.88 for each fine unit, or a total of $583.44. A fine office was established in the court for accepting fine payments and monitoring collections. Results indicated that the experiment was a success and the court enforced the sanction when offenders did not comply with the sanction. The program also generated revenue and increased collections. According to the Bureau of Justice Assistance (1996), average fine

Offense Level	Type of Offense	Number of Day Fine Units		
		Discount	Presumptive	Premium
Class A Misdemeanor	Assault 3			
	Substantial Injury: stranger-to-stranger	81	95	109
	Minor Injury: stranger-to-stranger	59	70	81
	Substantial Injury: acquaintances	38	45	52
	Minor Injury: acquaintances	17	20	23
Violation	Trespass	13	15	17
Class A Misdemeanor	Possession of Burglary Tools	42	50	58
Class B Misdemeanor	Petit Larceny			
	$1,000 or more	51	60	69
	$700-$999	42	50	57
	$500-$699	34	40	46
	$300-$499	25	30	35
	$150-$299	17	20	23
	$1-$149	13	15	17
Class A Misdemeanor	Criminal Possession of a Controlled Substance			
	Cocaine, heroin, PCP, LSD, other "street jobs"	42	50	58
	Valium, methadone, other pharmaceutical drugs	30	35	40
Violation	Unlawful possession of marijuana	13	15	17
Violation	Prostitution	13	15	17
Violation	Disorderly Conduct	13	15	17
Violation	Harassment	16	15	17
Class A Misdemeanor	Criminal Possession of a Weapon			
	Firearm	51	60	69
	Any other dangerous or deadly weapon	30	35	40

Source: Bureau of Justice Assistance, 1996.

Figure 7.6. Staten Island Day Fine Unit Scale for Selected Offenses

amounts rose by 25%, from $206 before the experiment (using fixed fines) to $258 while day fines were used. According to the same report, collection rates increased more than 10% after the day fine system was introduced; 85% of offenders paid day fines in full compared to 76% of offenders who had received fixed fines the year before.

Net Daily Income ($)	Number of Dependents (Including Self)				
	1	2	3	4	5
6	2.55	2.10	1.65	1.35	1.05
8	3.40	2.80	2.20	1.80	1.40
10	4.25	3.50	2.75	2.25	1.75
12	5.10	4.20	3.30	2.70	2.10
14	7.85	4.90	3.85	3.15	2.45
16	8.98	5.60	4.40	3.60	2.80
18	10.10	6.30	4.95	4.05	3.15
20	11.22	9.24	5.50	4.50	3.50
22	12.34	10.16	6.05	4.95	3.85
24	13.46	11.09	8.71	5.40	4.20
26	14.59	12.01	9.44	5.85	4.55
28	15.71	12.94	10.16	8.32	4.90
30	16.83	13.86	10.89	8.91	5.25
32	17.95	14.78	11.62	9.50	5.60
34	19.07	15.71	12.34	10.10	7.85
36	20.20	16.63	13.07	10.69	8.32
38	21.32	17.56	13.79	11.29	8.78
40	22.44	18.48	14.52	11.88	9.24
42	23.56	19.40	15.25	12.47	9.70
44	24.68	20.33	15.97	13.07	10.16
46	25.81	21.25	16.70	13.66	10.63
48	26.93	22.18	17.42	14.26	11.09
50	28.05	23.10	18.15	14.85	11.55
52	29.17	24.02	18.88	15.44	12.01
54	30.29	24.95	19.60	16.04	12.47
56	31.42	25.87	20.33	16.63	12.94
58	32.54	26.80	21.05	17.23	13.40
60	33.66	27.72	21.78	17.82	13.86
62	34.78	28.64	22.51	18.41	14.32
64	35.90	29.57	23.23	19.01	14.78
66	37.03	30.49	23.96	19.60	15.25
68	38.15	31.42	24.68	20.20	15.71
70	39.27	32.34	25.41	20.79	16.17
72	40.39	33.26	26.14	21.38	16.63
74	41.51	34.19	26.86	21.98	17.09
76	42.64	35.11	27.59	22.57	17.56
78	43.76	36.04	28.31	23.17	18.02
80	44.88	36.96	29.04	23.76	18.48
82	46.00	37.88	29.77	24.35	18.94
84	47.12	38.81	30.49	24.95	19.40
86	48.25	39.73	31.22	25.54	19.87
88	49.37	40.66	31.94	26.14	20.33
90	50.49	41.58	32.67	26.73	20.79
92	51.61	42.50	33.40	27.32	21.25
94	52.73	43.43	34.12	27.92	21.71
96	53.86	44.35	34.85	28.51	22.18
98	54.98	45.28	35.57	29.11	22.64
100	56.10	46.20	36.30	29.70	23.10

Source: Bureau of Justice Assistance, 1996.

Figure 7.7. Dollar Value of One Day Fine Unit, Staten Island, New York

Potential Benefits of Day Fines

Researchers at the Justice Management Institute and the Vera Institute of Justice have identified potential benefits of day fines (Bureau of Justice Assistance, 1996):

- **Offender Accountability**—Day fines have a retributive value; they are equally punitive to offenders, since they are based on income, and they match the seriousness of the offense. The offender is made to pay his or her debt to society.
- **Deterrence**—Day fines serve a deterrent value. They are meaningful economic consequences for criminal behavior.
- **Fairness**—Judges and other criminal justice officials are impressed by the equity of the day fine system. Although easier to use, the fixed fine is inherently unfair because amounts are based solely on the nature of the offense. Amounts are often too low to be meaningful to affluent offenders but high enough to exceed the ability of some offenders to pay and subjecting them to additional punishments.
- **Effective and Efficient Use of Limited System Resources**—Day fines are relatively inexpensive to administer compared with other intermediate sanctions. Although staff and computer resources are required to establish payment plans, monitor compliance, and take follow-up action when necessary, the resources needed are less than for virtually any other sanction. The use of day fines should free scarce and more costly prison, jail, and probation supervision resources for use with offenders who pose more of a risk to public safety.
- **Revenue**—Day fines can be more effective than fixed fines in generating revenue. As a source of net revenue, structured fines are more effective than sanctions involving supervision or incarceration.
- **Credibility of the Court**—The court has a strong capability for collection of fines. Offenders pay in full in a very high proportion of cases. In the small proportion of cases where fines are not collected, the court imposes a sanction that is roughly equivalent to the structured fine in terms of punitivness. When these conditions are present, the day fine is a meaningful sanction and the court sentence has credibility with the offender and the community.

RESEARCH ON FINES

Program Completion

Program completion refers to successful fine payment. It is common practice for a court to issue arrest warrants for offenders who do not pay the fines. Offenders might be penalized for noncompliance in the form of reprimands, community service orders, extended terms of probation or parole supervision, increased payments or fine amounts, and even short terms of confinement in jails (Parent, 1990b).

Some contend that the collection of fines is often problematic and as a result some judges do not make greater use of fines. This may be due in part to the courts' capacity for monitoring offenders who owe fines and for collecting outstanding fines. Collection is often a problem, either because there is no office to collect fines or because court officials and probation officers consider fine collection a low priority (Morris & Tonry, 1990). Proponents of fines and day fines point out that the sanction can be enforced relatively easily (Hillsman & Greene, 1992) especially when courts and other agencies develop a commitment to and systems for tracking and monitoring offenders. New Jersey has addressed the issue by devising a new system, the Comprehensive Enforcement Program, designed to increase completion rates.

Albeit limited, available research on day fines shows that offenders who receive day fines tend to complete the fine payments (MacKenzie, 1997). The research on New York's program indicated that about 77% of offenders paid the fines in full and only about 14% of all offenders ordered to pay day fines over one year failed to comply (Tonry & Hamilton, 1995). New York's experience with the Staten Island Day Fine Project shows that fine collection can be made more efficient, especially when judges take into account an offender's ability to pay when the fine amount is set (Winterfield & Hillsman, 1995). According to the Bureau of Justice Assistance (1996), courts can increase the likelihood of payment in various ways:

- Accept a variety of payment types, making it convenient for offenders to pay fines, including cash, personal checks, money orders, cashiers' checks, and credit cards;
- Enable payments to be made at local banks or check cashing outlets, police stations, sheriffs' offices, and probation departments, night boxes outside of the court, and payment by mail;

- Provide discounts for early payments, such as a 15% reduction for immediate payment as is the case in Bridgeport, Connecticut;
- Promptly track and follow up on situations of deferred or installment payments using postcards, letters, and telephone calls;
- Assess surcharges for late payment, such as a fixed amount or a percentage of the total owed for each month the payment is overdue; and
- Impose the fine in lieu of incarceration so that offenders realize that noncompliance leads to a more punitive penalty.

Recidivism

There is a limited amount of research examining the effects of traditional and day fines on recidivism, but the research that has been conducted suggests that using fines in addition to other penalties may be more effective in reducing recidivism than not using fines. According to MacKenzie (1997) three research projects addressed the impact of fines on recidivism. A study by Gordon and Glaser (1991) indicated that offenders who were ordered to a traditional or fixed fine with probation had lower recidivism rates than offenders who received only probation. Although the differences in rearrest were not significant, they do indicate that using fines in addition to probation does result in a reduction of recidivism. The two other studies focused on the effect of day fines on recidivism and report similar results. Research reported by Worzella (1992) indicated that there was no difference in recidivism between offenders who received day fines and a group receiving traditional fines; receiving day fines did not increase the chances of reoffending. In the third project (See Turner & Petersilia, 1996b), day fines were associated with reductions in technical violations and reoffending, which suggests that using day fines may be more effective in reducing recidivism than using other community correctional options without fines.

Net Widening

Day fines are used in only a few jurisdictions throughout the country and fines are rarely used as alternatives to incarceration (MacKenzie, 1997). Because of this, fines and day fines are not likely to reduce correctional populations or save taxpayer dollars. However according to Turner and Petersilia (1996a), day fines can be used as alternatives to incarceration with no increase in reoffending. And according to the Bureau of Justice Assistance (1996) structured day fines are less expensive than virtually all other criminal sanctions and if they were used more widely for low level offenders headed for jail, they would free jail space for more serious offenders.

Cost Effectiveness

Fines, and particularly day fines, have the potential of increasing court revenue when enforcement and collection are given high priority. Follow-up research by the Vera Institute of Justice on the Staten Island day fine program showed that day fines were used in 70% of cases traditionally handled by way of fixed fines and the average fine amount increased from before the system's inception, thereby yielding greater court revenue (Tonry & Hamilton, 1995).

Fines can also be beneficial when they are used to assist criminal justice systems and to meet some needs of crime victims. At the federal level, fines collected from criminal offenders are paid in most cases to the Department of Justice's Crime Victims Fund (U.S. General Accounting Office, 1998). Overall in 1996, federal courts imposed approximately $102 million in fines.

Behavioral Change/Treatment Effectiveness

There is scant literature on treatment effects of fines. Research by Allen and Treger (1994) indicates that probationers believe fines are intended in some ways to be rehabilitative and to serve deterrent functions. Fines can be rehabilitative when, through scheduled payment, offenders become more responsible and accountable for their behavior. Fines, especially day fines, serve a retributive function because they can be scaled according to the gravity of offenses. Furthermore, fines deprive offenders of some financial criminal gains and serve as a deterrent to criminal behavior.

RESTITUTION

BACKGROUND

Restitution requires that criminal offenders compensate victims, victims' families, or organizations designated by victims for harm caused by the crime. Money or property taken, damaged, or destroyed is returned and/ or restored through financial payment and to a lesser extent, service performed by the offender. Bodily and emotional harm is also considered for restitution. Restitution is commonly referred to as victim restitution and is the one criminal sanction that directly involves the victim in criminal punishment and directly addresses the needs of the victim. It is a form of punishment that may serve goals of deterrence, rehabilitation, retribution, and restoration.

Like the fine, restitution is also one of the oldest known penalties. It dates back to prehistoric clans and tribes requiring non-financial and restorative repayment to crime victims. In the later Middle Ages, restitution was used as a formal mechanism in response to criminal victimization when England introduced the wergild (or "man money") as a way to limit the blood feuds between relatives of murdered victims (Clear & Cole, 2003). Restitution soon fell into decline, as governments instead required offenders to pay fines rather than make financial restitution to victims of crimes.

It was not until the victims' rights movement in the 1970s that restitution became popularized in the United States according to Tobolowsky (1993). In the 1970s, the Law Enforcement Assistance Administration (LEAA) offered funding for the development of restitution programs nationally. A 1976 survey revealed 87 restitution programs for adults (Anderson, 1998). The President's Task Force on Victims of Crime and the Victim Witness Protection Act of 1982 spurred the growth of victim restitution programs in the United States (Tobolowsky, 1993; Allen & Treger, 1994). The act authorized restitution to crime victims as complete or partial punishment for criminal offending. By 1994, 29 states had instituted restitution. Today, every state incorporates some form of victim restitution. Texas, for example, operates at least 14 residential restitution centers (Jones, 2000). Federal courts also rely on the use of victim restitution. According to the U.S. General Accounting Office (1998), federal courts imposed about $1.5 billion in victim restitution. An offender ordered to pay restitution may be required to make a lump sum payment or be permitted to make installment payments over time.

TARGET POPULATIONS

Restitution is used mainly for property offenders who are able to make financial compensation to victims. It can be used in response to violent crimes, but the difficulty of estimating the financial value of physical and emotional injuries and ancillary loss to victims has traditionally limited its use for victims of violent crimes. This is not to say violent and repeat offenders are always excluded. Research on the sentencing practices of a Philadelphia judge from 1974 to 1984 found that about half of those sentenced to restitution were convicted of violent crimes (robbery and assault mainly) and had prior arrests and convictions

---

NATIONAL DEATH ROW INMATE RESTITUTION ART SHOW

Developed in 1998, Restitution Incorporated is a non-profit organization designed to assist offenders in making restitution to their victims. The organization sponsors the National Death Row Inmate Restitution Art Show. As part of the program, death row inmates from across the country use their creative gifts to make restitution by giving back to either the victims' families or to the communities that have been harmed by their crimes. As part of the program, prints of original inmate artwork are sold for $20. Funds collected are divided and distributed to the victims' families or to charitable organizations that have been designated by the inmates. As of March 2002, the inmate-artists distributed $644 to victims' family members and charitable organizations. The inmates receive no financial benefit from making restitution.

"Lion" © 1998
by Michael L. Fullwood
Death Row, Central Prison
Raleigh, North Carolina

Source: Restitution Incorporated. Used with permission.

Figure 7.8. Restitution Incorporated - National Death Row Inmate
Restitution Art Show

(Tonry & Hamilton, 1995). According to the U.S. Sentencing Commission (2000) (Figure 7.1), restitution without a fine was ordered in 14% of all felony sentencing guideline cases in 2000. It was ordered in both violent and nonviolent crimes: 53% of manslaughter cases, 66% of robbery cases, 74% of arson cases, 68% of burglary cases, and 62% of embezzlement cases. State conviction data for 1998 (Figure 7.3) reveal that restitution was ordered in 13% of violent offenses, 24% of property offenses, six percent of drug offenses, and five percent of weapons offenses. Restitution is also used with inmates sentenced to death (Figure 7.8)

Restitution Centers as Front-end and Back-end Alternatives to Incarceration

Restitution is rarely used as a sole penalty, but is typically used in conjunction with other sanctions, such as probation. The most common application of restitution is as a condition of probation. Restitution is typically a penalty that is imposed at sentencing and is frequently collected at the parole stage after offenders have served terms of confinement and have incomes through employment (Outlaw & Ruback, 1999). Restitution orders are becoming more common as an alternative to incarceration (Crew & Vancore, 1994). When used to divert offenders from jails and prisons, restitution often involves a period of stay in a community-based residential program where in addition to paying restitution, offenders must follow strict rules and regulations, and participate in programs such as community service, employment, and treatment. The following programs are examples of front-end and back-end alternatives to incarceration.

The Minnesota Restitution Center

The Minnesota Restitution Center, established in 1972, is a non-residential restitution program. It was designed for property offenders sentenced to two years or less in jail. As an early release mechanism, it requires that offenders must have served at least four months of their sentence to be eligible and must have the power to earn money over the remainder of their sentence to pay restitution. Chronic and dangerous offenders and those who could easily afford restitution are excluded. Among offenders who volunteer, restitution contracts are arranged with crime victims, offenders, and program staff after a review of official records of the crime (arrest report, presentence investigation, and court transcripts). This contract defines the type and amount of restitution and schedule of payments. An account for restitution is established at a bank where the offender deposits payments for the victim. Though considered a success, the program was disbanded with changes in sentencing policy (Cromwell & del Carmen, 1999).

Georgia's Residential Restitution Programs

Through LEAA funding, Georgia began residential restitution programs, which also operate as community service programs, in 1970. According to the Georgia Department of Corrections (2000), the programs operate as alternatives to incarceration and serve both probationers and parolees. Programs for probationers are front-end diversions and programs for parolees are back-end diversion programs. Groups of 20-40 nonviolent property offenders who can afford restitution are admitted to the program and remain there for up to five months. While there, they must work while paying restitution (Cromwell & del Carmen, 1999). Additionally, according to the Georgia Department of Corrections, residents must pay the state for room and board, fines, and medical expenses. They attend educational counseling and socialization programs, which include GED schooling, substance abuse treatment and classes on the impact of crime on victims. Upon release, diversion center residents continue on probation supervision under the control of the sentencing court. Over 1999, probationers paid $3.5 million in restitution. As reported by Cromwell and del Carmen, a 1999 study of the program showed a rearrest rate of 85% within 18 months of release; however, the public and policy makers continue to support the program, mainly because of its financial benefits.

South Carolina's Restitution Centers

South Carolina's restitution centers are located on the grounds of state prisons and serve nonviolent offenders who serve up to six months in the centers as a diversion from jail terms. Offenders are first evaluated for their suitability for employment then placed into jobs. They are transported to and from work at their own cost. Paychecks are sent directly to the centers and 75% is deducted for restitution, court fees, and other financial responsibilities of the offender, as well as room and board. As of 1995, 2327 offenders were admitted and paid $3.8 million in restitution and other fees. A resident who works for six months at a minimum wage job can pay between $3,000 and $4,000 in restitution. Other services include drug treatment, victim awareness, GED preparation, and mental health counseling (Anderson, 1998).

PROGRAM CHARACTERISTICS

Determining Restitution Amounts

The amount of restitution an offender pays a victim is based on several criteria. These criteria vary with the nature of the offense, number of

---

THE JEFFERSON COUNTY, TEXAS, RESTITUTION CENTER #1

Program Description
Located in Beaumont, Texas, the Restitution Center is a 36-bed facility for female felony offenders. It emphasizes employment, discipline, community service, parenting, self-esteem, and social skills. Although the Center is not a locked unit, residents are carefully monitored. Alcohol scans and pat down searches are performed on each resident every time she enters the Center. Drug tests are performed at least twice per month. The program aims to protect the community, to rehabilitate the offender, and to divert female offenders from incarceration. The Restitution Center is designed as a front-end diversion from incarceration.

Target Population
The program serves adult female felons, except those convicted of crimes against persons (committed a violent offense, caused bodily injury, or used a deadly weapon). District judges, with the help of the local probation department, determine which offenders will be admitted to the Center. Priority is given to offenders who owe victim restitution and who are in jail.

A Self-Paced System
Offenders are ordered to the Center for a period of three to twenty four months. Resident progress is self-paced. Employment, life skills and community service restitution are the key elements of this program. A reintegration program with six phases is used to develop and encourage pro-social behavior. The underlying assumption is that by providing social, professional and individual services to the residents, they will be better able to meet the diverse demands of the work place and return to the Center at the end of their work day. When not working at their jobs, residents are required to perform community service.

Employment is the Core
Residents must work a minimum of 40 hours per week. Most work 50 or more hours. A full-time employment specialist helps the residents with job placement and with maintaining employment. Life skills chasses include job search, application and interviewing, and job maintenance. Other treatment programming address topics such as self-esteem, relationships, money management, women's health, and victim's issues. Residents are provided with services for GED, literacy, substance abuse, parenting, anger management, and first aid/CPR. Residents also perform community service and handle the cleaning and maintenance of the center and grounds.

Resident Profile
The typical resident:
- ❑ Owes restitution of $5,000
- ❑ Has a least one child
- ❑ Has history of substance abuse
- ❑ Is a victim or physical or sexual abuse
- ❑ Has been employed less than three months over the previous year
- ❑ Has less than a high school education
- ❑ Referred to Restitution Center for failure to pay and report
- ❑ Offense is forgery, fraud, welfare fraud, credit card abuse, or other theft

Program Performance
Over Fiscal Year 1999, $98, 195 was paid to crime victims, $162,096 was paid in room and board, and $42,024 was paid to probation departments for supervision fees. Since 1998, the women of Center # 1 have consistently paid over $90,000 per year to victims.

Source: Jefferson County Community Supervision and Corrections Department. (n.d.)

Figure 7.9. The Jefferson County, Texas Restitution Center #1

---

victims, harm to victims, and other factors. In Texas, judges determine restitution amounts by considering: (a) the financial resources and earning ability of the offender, (b) the amount of loss sustained by the victim as a result of the crime, and (c) the willingness of the victim(s) to cooperate. An offender's ability to pay can be assessed using a financial statement that shows assets (such as bank accounts, securities, and real estate) and debts (such as rent, child support, and loans). The offender's financial needs are also considered. In the case of property crimes, the amount of loss suffered by a victim is straightforward, calculated as the fair market value of the property on the date of the damage, loss, or destruction. If the offense results in bodily injury to a victim, the court may order the offender to pay direct and indirect costs. This would include the cost of any immediate and subsequent necessary medical, psychological, and psychiatric care. Rehabilitation therapy and counseling services are examples of subsequent losses. The loss of future income is an indirect loss that can also be calculated. If the offense results in death to the victim, the court may order an offender to pay for funeral services (Gould Publications of Texas, Inc., 2002).

Collecting Restitution

Courts generally require an offender to make restitution within a specified period or in specified installments. Offenders who are on probation are usually required to make restitution no later than the end of the period of probation. In Texas, offenders must pay all restitution ordered within five years after the end of their imprisonment (Gould Publications of Texas, Inc., 2002). These and other conditions of payment, grace periods allowed, and consequences for non-compliance are usually established at sentencing and may be modified, for instance by paroles for offenders who are beginning to make the restitution after they have served prison terms.

The monitoring and enforcement of an offender's payment of restitution is handled by various agencies, such as sentencing courts, state and local corrections, and private agencies that contract criminal justice services. The enforcement of restitution conditions has presented difficulties, especially revocation proceedings for probationers and parolees. Because the United States Constitution bans imprisonment for debt, probation and parole officers may be reluctant to initiate revocation proceedings. Most jurisdictions permit about a three-month period before dealing with non-compliance, and often efforts are made to modify the order for restitution or to develop alternative arrangements (McCarthy, McCarthy, & Leone, 2001).

RESEARCH ON RESTITUTION

Program Completion

The payment of restitution on the part of offenders tends to vary. According to Davis and Bannister (1995) a 1991 study by the American Bar Association found that nonpayment rates ranged from 38% to 67%. Available research indicates that offenders tend to pay all or part of the restitution more frequently than not to pay any restitution. A Philadelphia study revealed that more than 60% of offenders paid all restitution (Tonry & Hamilton, 1995). Another Pennsylvania study (Outlaw & Ruback, 1999) found that 48% of the 127 offenders ordered restitution paid in full, 36% paid in part, and only 16% failed to pay. Research does indicate that most offenders do comply with the restitution order when efforts are made to facilitate repayment, such as reminder letters and telephone calls to offenders with outstanding debts (Davis & Bannister, 1995). Enforcing restitution may be particularly challenging for probation and parole departments, which have become increasingly strained with large caseloads of offenders.

Program completion can also be understood in terms of offenders' ability to successfully comply with requirements of restitution centers. Research in the late 1980s on seven residential restitution centers in Texas (Anderson, 1998) indicates that a large proportion of the 717 offenders in the program paid their debts. Completion rates were not particularly favorable, but this should be considered in light of the fact that half of the offenders in the group were deemed high risks for reoffending. Of the offenders discharged from the program for which findings were reported, 411 offenders (66%) failed because of technical reasons (failure to work, pay restitution, comply with rules and regulations, etc.) Updated information revealed that for the 16 centers that were operative in 1993, nearly half of the 1872 offenders completed the program, half were terminated for technical reasons, and few were terminated because of a new arrest. The high failure rate for technical reasons is probably due to the level of surveillance that detected noncompliance with program rules. The low failure rate for criminal conduct indicates that public safety was not diminished by the participation of offenders in the program.

Cost Effectiveness

Restitution is inexpensive to administer compared to most other sanctions (McCarthy, McCarthy, & Leone, 2001), including probation, parole, imprisonment, boot camps, and halfway houses. This is especially true when offenders successfully complete restitution. With the added costs of sanctions for noncompliance, costs associated with restitution will increase in cases when offenders fail to complete restitution. Since restitution is generally supported by the public and has important benefits to the victim, with serious attention paid to planning, selection of offenders, implementation, and enforcement, restitution can be a very useful sanction. However, because restitution pays victims and not the state or county, the actual money saved by the county or state is minimal. When restitution is used to divert offenders from jail and prison terms, as research suggests it does in Texas (Lawrence, 1990), restitution becomes a cost-effective alternative to incarceration.

Though offenders may benefit from restitution, through the individualized justice and the self-worth that may come through paying a debt and meeting a responsibility, victims of crime benefit directly. Especially since many victims are themselves financially disadvantaged, reimbursement may be essential to a victim's recovery from a criminal event. Also to the benefit of the victim, ordering offenders to pay restitution signifies the system's concern about the specific individual and may increase victims' satisfaction with the criminal justice system.

Recidivism

Restitution is said to be an effective means to reduce recidivism (Outlaw & Ruback, 1999). Research in the late 1970s showed that the recidivism rate for a group released from prison to a restitution center was four times lower than a similar group released on parole (Tonry & Hamilton, 1995). More recent research indicates that it is more effective than regular probation and incarceration (Rowley, 1990).

Net Widening

Research on diversion and net widening is virtually non-existent, probably because most restitution programs do not aim to divert offenders from prison. In Texas, however, the Texas Department of Criminal Justice, which oversees all correctional programs, has developed restitution centers aimed at diverting offenders from jail and prison terms. According to Anderson (1998) and Lawrence (1990), research in the late 1980s on seven residential restitution centers in Texas found that a large proportion of the 717 offenders who participated were being diverted from prison. Therefore, net widening was limited in these cases.

Behavioral Change/Treatment Effectiveness

Restitution may benefit offenders in various ways. In one way, restitution personalizes justice because the sanction is directly and meaningfully related to the offense committed. Offenders view the criminal justice system and society as responding directly to their behavior. Allen and Treger (1994) indicate that probationers perceive their restitution as a means for society to show disapproval (punishment). Restitution may also be rehabilitative. By fulfilling restitution orders, offenders may feel a sense of accomplishment and increased self-worth knowing they have made some reparation for the harm they caused. Restitution may also contribute to the development of personal discipline as a result of budgeting for restitution payments. According to Allen and Treger (1994) restitution is often perceived by probationers to be rehabilitative.

SUMMARY

Fines and restitution are the two monetary intermediate sanctions programs used in the United States. Fines require financial payment to the court and certain criminal justice or crime victims' funds and restitution requires compensation to crime victims. Monetary penalties are designed to deter crime, punish offenders, assist victims, and generate revenue to offset the costs of the criminal justice system. The use of these sanctions has increased significantly over the past 30 years, although they still seem to be underused, especially for serious offenders and as alternatives to incarceration. Two fines are distinguished: fixed fines and day fines. Fixed fines are based on the severity of crimes and day fines are based on the severity of crimes and the financial resources of offenders. Day fines are said to be more equitable and fair, although they have yet to be implemented on any significant scale. Enforcement of fines continues to be problematic in many jurisdictions. Despite its popularity overseas, the fine is not likely to become a viable alternative to jail or prison incarceration in the United States. Although research indicates that fines can be used effectively as alternatives to incarceration, they are used overwhelmingly for less serious offenders and as a supplement other sanctions, such as probation.

Restitution has widespread support because it addresses the needs of crime victims and aims to hold offenders accountable for their crimes. It involves compensation on the part of the offender to the victim, the victims' families, or to charitable organizations designated by the victim. It is used for property and violent offenders and mainly as a condition of probation or a supplemental penalty to incarceration. The enforcement of restitution can be improved using very simple techniques, such as reminder letters and telephone calls to offenders with outstanding debts.

 **CHAPTER 8**

Community Service

BACKGROUND

Community service is compulsory, free, or donated labor performed by an offender as punishment for a crime. The requirement of an offender to perform community service is often referred to as a community service order. An offender under a community service order is required to perform labor for a certain length of time at charitable not-for-profit agencies, such as domestic violence shelters, or governmental offices, such as courthouses. The work is completed within a proscribed time period, such as six months. Community service is closely aligned with restitution in that the offender engages in acts designed, in part, to make reparation for harm caused by his or her criminal offending, but these acts are directed to the larger community in the form of good works rather than to the victim alone. The main idea is that the work an offender performs is unpaid and benefits the community in some meaningful way. Community service addresses several important goals:

- **Punishment and Accountability**—Community service holds offenders accountable for the harm they have caused to the community by setting them to instrumental tasks. The assumption is that the community is a secondary victim indirectly affected by the crime. Community service deprives the offender of free time and places an obligation on him or her to work.

- **Restoration and Reparation**—A philosophy underlying community service is restorative and reparative in nature. Restorative justice practices seek to benefit the victim, the community, and the offender. Community service allows offenders to repair some harms they have caused and to provide tangible benefits to the community. Offenders' labor can improve the quality of life in communities and provide a valuable resource to government and not-for-profit agencies.
- **Restitution**—Good deeds on the part of an offender in the form of unpaid service to the community become an alternative to financial payment to the victim.
- **Rehabilitation**—Community service can assist offenders in developing a sense of responsibility, self worth, and motivation for legitimate work.
- **Victim Involvement**—Community service often provides victims a voice by recommending the type of community service that could be performed by an offender.

Community service is a fairly recent innovation. The first documented community service program in the United States began in Alameda County, California, in the late 1960s when traffic offenders who could not afford fines faced the possibility of incarceration (Anderson, 1998; McDonald, 1986). To avoid the financial costs of incarceration and individual costs in the lives of the offenders (who were often women with families), physical work in the community without compensation was assigned instead. The idea took hold and the use of community service expanded nationwide through the 1970s. It was promoted by the idea of "symbolic restitution," whereby offenders pay back for harms they have caused symbolically through good deeds in the form of free labor benefiting the community (McDonald, 1992). During the late 1970s, many community service programs were started with grants from the Law Enforcement Assistance Administration (LEAA) (Krajick, 1982). Then in the 1980s the logic for its use became punishment and incapacitation (Morris & Tonry, 1990). During the 1980s, with the shift in correctional focus from rehabilitation and reintegration to punishment and incapacitation, community service became known as an intermediate sanctions program.

Today, community service is used in every state (Tonry & Hamilton, 1995) and at the federal level. Lacking a national survey it is impossible to pinpoint the number of community service programs nationwide or the number of offenders with community service orders. According to a survey by the Bureau of Justice Statistics (Durose & Langan, 2001), six percent of all felony offenders sentenced in state courts in 1998 received a community service order in addition to their jail or prison terms. This amounts to more than 55,500 offenders. Nearly 25% of adults under the community supervision of jails in 2001 (17,561) were required to perform community service (Beck, Karberg, & Harrison, 2002). And about one-fourth of all DWI offenders on probation in 1997 (more than 109,000 persons) were required to perform community service as a condition of probation (Maruschak, 1999). In Maryland, 32,487 offenders received community service orders during 2001 (Maryland Division of Parole and Probation, n.d.). In California, 10,000 offenders are sentenced each month to community service (Krajick, 1982). Community service is a popular sanction in Texas, according to recent research by Caputo (2002). According to that research, probation administrators indicated that in some counties at least 75% of adults on probation had a community service order and in every jurisdiction at least 25% of adults had a community service order. In 21 Texas counties all probationers were also ordered to perform community service. According to state data, approximately 197,485 adult defendants participated in community service projects during fiscal year 2000 in Texas (Ramirez, n.d.). The use of community service has increased in Texas over the past five years; it has grown at about the same rate (70%) as probation or at a higher rate than probation (24%).

Community service is commonly used in other countries, often as an alternative to incarceration. It was introduced for offenders convicted of offenses punishable by imprisonment in England and Wales in 1975 (Joutsen & Zvekić, 1994) and New Zealand in 1981 (Challinger, 1994). In England and Wales, for instance, nearly 40,000 offenders received community service orders in 1990 (Great Britain Home Office, 1992). It is used in a host of European countries including Denmark, France, the Netherlands, Poland, Portugal, Sweden, Switzerland, Russia, and Yugoslavia (Joutsen & Bishop, 1994). Community service is used as an alternative to imprisonment in Africa (Odekunle, 1994), Latin countries such as Mexico and Brazil (Carranza, Liverpool, & Rodríguez-Manzanera,

1994), Scotland (McIvor, 1993), and Canada (Department of Justice, Sentencing Team, 1994). It is available in every Australian jurisdiction (Challinger, 1994), but still in its experimental states in Asia (Sugihara, et al., 1994).

TARGET POPULATIONS

Community service is ordered for various types of offenders including adults and juveniles, males and females, felons and misdemeanants, lower risk and higher risk offenders, probationers, and offenders who are incarcerated. Characteristics of adults with community service orders are similar to the characteristics of adults on probation generally. The typical probationer performing community service in 2000 in Texas was white, male, Hispanic, and was assigned to regular supervision (Caputo, 2002). The race and gender characteristics are consistent with national statistics of probationers over 2001 (Glaze, 2002). In Texas, half of the probationers with community service orders were felons and half were misdemeanants.

For the most part, community service is applied to nonviolent offenders, such as shoplifters and persons convicted of low-level drug possession offenses. In Texas, drug offenders and theft offenders are most commonly ordered to community service (see Figure 8.1). Community service is used more often for violent/assaultive offenders than for traffic/public order offenders and probation/parole violators (Caputo, 2002). According to the U.S. National Highway Traffic Safety Administration (2001) 23 states and the District of Columbia have implemented state laws requiring community service options (in addition to other penalties) for the second and subsequent convictions for driving while intoxicated or driving under the influence of alcohol. They include Alabama, Arizona, Arkansas, Colorado, Florida, Hawaii, Indiana, Idaho, Iowa, Kentucky, Maine, Michigan, Mississippi, Nebraska, Nevada, New Hampshire, New Jersey, North Carolina, Oklahoma, Pennsylvania, Utah, Virginia, and Washington.

In some jurisdictions, certain types of offenders and offenders convicted of certain offenses are excluded. In New York offenders with a sex offense conviction are excluded (New York State Division of Probation, n.d.) and in Texas offenders convicted of certain intoxication-related offenses (driving, flying, and boating while intoxicated,

	Number	Percent
How commonly theft offenders do community service		
Never/rarely	1	1%
Sometimes	25	29%
Most often	61	70%
How commonly violent/assaultive offenders do community service		
Never/rarely	3	4%
Sometimes	34	39%
Most often	49	57%
How commonly traffic/public order offenders do community service		
Never/rarely	25	30%
Sometimes	25	30%
Most often	33	40%
How commonly traffic/public order offenders do community service		
Never/rarely	25	30%
Sometimes	25	30%
Most often	33	40%
How commonly drug offenders do community service		-
Never/rarely	-	
Sometimes	25	29%
Most often	61	71%
How commonly probation violators do community service		
Never/rarely	17	20%
Sometimes	35	41%
Most often	33	39%

Figure 8.1. Community Service Profile by Offender/Offense in Texas: Results of a 2001 Survey of Probation Personnel

intoxication assault, and intoxication manslaughter) are excluded (Gould Publications of Texas, Inc., 2002). Disabled and seriously ill offenders as well as sex offenders are sometimes unofficially excluded in Texas (Caputo, 2002).

The best way to understand the different ways in which community service is used is by considering how it is combined with other punishments. Figure 8.2 illustrates three common sentencing models for the use of community service in the United States. It is likely that most states employ all three models.

COMMUNITY SERVICE MODEL 1	COMMUNITY SERVICE MODEL 2	COMMUNITY SERVICE MODEL 3
Community service is a sole punishment for very minor offenders	Community service is a front-end diversion from incarceration	Community service is a probation enhancement tool

Figure 8.2: Three Common Community Service Models

Community Service as a Sole Penalty

First, community service is used as a sole penalty usually for very minor and first-time offenders, for instance traffic violators. In this way, community service becomes an alternative to probation or to fines (and even fine default) and is not used as an intermediate punishment (one between probation and incarceration). In California, for instance, certain offenders who commit very minor offenses and for whom paying a fine would be a hardship may be ordered to perform community service instead of paying a fine (Gould Publications, Inc., 2002).

Community Service as a Supplemental Sanction

Second and most commonly, community service is used as a special condition of probation or parole. In this way community service is not a sole sanction, but part of a sentencing "package." This is the case at the federal level where federal offenders sentenced to probation may receive a community service order as a special condition of probation. In fiscal year 2000, nearly 5,600 federal offenders were ordered to perform community service as part of a probation sentence. For these offenders, the courts ordered more than one million community service hours (Administrative Office of the Courts, 2001). Federal offenders sentenced to prison may also receive an order requiring community service following imprisonment and when the offender is on parole supervision. According to the research by Caputo (2002) community service is used most often or always as a supplement to probation supervision in Texas, or in other words as a special condition of probation (Figure 8.3).

Community Service as an Alternative to Incarceration

Third, community service may be used in the place of incarceration as an intermediate sanction. Although it is commonly used as an alternative

	Number	Percent
Proportion adults under supervision with community service orders		
Less than 25%	-	-
25% - 50%	6	6%
51% - 75%	15	18%
More than 75%	43	51%
All	21	25%
How commonly community service is used as jail alternative		
Never	8	9%
Rarely	17	20%
Sometimes	24	28%
Most often	35	41%
Always	2	2%
How commonly community service is used as a sole sanction		
Never	46	53%
Rarely	33	38%
Sometimes	6	7%
Most often	2	2%
Always	-	-
How commonly community service is used as a condition of probation		
Never	-	-
Rarely	-	-
Sometimes	5	6%
Most often	57	66%
Always	24	28%
Growth of community service over the past five years		
Increased about the same rate as probation	57	70%
Increased at a higher rate than probation populations	20	24%
Decreased while probation populations have increased	5	6%

Figure 8.3. Characteristics of Community Service Sentencing in Texas: Results of a 2001 Survey of Probation Personnel

to jail in European countries, community service is rarely used in this way in the United States. (See McIvor, 1990, 1993; Pease, 1985.) In fact, Tonry (1996, p. 121) calls it "the most underused intermediate sanction".

When community service is used as an alternative to incarceration it is generally used for misdemeanants in the place of jail rather than for felons in the place of prison. For instance, the Community Service Sentencing Project (CSSP) based in New York City serves upwards of 1,000 repeat misdemeanants who would be normally sent to jail for up to six months. According to research by the Vera Institute of Justice (Caputo, 2000; Caputo, Young, & Porter, 1998c; 1998b; Young, Porter, & Caputo, 1999) the offenders have persistent involvement in low-level offending. Sixty-five percent of a group of 146 offenders studied had at least 10 prior adult arrests, 74 percent had five or more misdemeanor convictions, 47 percent had 10 or more misdemeanor convictions, and 69 percent had at least one felony conviction. Many of the misdemeanor convictions were for property crimes, primarily petty larceny (for instance, shoplifting). In Texas, community service is used as an alternative to jail terms for adults sometimes (25%), most often (41%) or always (2%). There, 85% of probation administrators surveyed support the use of community service as an alternative to jail incarceration (85%) for low-level nonviolent offenders (Caputo, 2002).

Community Service in Conjunction with Incarceration

Fourth, community service may be used in conjunction with incarceration. Jails and to a lesser extent prisons may operate community service work crews composed of inmate workers. Removing litter from roads and highways and other public service work projects are common. In Kentucky, minimum-security nonviolent jail inmates perform community service in work crews supervised by staff of the Boone County Jail (Boone County Jail, n.d.). The Department of Rehabilitation and Correction in Ohio (Wilkinson, 2000) reports that state prison inmates in Ohio worked 4.2 million hours of community service in 1999. Not all jail and prison inmates are eligible for participation. Violent inmates, inmates who represent escape risks, and those in disciplinary segregation or other restricted housing may not be eligible to participate.

PROGRAM CHARACTERISTICS
Community Service Orders

Community service orders can range from very short terms, such as 20 hours, to more than 1000 hours. In Texas over fiscal year 2000 the typical order for misdemeanants was 60 hours and the typical order for felons was 230 hours (Caputo, 2002). Generally, the number of hours or days an offender is ordered to perform community service varies with the nature and seriousness of the offense, the offender's prior criminal record, and extra-legal factors such as family and work responsibilities.

In some jurisdictions, such as in Texas, the employment status of the offender is an important consideration in the determination of community service orders. According to the Texas Code of Criminal Procedure, offenders who are employed cannot be ordered to more than 16 hours of community service weekly and unemployed offenders cannot be ordered to more than 32 hours weekly (Gould Publications of Texas, Inc., 2002).

The framework for determining the duration of community service orders (hours or days) differs across jurisdiction and often within jurisdiction for similar types of offenders. When judges decide a community service order is appropriate, they usually have flexibility in determining its duration, relying on a range of hours that are legislatively proscribed for certain offense levels, such as misdemeanors and felonies.

Most often, the duration of a community service order is calculated against a fine or term of incarceration that could have, or presumably would have, been imposed. In the case of using incarceration to determine duration of community service, jurisdictions employ a formula equating hours of community service with jail time that is "displaced" (e.g., could have been imposed). For instance, in Texas eight hours of community service work replaces one day of incarceration (Gould Publications of Texas, Inc., 2002). Oregon's sentencing guideline system authorized an exchange of one day's confinement for 16 hours of community service (Tonry, 1997).

Determining duration of community service based on an alternative fine amount involves a calculation of the monetary value of labor (the standard minimum wage for instance) against the total fine amount. The result is the number of hours an offender must work to "pay off" the fine.

Another model for determining duration of community service involves a fixed or "flat" sentencing system. The Community Service Sentencing Project in New York City relies on such a system and other programs probably do as well, but this appears to be the exception. At CSSP, offenders who are expected to receive terms of 20 to 45 days in jail receive 10 days (70 hours) of community service and those facing 46 to 180 jail terms receive 15 days (105 hours) as the main punishment for crimes.

Community Service Work Sites

As part of the community service order, offenders perform work at an agency or organization that is approved by the court, the probation department, the parole department, or the organization overseeing the community service order. The agencies at which offenders perform community service work are referred to as worksites or host sites. According to the research by Caputo (2002) these worksites are nearly always not-for-profit or charitable agencies as well as government agencies. A written agreement between the worksite and the correctional agency would outline information such as the procedures for placement and supervision of offenders and the nature of community service work that would be performed. Very rarely are for-profit agencies used and in some states, such as in Texas, private agencies are excluded from involvement (Gould Publications of Texas, Inc., 2002). Common worksites include: community organizations, hospitals and nursing homes, animal shelters, churches, Goodwill, food pantries, schools, humane societies, city parks, senior citizen centers, Boys/Girls Clubs, Salvation Army, as well as township and city agencies such as courthouses and fire departments. According to the Administrative Office of the United States Courts (1981), community agencies should meet the following criteria:

- The organization must be nonprofit, tax exempt, and not primarily politically partisan.
- The organization must not discriminate in the acceptance of volunteers.
- The organization must serve valid community needs in an appropriate manner and must have a demonstrated ability to use volunteers effectively.
- If the organization is a membership organization, the primary purpose of the organization must not be to serve the economic or social needs of the members.
- The agency must have a "job description" for the work performed by each community service worker, and the performance of the job must not seriously jeopardize the safety or health of the offender or the community.
- The work performed by offenders for those agencies should not displace paid workers and should consist of duties and functions

that would not have otherwise been performed without volunteer workers.

The Administration of Community Service

Community service may be administered and managed by a variety of criminal justice agencies, such as law enforcement offices, courts, jail and prisons, parole departments, probation departments, and through private agencies. Since community service is used mainly as a condition of probation most agencies that supervise offenders who do community service are probably probation departments.

Some probation departments have developed special units responsible for placing offenders into community service work positions and for overseeing offenders' compliance with community service orders (Caputo, 2002). In Texas the units are referred to as Community Service Restitution Units and are typically composed of a three-member staff, generally full time workers who are responsible for managing community service restitution in the department. Community Service Restitution Coordinators oversee such duties as:

- Providing community service orientation to offenders, assigning a worksite based on job skills, employment/unemployment status, transportation, and health issues;
- Coordinating with worksite agencies to maintain communications to monitor community service activities;
- Maintaining the count of community service hours worked;
- Reporting noncompliance to probation supervision officers when offender fails to report to worksite, fails to adhere to community service rules, or commits any other unacceptable behavior;
- Monitoring offenders' program completion.
- Maintaining annual calendar of scheduled activities and community service projects;

Other correctional departments rely on individual probation officers to manage and enforce community service orders. Agencies that use a specialized unit for overseeing community service are more likely to formalize the placement of offenders into work positions and supervise offenders while they are at the worksites. Some jurisdictions contract with private agencies to administer and oversee community service and then to report back on the progress of offenders who are ordered to perform community service. The Community Service Sentencing Project is one such agency that contracts with the city of New York to place offenders into work positions, supervise offenders while they perform the work, take action in case of noncompliance, and report to the courts on the progress of offenders ordered to community service. The program is described in detail in Figure 8.4.

Placement and Monitoring of Offenders

Once community service is ordered, offenders must be placed into a community agency worksite and the community service must be

---

THE COMMUNITY SERVICE SENTENCING PROJECT (CSSP)

Program Description
CSSP is nonresidential alternative to incarceration for non-violent adult repeat misdemeanor offenders who would otherwise serve jail terms of up to six- months. Offenders perform up to 15 days of community service in poor neighborhoods throughout New York City. CSSP is run by the Center for Alternative Sentencing and Employment Services (CASES). CSSP was developed as a demonstration project by the Vera Institute of Justice in 1979 in Bronx, NY and transferred to CASES in 1989 where it was expanded to Queens, Manhattan, and Brooklyn and served upwards of 1,000 annually.

Selection of Participants
CSSP operates in the Criminal Courts of the Bronx, Brooklyn, Manhattan, and Queens. Using empirically-based criteria which identify offenders as "jailbound", CSSP court representatives screen eligible cases and advocate before judges for the placement of offenders in CSSP. Offenders placed into CSSP have plead guilty to the misdemeanor offense and receive a conditional discharge which requires either 10 or 15 days of community service under the supervision and direction of CSSP staff. Offenders facing jail terms of 20 to 45 days received a 10-day community service order (called Model A sentences) and offenders facing 46 to180 day jail sentences received a 15-day order (called Model B sentences).

Three Units Assist Participants
Approximately 40 CSSP staff are organized into three main units. "Site Unit" staff supervises the community service work, records attendance, work hours, and infractions, and evaluates participants' performance, behavior and attitude after five and then ten workdays. Retired law enforcement officers comprise the "Compliance Unit" and encourage attendance by making work site and home visits and daily telephone calls. They also serve arrest warrants for participants who have violated conditions of CSSP. Although CSSP contains no treatment component and does not intend to change offenders' behavior in any way, it does help offenders with basic needs, such as food and clothing. This "Support Services Unit" also provides referrals for services related to legal issues, education and employment, substance abuse treatment, as well as medical and mental health.

Daily Schedule of Activities
The community service work is highly structured. Each weekday morning participants report to a centralized location (usually at a housing project) where they are provided breakfast and the day's schedule of activities. Then participants are transported by CSSP staff in teams to worksites throughout the city where they perform various types of community service work. Worksites consist of nonprofit organizations. Most of the work involves physical labor. Participants are supervised by CSSP staff at the worksites at all times.

Supervision of Participants
CSSP participants are supervised each day while they are performing community service and are required to abide by a set of rules and regulations during non-working hours.

Program Performance
Research on CSSP in 1986 and in 1998 suggests that CSSP is a successful program. The research published in 1998 by Douglas McDonald show communities benefit from the work performed, judges viewed the program favorably, participants did not have higher rates of reoffending compared to jail inmates. The more recent research indicated rates of completion were favorable (upwards of 75%) and many offenders believe community service helped them in various ways.

Source: Caputo et al., 1998b, 1998c; McDonald, 1986.

Figure 8.4. The Community Service Sentencing Project (CSSP)

monitored. There is variation in this process of placement, monitoring and supervision, and terminating, but we can identify two broad placement models. One model requires offenders to take an active role in their own placement, for instance choosing a worksite from a list of approved agencies and arranging a work schedule with the agency. A second model for placement of offenders involves a referral process where correctional staff (such as staff of a community service division within a probation department) place offenders. Community service is more formalized in some departments; for instance a number of probation departments in Texas operate specialized community service units with staff dedicated to the placement and monitoring of offenders with community service orders.

Depending on the formalization of a community service program, offenders with community service orders may be supervised at the worksites by correctional staff (such as probation officers assigned to community service work crews). In such programs, monitoring of offender performance and compliance with the community service order should be rather straightforward. Not all probation and parole departments operate a specialized community service unit. Rather, individual probation and parole officers with supervision caseloads are responsible for monitoring the compliance of offenders with community service orders on their caseloads. This would involve close contact by the officer with the offender and the worksite agency.

Treatments and Services for Offenders

Some correctional agencies provide some form of treatment and services for participants in community service programs. For instance, the Community Service Sentencing Project has a special unit that provides in-house and referral services for family, medical, and social problems as well as food, housing, and clothing to participants as necessary. The treatment needs of participants are evaluated at program intake and referrals are made to appropriate agencies and programs throughout the city (Caputo, Young, & Porter, 1998b, 1998c).

The most obvious treatment need of probationers with community service orders in Texas is alcohol abuse. Drug abuse and financial difficulties are also impacting more than half of adults with community service orders. Mental illness is the only problem that is observed in fewer than 25% of the population. Most treatments and services are provided through referral to outside agencies and address alcohol abuse, drug abuse, education, and financial management difficulties. Most departments do not provide treatments or services for legal issues and childcare either through referral or to outside agencies (Caputo, 2002).

Type of Work Performed

Community service involves a variety of different types of work. The work that offenders perform depends on the offenders' work skills and the needs of the worksite agencies. Research by the Vera Institute of Justice on the Community Service Sentencing Project (Caputo, 2000; Caputo, Young, & Porter, 1998b, 1998c; Young, Porter, & Caputo, 1999) indicates that all of the work performed by a group of offenders in 1998 involved physical labor, both skilled and unskilled. Most included carpentry (building bookcases) and janitorial maintenance (painting, floor waxing, and graffiti removal). Some of the work involved the restoration of a church, painting a social service building for children, and assisting residents of a nursing home with daily maintenance chores. Community service in Texas also involves physical labor most often. Outdoor maintenance and debris removal is the most popular. Rarely do offenders perform clerical and human or social service work (Caputo, 2002). Community service work has some common elements:

- The work is uncompensated
- The work must be completed within a specific amount of time
- The work is performed during an offender's leisure time
- The work is performed at charitable or government agencies
- The work is determined by the judge, a probation/parole official, and the needs of the work agency

Most offenders with community service orders work at their own pace, according to a schedule and often alone. They are frequently supervised at the worksite by the worksite staff especially when they work individually (Caputo, 2002). Participants in more formalized programs may be required to work on a prearranged schedule or on work crews with other offenders also performing community service. The "Weekend Work Order" is one such program in Ulster County, New York. It was developed for felony DWI offenders and requires offenders to work on crews each Saturday and Sunday to perform community service under the direction of a corrections officer from the Sheriff's department (Cappillino, 1993).

PROGRAM EXAMPLE:
THE COMMUNITY SERVICE SENTENCING PROJECT

The Community Service Sentencing Project (CSSP) is the most well-documented program in the United States. It began in 1979 as a Vera Institute of Justice demonstration project in Bronx County, New York. With staff stationed in court to select eligible offenders and advocate for their release, its population would include offenders likely to receive lesser penalties and offenders likely to receive jail terms. Offenders selected for participation received a conditional discharge, requiring they complete 10 days (70 hours) of physical labor under the supervision of Vera Institute staff. As a middle range sanction, CSSP was supported by city officials who were faced with an increase in jail populations and criticism that punishment for offenders was often too lenient. About 400 offenders participated over the first two years and nearly 90% completed successfully (Vera Institute of Justice, 1981).

By 1983, CSSP had expanded and was serving more than one thousand offenders annually. To the benefit of CSSP, research reported by McDonald (1986) indicated that offenders were successfully being diverted from short jail terms to the project and that rates of rearrest for CSSP participants were no higher than for a comparison group of offenders who were incarcerated.

The Center for Alternative Sentencing and Employment Services (CASES) assumed program operations in 1989 and CSSP expanded throughout New York City. A Site Unit supervised the community service work, recorded attendance, work hours, and infractions, and evaluated the performance, behavior, and attitude of offenders after five and ten workdays. A Compliance Unit (comprised exclusively of retired law enforcement officers) encouraged attendance through daily telephone calls and unannounced home and worksite visits. A Support Services Unit assessed participants' needs and provided assistance with food, clothing, shelter, and transportation, as well as out-of-program referrals for treatment and other services. Essentially, CSSP staff did whatever it could reasonably do to facilitate offenders' successful completion of the program. Over time, the program was restructured to operate exclusively as an alternative to jail terms of up to six months and added a 15-day community service option.

In mid-1997, the Central Court Screening Service (CCSS) of the New York Criminal Justice Agency (CJA) assumed the role of selecting offenders into the program using empirically based criteria and then liaising between courts and the program. Once criminal defendants were identified as "jailbound" (likely to be given jail terms upon conviction), a fixed sentencing system was applied. Offenders facing jail terms of 20 to 45 days received an 8-, 10-, or 12-day community service order (called Model A sentences). Offenders facing 46- to180-day jail sentences received a 15-, 18-, or 22-day order (called Model B sentences). The scheme was eventually simplified to the 10-day order under Model A and the 15-day order under Model B. As of this writing, CASES has again taken over selection of offenders.

According to research by the Vera Institute in the late 1990s (Caputo, 2000; Caputo, Young, & Porter, 1998b, 1998c; Young, Porter, & Caputo, 1999) CSSP participants are predominately male, have substance abuse, medical, and employment problems, and have persistent involvement in low-level offending. About 65% of a group of offenders in CSSP had at least 10 prior adult arrests, 74% had five or more misdemeanor convictions, 47% had 10 or more misdemeanor convictions, and 69% had at least one felony conviction. The misdemeanor convictions were typically for crimes such as petty larceny (for instance, shoplifting). As many as 75% completed their community service orders successfully and failures were most often rule-related and not due to the commission of new crimes. Additionally, members of community agencies reported favorable views of the program and the work performed by the offenders. This research indicates that community service can be used successfully with the low-level repeat offender.

CSSP appears to differ from the typical form of community service with respect to its offender population, structure for establishing duration of community service, supervision responsibilities, and administration. First, it supervises the higher-risk offender as an intermediate punishment whereas most community service sentences are handed down as alternatives or additions to probation. Second, it relies on a fixed sentencing structure, whereas other jurisdictions probably determine duration of community service based upon possible fines or terms of imprisonment. Third, it is operated by a not-or-profit agency that manages and directly supervises the community service work, whereas typically, probation departments manage offenders on community service but do not supervise their work directly.

RESEARCH ON COMMUNITY SERVICE

Program Completion

Program completion refers to the completion of sentenced hours or days of community service, or in other words completion of the community service order. Rates of completion are generally favorable. According to Krajick (1982), 85% to 95% of offenders with community service orders complete their sentences. McDonald (1986) reported completion rates of 50% to 85% for offenders in the Community Service Sentencing Project in the mid-1980s. Recent research on the program found that completion rates were about 74% (Caputo, 2000; Caputo, Young, & Porter, 1998b, 1998c; Young, Porter, & Caputo, 1999). Anderson (1997) reported a rate of 85% for adults in New Jersey and an 80% rate for offenders in an Indiana program. On average, 71% of Texas probationers with community service orders in 2000 completed their community service orders successfully and 75% completed probation successfully.

Community Service Sentencing County of Erie, NY

The Community Service Sentencing operates through the probation department and is used for misdemeanants and felons. In addition to developing work sites, placing and monitoring offenders, the program also provides many support services, such as for problems relating to drugs and alcohol. In 1994, a total of 550 offenders participated in the program. During 1994, offenders performed 42,074 hours of community service. The program reports a successful completion rate of 85% for 1994.

Field Services Program, Clarksville TN

The Tennessee Department of Corrections Field Services Program was implemented in 1985 and is run by thirteen Work Project Coordinators. Coordinators place offenders into work sites and monitor the offenders' performance in the community service placement. In 1989 and in 1990, 500 offenders participated in the program. The program reports a 64 percent success rate. Two percent of the offenders who successfully completed the program committed new crimes compared to 10% that did not successfully complete the program.

Oklahoma County Community Service, Oklahoma City, OK

Established in 1983, the program places and monitors offenders with community service orders. Participants may also use the "Literacy Council" to learn to read and write as their community service requirement. In 1994, 2,972 adult offenders were ordered to perform 230,972 hours of community service.

Court Community Service Program, Marietta, GA

This Community Service Program was initiated in 1980. The project actively develops community service slots in addition to monitoring offenders in placements. It also offers services to participants, such as job development services, work skills training, and psychological counseling. In 1990, 136 adult offenders participated and completed a total of 24,960 hours of community service. The program reports a completion rate of about 66%.

Source: Schneider and Finkelstein, 1998.

Figure 8.5 Community Service Program Examples

Although the evaluation literature is quite modest, two research projects indicate that participants in community service programs who do not complete the community service order successfully generally fail as a result of rule violations rather then as a result of a new crime. Participants in the Community Service Sentencing Program in the late 1990s who did not complete failed mainly because they did not perform the days of community service ordered by the court (Caputo, 2000; Caputo, Young, & Porter, 1998b, 1998c; Young, Porter & Caputo, 1999). Also for Texas adult probationers (See Figure 8.6), failure to complete hours ordered was the most common reason cited by probation administrators for noncompliance with community service in 2000 (Caputo, 2002).

	Never/Rarely	Sometimes	Most Often
Failure to complete hours ordered	21%	44%	35%
Poor performance at worksites	58%	41%	1%
Negative attitude/behavior at worksites	47%	51%	2%
Probation revocation for new arrest	5%	81%	14%
Probation revocation for technical violation	11%	82%	7%
Early/successful probation completion	70%	27%	3%
Transfer out of jurisdiction	22%	77%	1%
Incarceration	12%	82%	6%

Figure 8.6. Reasons for Offender Noncompliance with Community Service Orders in Texas: Results of a 2001 Survey of Probation Personnel

For community service to be an effective sanction it must be enforced. Lax enforcement can be especially problematic, because when offenders fail to comply with the community service order and are not held accountable, community service loses credibility. The Vera Institute of Justice research on the community service sentencing program (Caputo, et al., 1998c) shows that the program initiates court action in every case of noncompliance by issuing arrest warrants. Additionally, administrators of probation-based community service programs in Texas tend to disagree that lax enforcement is an issue, but indicate that an important problem is that criminal justice officials (such as judges) do not take community service seriously enough (Caputo, 2002).

Recidivism

1984 research on CSSP (McDonald, 1986) estimated the impact of program participation on subsequent criminality. Overall, 43 percent of a group of almost 500 had been rearrested, most within three months and the remainder within six months of program completion, and mainly for property crimes. These results were compared to those for a group of offenders who were eligible for the program, but had instead received jail terms. The rearrest rates of the two groups were not significantly different. The researchers concluded that although neither sanction was particularly effective at reducing subsequent criminality, CSSP did not increase risk.

Recent research on state prison inmates involved in community service project suggests that the more hours of community service participation the less likely an inmate is to become reincarcerated (Wilkinson, 2000). Other research has shown that offenders with community service had lower rates of recidivism than those with prison sentences (Pease, 1985)

Net Widening

Community service is rarely used as an alternative to incarceration in the United States and therefore is unlikely to reduce correctional crowding or costs (Immarigeon, 1986) and may increase net widening. Programs that claim to divert offenders from incarceration but instead draw participants from probation or other lesser sanctions would be contributing to net widening. In 1984, Douglas McDonald and his colleagues at the Vera Institute of Justice evaluated the extent to which the nationally recognized CSSP was drawing offenders from jail or contributing to net widening (McDonald, 1986). Researchers used comparison groups to estimate the probability and length of jail sentences for the offenders if the community service program had not been available. Results suggested that the proportion of participants who would have received jail terms was less than 50 % in the Bronx and in Brooklyn, and 60% in Manhattan. Vera researchers concluded that in the Bronx and Brooklyn, prosecutors had a more active role in screening and selecting cases while in Manhattan, judges were more involved. Based on these findings, selection procedures were modified to increase the likelihood of diversion.

Cost Effectiveness

Correctional dollars are often saved when community service is used as an alternative to incarceration. In a study of a federally run program in

Georgia, Majer (1994) reported prison cost savings into the millions. Most research assessing cost benefits of community service involves the economic value of community service work that is "donated" to communities, because the real value of community service lies in the benefits it provides to communities. Vera Institute researchers estimated that 60,000 hours of labor had been provided to the community in 1984 by participants of the Community Service Sentencing Project and that if participants had been paid the minimum wage of $4.50 per hour, the labor performed was worth upwards of $270,300 (McDonald, 1986). In Texas, more than nine million hours of community service were completed throughout the state in 2000. Using the minimum wage figure of $5.15 it is calculated that services worth a total of $46,907,770 have been contributed to the community through community service (Ramirez, n.d.).

Behavioral Change/Treatment Effectiveness

Offenders tend to have favorable views of community service and the work they perform (Allen & Treger, 1990). In fact, some offenders continue working in the same setting even after completing the order (Majer, 1994). Research indicates that participation in community service does benefit offenders particularly through the work structure and routine (Caputo, 2000; Caputo, Young, & Porter, 1998b, 1998c; Young, Porter, & Caputo, 1999) and in terms of developing a work ethic, prosocial attitudes, prosocial relationships, and responsibility/accountability (Caputo, 2002).

SUMMARY

Community service is the only sanction that directly involves the community in corrections. Offenders with community service orders work for the benefit of communities and the services provided are thought to contribute to a better quality of life in communities. The idea of offenders performing physical labor without compensation is generally supported by the public (Tonry, 1996). When enforced properly, community service can serve as meaningful punishment for misbehavior; quality of life in communities can be improved, and community members can feel that they have played a role in criminal justice. To the benefit of offenders and their families, community service is less intrusive than most other sanctions and with structured work routines, it may prove beneficial in the lives of offenders. Even if a community service program does not aim to treat their needs, when offenders remain in their communities performing unpaid labor as a criminal sanction, they are able to maintain their familial, social, and work-related responsibilities and ties. When available to replace short jail terms, especially for repeat, but minor property offenders whom the system finds hard to deal with, community service sentencing may also bring relief to overcrowded jails.

CHAPTER 9

Halfway Houses

BACKGROUND

Halfway houses are community-based residential facilities designed to limit the freedom of offenders while seeking to reintegrate them into society through employment and other services. They are used primarily to help inmates who are being released from prisons make the often-difficult transition from confinement to the community. Halfway houses are also referred to as adult residential centers, community residential centers/programs, community corrections centers, community release centers, parole residential centers, transitional centers, and residential community correctional facilities. Halfway house facilities are located within communities, were often once private residences, and are designed to "blend in" with the community.

Participation in halfway houses requires 24-hour supervision and offers offenders access to treatment and other rehabilitative services. Participants are permitted to leave the house with restrictions for work, education, and other responsibilities and they generally spend the evenings at the halfway house. Given its residency condition, a halfway house provides more structure and supervision than a typical probation or parole program, but is not as secure as a jail or prison.

When used to provide punishment and structured supervision for offenders, such as those who are directly sentenced for a crime to a halfway house, halfway houses are often referred to as "halfway-in" facilities. The "halfway-out" facilities are the most popular form of the halfway house and are used to assist in the reintegration of inmates from confinement to community life. As the name suggests, these halfway houses are halfway between prison and freedom. Thus, halfway house residents have greater autonomy and responsibility than inmates, but less independence than ordinary citizens. The logic of these programs is that offenders, especially prisoners awaiting release, need stability in their lives as well as assistance with reestablishing themselves into conventional society. By providing offenders a structured and supportive environment, where their basic necessities are provided, halfway houses should allow offenders to take charge of their lives and futures.

Halfway houses originated in England and Ireland in the early 1800s and today are used throughout the world. The earliest halfway houses in the United States were developed in the 1840s by the Quakers in an effort to assist offenders who were released from prison (Clear & Dammer, 2000). Most early halfway houses were run by charitable organizations (Latessa & Travis, 1992). Although the use of halfway houses went through a period of decline during and after the Great Depression (1930s–1940s), they were popularized by a national halfway house movement, which began in the 1950s and continued through the 1960s. This movement was spawned by the increased use of parole. Paroling authorities wanted to ensure that inmates would have jobs and an ability to support themselves before being fully released from correctional custody. As such, halfway houses were primarily used as "halfway-out" programs for parolees. It was believed that transitional support services, such as job placement, would reduce the likelihood of parolee recidivism. The success of the programs and the development of the International Halfway House Association in 1964 (later renamed the International Community Corrections Association) led to the institutionalization and expanded use of halfway houses for adults as authorized in the Federal Prisoner Rehabilitation Act of 1965. By the 1960s, states also began to use halfway houses for offenders at sentencing, or as a front-end alternative to incarceration. The so-called "halfway-in" houses were created for adult probationers and other offenders as diversions from the criminal justice system (McCarthy, McCarthy, & Leone, 2001.). Beginning in the 1970s, the support for these programs dwindled with the move to get tough on crime and many programs lost funding. With the increased attention paid to the reentry of prisoners to communities, the 1980s saw a growth in programs, especially those for parolees. By 1989 there were 839 facilities serving adult offenders (Knapp & Burke, 2000).

More recent research on halfway houses for inmates in state and federal prisons found that 11 states operated 72 halfway houses at the start of 2000. The Iowa correctional system operated the most halfway houses (21) followed by Michigan (18) and Pennsylvania (14). In Iowa, more than 16% of all inmates were housed in halfway houses at the start of 2000. Many of these states as well as others housed their inmates in halfway houses operated by private agencies. In total, 22 states housed inmates in 961 halfway houses, which were operated by private agencies. Ohio alone housed 6,150 inmates, or 13% of its total inmate population. Alaska had the highest proportion of its inmates (23%) in halfway houses (Camp & Camp, 2000). Compared to state systems, the Federal Bureau of Prisons offers more release preparation programming and makes greater use of halfway houses. In 2000, the BOP had contracts with 282 halfway houses, which served 18,113 inmates, about 45% of all inmates released that year (U.S. General Accounting Office, 2001). These statistics refer to halfway houses used for inmates and do not reflect the hundreds of halfway houses designed for probation and pretrial populations throughout the country. Consolidated statistics regarding the actual number of offenders placed in halfway houses are unavailable. However, population statistics from several states and the federal system indicate that thousands of inmates do participate in halfway houses annually.

TARGET POPULATIONS

Halfway houses serve both women and men and some halfway houses are coed facilities. Most programs serve populations of offenders with drug and alcohol problems and tend to exclude violent and sex offenders (Knapp & Burke, 1992). As Figure 9.1 illustrates, each type of halfway house facility targets more than one offender group. "Halfway-in" facilities are used as a front-end alternative to incarceration and halfway-out facilities are used as a back-end alternative to incarceration. In addition, halfway houses may also be used as pretrial release facilities. Many existing halfway houses draw participants from more than one population, such as offenders who are directly sentenced to halfway houses and offenders who have violated probation and have been resentenced to the halfway house.

"HALFWAY IN" HOUSES		"HALFWAY OUT" HOUSES	
Halfway house is used as a front-end alternative to incarceration.		Halfway house is used as a back-end alternative to incarceration.	
Primary purpose is punishment, accountability, and supervision.		Primary purpose is reintegration, supervision, and assistance.	
Used as a Direct Sentence	**Used as a Graduated Sanction and Probation/Parole Enhancement Mechanism**	**Used as a Pre-Release Mechanism**	**Used as an Early Release Mechanism in Conjunction with Parole**
Offenders who are directly sentenced by the court to the halfway house as an alternative to incarceration.	Participants of programs, such as probation and parole who are reassigned to halfway house for violations and special needs.	Inmates nearing the end of their sentences who are "pre-released" into the halfway house before final release.	Inmates nearing the end of their sentences who are released early from jail or prison and placed into the halfway house usually as a condition of post release supervision (parole).

Figure 9.1. Two Halfway House Models

"Halfway-In" Houses as Front-End Alternatives to Incarceration

Halfway House Placement as a Direct Court Sentence

Halfway houses, like other intermediate sanctions, are often used as a direct court sentence for offenders who are in need of a more punitive and restrictive sanction than probation or other intermediate sanctions. "Halfway-in" houses serve this population and provide punishment and supervision as an alternative to incarceration. The placement into a halfway house may be used in conjunction with probation or other intermediate sanctions. For example, a halfway house participant may also be required to perform community service. An offender sentenced directly to a halfway house program typically presents a greater need for the structure, supervision, and supportive services offered by such a facility. For example, a repeat property offender with a poor employment history and chronic drug problem may benefit from the employment training and/or placement and substance abuse treatment services that many halfway house facilities provide.

Halfway House Placement as Graduated Sanction or to Enhance Probation and Parole

In addition, "halfway-in" houses are also used as a graduated sanction resulting from failure in another program. For instance, if a participant in an intensive supervision program was repeatedly violating his curfew and was not regularly attending his job, that offender might be placed into a halfway house facility rather than jail or prison. The halfway house setting provides around-the-clock monitoring and may help to ensure compliance with various conditions, such as employment, restitution, and treatment. "Halfway-in" houses are also used as enhancement models for probationers and parolees who might not have violated conditions, but who could be helped by the residency and other requirements of the halfway house. The Kalamazoo Probation Enhancement Program is one such example (See Figure 9.2).

A halfway house used to enhance regular probation

Program Description

KPEP is a privately operated halfway house in Michigan. It is a probation enhancement halfway house intended to provide probationers who have been convicted of nonviolent crimes with a highly structured and residential experience. The emphasis is on helping participants obtain and maintain employment.

Four Program Components

KPEP offers a range of programming in-house and through referral to other agencies:
- employment skills classes which aim to build job seeking skills and skills for continued employment
- job club, a peer support group for participants who are seeking employment or who have recently acquired employment
- basic life skills classes which focus on practical skills such as income budgeting
- GED classes
- Substance abuse counseling
- Vocational training

Four Program Phases

The facility incorporates phases or levels of supervision. Newly admitted participants begin at level one and proceed through the program to level four, which prepares participants for release. The levels vary in the nature of goals to be achieved as well as the intensity of supervision, responsibilities, and the level of privileges. Participants graduate through phases when they have accomplished the goals outline for each phase. For example, participants must have a job in hand before they can proceed to level two. KPEP staff keep record of participant progress through the use of a point system. Points are rewarded for forward moving progress and retracted for disciplinary and other reasons. Participants spend about 20 weeks in the program and are then released to regular probation.

Program Requirements

Participants must abide by a variety of conditions. Rule infractions may result in point demotions (which affect a participant's progress in the levels or phases of the programs) as well as termination.
- Adhere to in-house rules, governing personal hygiene, care of facility (chores), and interaction with other participants
- Adhere to out-of-house rules, such as curfews, refraining from the use of alcohol and drugs.
- Submitting to random urinalysis

Source: Hartmann, Friday, and Minor, 1994

Figure 9.2. The Kalamazoo Probation Enhancement Program (KPEP)

"Halfway-Out" Houses as a Back-End Alternative to Incarceration

The most common use of the halfway house is as a back-end diversion from incarceration (Knapp & Burke, 1992). According to recent statistics, 97% of inmates in confinement will eventually be released from prison and will return to communities (Parent & Barnett, 2002). It is well documented that inmates face significant hardships upon release from prison, such as broken ties to the community, drug and alcohol abuse, problems with gaining employment, and problems adjusting to community life. An offender's failure on post-incarceration supervision is most likely to occur in the first three months of release (U.S. General Accounting Office, 2001). The halfway-out facilities aim to address the difficulties faced by inmates upon release and to reduce the likelihood of their recidivism by providing supportive services, including job placement, drug/alcohol treatment and mentoring. Whereas accountability, punishment, and supervision are the focus of "halfway-in" houses, reintegration is the focus of "halfway-out" facilities. Inmates may be placed into halfway houses as a form of pre-release and as early release (See Figure 9.2). The overriding goal of "halfway-out" houses is to help ease the transition of jail and prison inmates back into the community. Figure 9.3 illustrates the use of halfway houses for federal inmates.

Halfway House Placement as a Pre-Release Mechanism

Inmates who are selected to participate in halfway houses as a form of pre-release are still considered inmates and are placed into a halfway house when they are nearing the end of their sentence. The inmate has not been officially released from prison onto parole supervision and is subject to return to the custodial institution for violating the specified conditions of his or her contract. Once the inmate has successfully completed the remaining time in his or her sentence at the halfway house, he or she would then be released from the authority of correctional institutions and most likely placed on parole.

Halfway House Placement as a Form of Early Release from Confinement

Inmates who are placed into halfway houses as a mechanism for early release are inmates nearing the end of their sentences and who have qualified for early release. As part of their supervision (on parole) and

---

A System of Back-End Halfway Houses

Program Description
The federal Bureau of Prisons (BOP) is responsible for the incarceration of offenders who are convicted and sentenced for federal offenses. Compared to many state corrections systems, the federal system emphasizes the reintegration of offenders into the community. The federal system incorporates a three-phase system to prepare inmates for reintegration. Reintegration begins immediately upon incarceration (phase one) through treatment and other programming. During the second or transitional phase, inmates are released to a community-based halfway house for a period up to the final 180 days of the sentence. During the final phase, offenders are released to a three-five year period of community supervision by probation officers. In 2000, the BOP had contracts with 282 halfway houses, which served 18,113 inmates, about 45% of all inmates released that year. Halfway houses are also used at the federal level for other groups of offenders, such as federal probationers and Parolees for those who need more assistance and supervision than can be provided by community supervision.

Program Eligibility
Federal inmates are screened for halfway house eligibility within 11 to 13 months of their release from prison. The following inmates are ineligible: sex offenders; deportable aliens; inmates undergoing inpatient medical or psychiatric treatment; inmates serving sentences of six months or less; inmates who refused to participated in a Release Preparation Program; and inmates who are considered a significant threat to the community.

Program Requirements
- Comply with an individualized program plan. Halfway house staff prepare an individualized program plan for participants within two weeks of their arrival at the halfway house. This plan includes treatment needs and a time frame for achievement of goals. Approximately 40% of BOP halfway house residents are involved in drug treatment programming during their stay.
- Secure and maintain full-time employment. The halfway houses assist participants in finding suitable employment and assist them in maintaining employment while at the halfway house. Those who do secure employment may be returned to prison. Research shows that participants usually secure jobs such as clerks, mechanics, laborers, fast food workers, cooks, painters, janitors, and secretaries and most participants earn more than $5.00 per hour.
- Abide by the rules of the halfway house, such as curfew.
- Submit to urine testing.
- Pay a fee of about $4.41 daily for room and board.

Program Completion
The BOP specifies that the maximum length of time to be spent in a halfway house is six months (180 days). The average halfway house stay in 2000 was 104 days. About 90% of BOP inmates successfully complete their transitional living period in a halfway house and are released to community supervision. Those who do not complete the program successfully are returned to federal prison. Usually 90 days before being released from the halfway house, the Probation Office is contacted and assigns a probation officer to supervise the offender upon release.

Source: U.S. General Accounting Office, 1999; 2001.

Figure 9.3 Halfway House Facilities in the Federal Bureau of Prisons

as a condition of their release, these inmates may be required to live in a halfway house for a designated period of time (e.g., 3 months). Upon successful completion of this stay in a halfway house facility, the offender is likely to remain on regular or intensive parole supervision within the community. If the parolee fails to abide by the rules/regulations of the halfway house, and thereby fails to meet the conditions of his parole, it is likely that his parole release would be revoked and he would be sent back to prison. This type of placement differs from the pre-release placement in that inmates sent to halfway houses in this way have already been granted early release from prison whereas pre-release inmates are placed into halfway houses as an initial release option, which is then usually followed by release on parole.

Michigan's Community Residential Programs are a set of halfway houses geared toward the needs of male and female prisoners nearing the end of their prison terms and who are eligible for parole release (Michigan Department of Corrections, n.d.). Some of the participants reside in the halfway house with surveillance and supervision 24 hours a day, seven days a week, while others are placed on electronic monitoring in their homes. Participants are selected from among the minimum-security prison population. Prisoners who are excluded are those with histories of sex and assault-related offenses, drug trafficking, organized crime, long criminal histories, serious mental illnesses, prisoners serving life terms, and prisoners who are prone to violence. Once admitted, participants must secure and maintain employment, remain alcohol and drug free, and pay for room and board during their residences, which last about six months. Participants may be returned to prison for violations of rules. Participants who successfully complete are released to parole supervision.

PROGRAM CHARACTERISTICS

Halfway houses are residential facilities that offer assistance in the form of job readiness and placement, and treatment such as substance abuse counseling. They provide 24-hour supervision, monitoring of participants while on pass, at work, or attending treatment programs, and require strict curfews, adherence to house rules, and drug testing. As opposed to staff in other forms of intermediate sanctions, halfway house staff have daily contact with participants. Halfway houses are residential facilities, but are less secure than jails and prisons, since participants are allowed to leave the house, albeit with restrictions and curfews. Participants are reintegrated into communities mainly in their access to the community and its resources.

Halfway houses differ from one another in size, structure, and programming. As such, there is no single program model. A national survey of 647 halfway houses (Knapp & Burke, 1992) found that facilities ranged in size from 10 to 200 beds, privately operated facilities were smaller than state run houses, and female facilities were more often located in urban areas and converted from single or multiple family dwellings. Important characteristics of halfway houses are outlined below.

Two Program Models: Supportive and Intervention Halfway Houses

Halfway houses may be designed as supportive programs or intervention programs (McCarthy, McCarthy, & Leone, 2001). Supportive programs have a limited amount of direct services for participants and tend to act more as resource brokers. Thus participants receive most services through community-based agencies for help with their needs. Supportive halfway houses tend to employ a small number of semi-professional staff, since the focus is on transitional housing and less on the provision of direct services. Offenders and inmates with significant treatment needs would not be appropriate for such halfway houses. Intervention halfway houses, on the other hand, are highly structured programs that provide a variety of services directly to participants. The larger and more professional staff act as caseworkers and work to meet the needs of offenders and released inmates who have significant problems. Most halfway houses share characteristics of each model and fall somewhere in the middle (Latessa & Allen, 1999).

A Focus on Reintegration

Halfway houses are different from other intermediate sanctions in their emphasis on temporary housing and special needs of offenders who are returning to the community. Inmates who serve long periods of confinement face the strangeness of reentry (Clear & Cole, 2003) in their transition from living in a total institution in which their autonomy, freedom, and responsibility are limited to community life in which they are expected to function as normal citizens. Released inmates are thought to be ill equipped to make this transition successfully. Halfway houses aim to assist in offender reintegration by providing basic necessities, a structured environment, and a variety of services in a community-based setting. The provision of employment services is a foundation of halfway houses. Other core programming in halfway houses includes services related to education, finances, life skills, cognitive groups, anger management, mental health, and substance abuse.

Halfway houses focus heavily on vocational and employment issues. Most require participants to secure and maintain employment or risk termination. The logic is that having a job and earning an income is a first step in becoming self-sufficient. Some agencies work to secure potential employment opportunities for their participants with local employers and help participants maintain these positions. The Bureau of Prisons is one such agency. It requires that halfway houses used for federal offenders and inmates develop meaningful employment opportunities through community outreach and then help participants find and maintain employment. The BOP's research of participants in halfway houses found that 83% did find employment in diverse positions, such as painters, secretaries, and clerks (U.S. General Accounting Office, 1991).

Substance abuse is a common problem among criminal offenders and it is presumed to be one of the key factors for the high rates of failure on parole. According to recent research on participants in Ohio halfway houses (See Figure 9.4), most participants present substance abuse problems and other needs, including employment assistance and housing. And most participants were offered and did participate in the necessary treatments. According to a national survey of halfway houses, more than 90% of halfway houses provide alcohol and/or drug abuse services for participants (Knapp & Burke, 1992). Federal programs do not emphasize substance abuse treatment, as illustrated by findings from a recent survey showing only 40% of federal halfway house participants were involved in such programming (U.S. General Accounting Office, 2001).

Specialized Services for Distinctive Populations

While some halfway houses offer a similar set of services for a general population of participants, such as job readiness and placement and substance abuse counseling, others provide a specific set of services for particular offender populations. For instance, the Women's Prison

Type of Treatment	Percent of participants with need	Percent of participants who participated in treatment
Academic training	28%	14%
Vocational training	24%	8%
Employment assistance	79%	76%
Housing	51%	66%
Substance abuse counseling	77%	88%
Alcohol abuse counseling	66%	84%
Mental health counseling	20%	15%
Anger management	28%	34%

Source: Lowenkamp & Latessa, 2002

Figure 9.4. Programming Needs and Participation for
Ohio Halfway House Participants

Association & Home, Inc. (WPA) is a nonprofit agency that operates halfway houses designed to meet the special needs of female offenders and released female inmates. Its halfway houses emphasize independent living skills, self-empowerment, peer support, and participation in family and community life. WPA operates two halfway houses for two distinct populations of women offenders (See Women's Prison Association & Home, Inc., n.d.).

Hopper Home is a 16-bed front-end alternative to incarceration for adult female offenders. It is a "halfway-in" house providing residence and intensive day, evening, and weekend services to women who are facing at least four months in jail and who are not active substance abusers. These women are referred to the program by the criminal courts. While at Hopper Home, participants are supervised around the clock and required to participate in treatment and other services. WPA also operates the Sarah Powell Huntington House for homeless women who are released from jails and prisons in New York and who have children. This "halfway-out" house provides transitional housing and a comprehensive set of services designed to help women reunite with their families and build stability in their lives. This program is unique in its emphasis on rebuilding family relationships. The house accommodates 19 families as well as women living alone in 28 apartments. While at the halfway house, women are supervised 24 hours each day and are required to remain drug-free during their stay, which ranges between six and 18 months. Participants receive comprehensive assessments upon intake and continued case management throughout their stay. Substance abuse relapse prevention, HIV/AIDS education and services, peer support, education, independent living skills training, educational and vocational referrals, as well as permanent housing placement are offered to participants. The program also provides on-site child care and promotes family visits and activities, family reunification, and ongoing support services for the entire family.

Location of Halfway Houses

Halfway houses are designed, in part, to help offenders and inmates reintegrate into communities. Therefore, halfway houses should be located in community settings where participants have access to community resources, such as housing and employment services. Additionally, offenders should be placed into halfway houses in the communities where they expect to live upon release. In most states, halfway houses are located in urban, metropolitan, and rural settings. Latessa and Allen (1999) make important distinctions between urban and rural facilities.

The most numerous and diverse of all halfway houses are those located in metropolitan settings. Because of the wide range of community resources in urban areas, metropolitan halfway houses tend to rely heavily on community services, such as for drug treatment. Halfway houses located outside of metropolitan areas and in rural settings are smaller than urban programs. They face the challenge of helping inmates successfully reintegrate into communities, because the employment opportunities and other services in rural areas tend to be limited. A critical issue related to the placement of halfway houses in communities outside of urban areas is the potential for community resistance. The "NIMBY" (Not In My Backyard) syndrome refers to the idea that although community residents and community groups may support rehabilitation, they oppose programs that bring criminal offenders into their communities (for reasons related to fear, a worry about declining property values, and diminished quality of life). The extent to which communities oppose existing halfway house facilities is unclear. The Bureau of Prisons has enjoyed productive relationships overall with communities (U.S. General Accounting Office, 1991).

The Halfway House Experience

The programming and case management of offenders in halfway houses begins once eligible offenders are selected and transferred to halfway houses. New participants are oriented to the halfway house and its rules. Staff typically prepare a plan of action for individualized treatment that the participant follows during his or her stay. This plan may take the form of a contract that specifies participant and staff responsibilities. The plan also identifies halfway house rules and regulations. Rules include: observe curfew, check in and out, complete chores, attend treatment as specified, secure and maintain employment, pay economic sanctions, pay a supervision fee, remain drug- and alcohol-free, and submit to drug and alcohol testing. Once the plan is developed, participants begin receiving treatment and services. Progress reviews of the plans are ongoing. In most houses, participants are assigned to counselors who review plans and progress, encourage participants, and make modifications to the plans when necessary. Length of stay and release status vary by halfway house, the participant's progress, and the participant's legal status (McCarthy, McCarthy, & Leone, 2001).

RESEARCH ON HALFWAY HOUSES

Program Completion

Halfway house completion rates appear to be favorable. Research by the U.S. General Accounting Office (2001) on federal halfway houses revealed that about 90% of participants successfully completed and research on Ohio's halfway houses found that 64% completed successfully. Research comparing completion rates for halfway house participants to ISP participants in Colorado (English, Pullen, & Colling-Chadwick, 1996) also showed favorable results; completion rates were slightly higher for halfway house participants (55%) compared to ISP participants (50%). Technical violations appear to be a more common reason for program termination than rearrest. Since halfway houses focus heavily on employment and require participants to secure and maintain employment, failure to gain employment could be considered a technical violation. Additionally, absconsion and escape are also violations of halfway houses and a violation of curfew may fall into that category even when a participant eventually returns to the halfway house. Research on Colorado's halfway houses found that failure to complete halfway houses was significantly related to unemployment and not new arrests. In fact, only three percent of halfway house participants committed new crimes while residing at the facility. According to Knapp and Burke (1992), because halfway houses are more secure and intrusive than many other intermediate sanctions, a return to or placement in jail or prison would seem to be the most likely response to violations, including technical violations.

Recidivism

There has been minimal research conducted on the effectiveness of halfway houses at curbing recidivism and the research shows mixed findings. A review of research studies on halfway houses by Latessa and Allen (1982) found that in some cases halfway house participants had lower recidivism than offenders who did not participate, while other studies found that recidivism rates were not different. Overall, halfway house participants appear to do no worse than offenders who receive other correctional options. It does appear that successful completion of the halfway house experience is associated with a lower rate of reoffending. For example, a study of Colorado halfway houses indicated that most of the halfway house participants (73%) who successfully completed the halfway house experience did not commit new crimes during the one-year follow-up period (English, Pullen, & Colling-Chadwick, 1996). A seven-year follow-up study in Michigan also reported that those who completed successfully were less likely to commit new crimes than those who did not complete successfully (Hartmann, Friday, & Minor, 1994). The reason for this appears to lie in the effect of treatment. A study of halfway houses in Ohio used multivariate statistical analyses to identify the impact of halfway house participation on reoffending and found a significant treatment effect; that is, participation in halfway houses was helpful for reducing reoffending compared to other community sanctions (Lowenkamp & Latessa, 2002).

Net Widening

Research on the impact of halfway house placement on net widening is undeveloped. The pre-release and early release programs would have the most impact on reducing correctional crowding and costs, since participants are selected from prison populations. Front-end programs that are successful in meeting offenders' treatment needs may also have an impact on correctional populations, especially when treatment has a positive effect on participants' lives.

Cost Effectiveness

Halfway houses are less costly than institutional placements. Because they are residential facilities, they are more expensive to operate than other intermediate sanctions, however. For example, in 1999, a stay in a halfway house cost approximately $50 per offender for each day, while imprisonment cost about $58 each day per inmate. On average, traditional probation or parole cost slightly more than $3 per offender each day, while intensive supervision probation/parole was about $10 each day for each participant (Camp & Camp, 2000).

Behavioral Change/Treatment Effectiveness

Although much more evidence is necessary to draw firm conclusions, it appears that halfway houses are somewhat successful in meeting their treatment and reintegration goals (Latessa & Allen, 1982, 1999). Latessa and Travis (1991) compared a group of halfway house residents with a similar group of felons on probation. The halfway house group was more likely to have had drug, alcohol, and psychiatric problems, suggesting a need for greater treatment than the probationers. The researchers found that the halfway house participants did receive significantly more services and treatment than offenders who were on probation. In terms of recidivism, there was no significant difference between the two groups: the probationers and halfway house residents had roughly equal recidivism rates. Given that the halfway house residents had more extensive problems and needs, yet reoffended at roughly the same rate as the probationers, it appears that the programming offered through the halfway house was somewhat effective in curbing recidivism. The researchers concluded that the halfway house does appear to have effectively addressed the offenders' multiple and extensive needs.

Additional research on federal halfway houses (U.S. General Accounting Office, 1991) indicated that a very high percentage of inmates (83%) transferred to halfway houses had found jobs in the communities in which they expected to live upon release from the halfway houses. Other research indicates that halfway houses have been successful in the maintenance of offenders' community ties (Latessa & Allen, 1999). The treatment and services received by halfway house participants and the ability to secure employment as well as maintain important connections in the community may be significant factors in rehabilitating offenders and a benefit of halfway houses.

SUMMARY

Halfway houses and other community-based programs used for inmates upon release that target the needs of inmates will be viable programs given a growing public concern about the high recidivism rates of parolees and the lack of services in place to address their reentry needs. Given that the number of offenders who are reincarcerated for parole violations continues to increase and that such reincarcerations are a growing proportion of all prison admissions, greater attention to aftercare services may be a viable step towards addressing this problem. Many states and the federal system are experimenting with new reentry initiatives, which are designed in part to provide structured and directed treatment and services to inmates released from incarceration much like halfway houses. These initiatives target inmates for programming while they are still incarcerated and continue the programming when inmates are released to residential community-based facilities. This new breed of transitional community alternative is a step in the right direction for reducing the risk of reoffending among released prisoners through reintegration programming.

PART III

The Future of
Intermediate Sanctions Programs

**CHAPTER 10**

Conclusion

SUMMARY OF RESEARCH ON INTERMEDIATE SANCTIONS

Intermediate sanctions have not been established long enough for researchers to determine their overall effectiveness. While some important and comprehensive evaluations have been conducted, much more research is necessary. Some of the research is favorable, for instance with respect to fine payments, completion of community service, and day reporting centers. Other research raises doubts about the effectiveness of intermediate sanctions, such as the effectiveness of military boot camp models and intensive supervision programs focusing on control and monitoring. Overall, the research to date has indicated that intermediate sanctions are not the panacea they were once promoted as being. The following overall conclusions can be drawn:

Very few offenders have participated in intermediate sanctions.

Although intermediate sanctions have proliferated over the past ten years, relatively few offenders who could have been placed have participated in these programs. According to Petersilia (1999), less than six percent of the total adult probation and parole population is participating in intensive supervision programs. Only about one percent of probationers and parolees are under electronic monitoring. On a typical day, there are no more than about 10,000 participants in boot camp programs. As to day reporting centers, somewhere around 15,000 offenders are participating. In total, according to Petersilia, it appears that at most, 10% of probationers and parolees participate in intermediate sanctions. Because of the small number of offenders who participate, there has been no appreciable reduction in prison and jail populations.

Many intermediate sanctions have been poorly implemented and inadequately funded.

Poor implementation and failure to operate programs as they were designed has been problematic (Petersilia, 1999). Research has shown that intermediate sanctions are typically used for probationers and not populations for whom the programs are designed. Vague targeting and selection criteria as well as reluctance to place higher-risk offenders into intermediate sanctions have contributed to this problem. Additionally, weak and insufficient offender monitoring and enforcement functions have often led to ineffective supervision and consequently a higher likelihood of failure among participants. Inadequate funding is thought to be the likely cause of this problem.

Front-end intermediate sanctions are subject to net widening.

In large part, intermediate sanctions are not being used for the offenders that they are designed for: those offenders otherwise headed for jail or prison. They are too often filled with the incorrect offender populations or offenders who would otherwise have received a lesser sanction, such as probation. When filled with offenders likely to receive a less intrusive and costly sanction, intermediate sanctions are used inappropriately and "widen the net" of correctional control. This increases the burden of punishment and correctional cost and fails to have any favorable impact on correctional populations. For impact on correctional crowding and new prison admissions to be realized, the targeting and selection for intermediate sanctions must be stringent and capture jail and prison-bound offenders. Back-end intermediate sanctions, especially large programs such as New York's boot camp prison, do divert offenders from jail and prison terms appropriately and therefore have some impact on correctional crowding and costs. Intermediate Sanctions represent a viable alternative to incarceration for many different types of offenders. This system of sanctions should be the focus of continued research and development to better understand, improve, and expand this essential set of correctional alternatives.

Misuse of intermediate sanctions compounds problems resulting from failure due to technical violations.

Termination from intermediate sanctions is due mainly to technical violations rather than the commission of new crimes. This is good news for public safety. It is generally agreed that failure as a result of technical violation results primarily from the intensive monitoring and control that reveal more violations, rather than a higher volume of actual violations among offenders. In other words, offenders in intermediate sanctions probably do not commit more technical violations than probationers or parolees, but they are more likely to be detected and punished when they do. When offenders who are not in need of imprisonment and who would be adequately supervised on regular probation or parole are placed into intermediate sanctions, technical program failures become much more concerning. When they fail as a result of rule violations, their punishments are typically more severe and when these punishments involve incarceration, intermediate sanctions work against attempts to reduce correctional populations and costs. In sum, the more stringent surveillance uncovers more violations and when these failures involve the "incorrect" population, the situation is more problematic.

Completion rates appear to be at least acceptable for most intermediate sanctions.

It is difficult to generalize across programs for a number of reasons, including the differences in populations of offenders who participate in intermediate sanctions and the structure of programs. Overall, however, research suggests that most offenders complete programs. Programs that incorporate treatment and other programming to assist participants appear to be more successful than programs that focus on surveillance. For most programs, participants fail to complete usually as a result of a technical violation rather than the commission of new crimes. On the whole, most programs do not appear to increase public safety risks.

Intermediate sanctions are less costly than jail and prison, but long-term cost effectiveness is uncertain.

There has been modest research conducted on the cost effectiveness of intermediate sanctions. Most of the research in this area has focused on average daily costs associated with different penalties. Using this method, intermediate sanctions are much less costly than incarceration and usually more costly than regular probation or parole. The reader should know that costs will vary with the organizational structure and size of the agency operating the intermediate sanction, the program's offender capacity, its length, and so on. Programs that are well managed do appear to provide a cost-effective way to supervise offenders as an alternative to incarceration. The long-term costs of intermediate sanctions compared to prison and jail incarceration are unknown. The literature would benefit from a long-term study encompassing costs associated with post-program arrest and the associated cost of court processing, detention, representation, and resentencing to jail, prison, an intermediate sanction, probation, or some other sanction.

Intermediate sanctions are usually no more effective at reducing recidivism than probation, parole, or incarceration.

Overall, recidivism for offenders sentenced to intermediate sanctions is comparable to recidivism for offenders sentenced to incarceration and probation. Rates are neither higher nor lower. Especially considering the destructive impact of incarceration on individuals and families and the cost of incarceration to taxpayers, this is not always thought to be a negative finding, especially when the offenses are less serious. Ultimately the success of any correctional program is measured against public safety. Even when many offenders succeed after having participated in an intermediate sanction and their participation creates other benefits, the exception becomes a basis for skepticism. When offenders commit new crimes, public safety is diminished.

The surveillance and control mechanisms of intermediate sanctions are not alone effective at reducing reoffending.

The control and surveillance mechanisms of some intermediate sanctions such as home confinement and intensive supervision programs are not alone enough to reduce recidivism. Increased contacts between offenders and staff, more stringent restrictions over behavior, and other controls such as urine testing cannot reduce offending by themselves. Instead, these mechanisms of control must be situated within well-designed programs. Additionally, programs emphasizing structure, discipline, and challenge, such as boot camp programs that emphasize the military model have been found to be ineffective (MacKenzie, 2000).

Intermediate sanctions combining surveillance and treatment are the most effective at reducing recidivism

Without a treatment component, any sanction is unlikely to change offender behavior or reduce recidivism. According to Petersilia (1999), regardless of type of program, research has shown that intermediate sanctions that combine treatment such as substance abuse treatment and vocational services with surveillance best reduce recidivism compared to programs that lack treatment components. Programs that assist offenders in developing work skills and with education, for example, have been found to be effective at reducing recidivism (MacKenzie, 2000).

THE FUTURE OF INTERMEDIATE SANCTIONS

Research has identified several problems with intermediate sanctions that can be corrected, as well as several important components of programs that make their continued expansion promising. Based upon research, many programs are being redesigned to become more effective at meeting their goals. When large enough, adequately funded and implemented with community input and support, and when structured around principles of effective treatment, intermediate sanctions do have the potential of meeting important goals. They have the potential of diverting certain offenders from jail and prison and therefore minimizing troublesome effects of incarceration on offenders, families, and communities, and at the same time helping offenders deal with problems in their lives, minimizing harm to the public, and moving toward managing correctional crowding and costs. The following recommendations should prove useful for the future of intermediate sanctions.

Intermediate sanctions should be incorporated into existing sentencing schemes with specific standards for their use as equitable substitutes for jail, prison, and probation sentences.

While some states' sentencing guidelines incorporate standards for the use of intermediate sanctions, many guideline systems remain concerned only with meting out jail and prison terms. States should incorporate intermediate sanctions into a menu of sentencing options through the use of exchange rates consistent with the principle of interchangeability (Clear & Dammer, 2000). Interchangeability refers to the use of various types of correctional options that are considered equivalent and therefore can be used interchangeably. For instance, a three-month jail sentence may be equivalent to and therefore substituted for a sentence of two years probation, community service, and fines. Washington, Pennsylvania, North Carolina, and Ohio have sentencing guidelines that incorporate intermediate sanctions. These systems assist judges in determining fair and equivalent penalties for offenders as alternatives to probation and confinement. Providing judges and other decision-makers, such as paroling authorities, with such a mechanism may prove useful for increasing the use of intermediate sanctions in a way that is fair and equitable.

Systems should devise stringent offender targeting and selection criteria to include the types of offenders who would benefit from intermediate sanctions and to eliminate those who would not be appropriate for placement.

Targeting offenders who are bound for jails or prisons and who do not pose too high a risk to the community should have favorable effects on prison and jail populations and correctional costs, especially when offenders successfully complete programs. To reduce the problem of net widening, states and the federal system should devise stringent targeting and screening mechanisms that are intended to ensure that intermediate sanctions admit offenders who are bound for jail or prison in the absence of placement into an intermediate sanction. Some jurisdictions such as New York have based targeting mechanisms on sophisticated statistical analyses that serve to identify case factors (such as offense severity and criminal history) that predict custodial sentences. The case factors found to predict the likelihood that an offender would receive jail or prison are then used, in part, to select offenders for placement into intermediate sanctions.

Programs should distinguish among potential participants in their risk to reoffend and match their risk to the appropriate level of supervision and programming.

One way to address the public safety issue is to assess future dangerousness by incorporating risk assessments into the client selection process. Higher risk offenders require more intensive services while lower risk offenders require fewer services. It has been suggested that increasing the level of supervision and monitoring of lower-risk offenders actually increases recidivism (Bonta, 1997). It is important for judges and other decision-makers to calculate as best as possible the risk a potential participant poses to the community and then choose among available sanctions, perhaps combining several intermediate sanctions and incorporating incarceration when appropriate to achieve a better incapacitation effect.

Intermediate sanctions should receive additional and consistent funding so that they can serve more offenders and maintain surveillance/monitoring mechanisms to meet public safety needs.

Programs such as community service and monetary sanctions are underdeveloped in the U.S. These and other intermediate sanctions should be expanded if they are to achieve their full potential. They will become increasing popular as long-term prisoners are being released from prisons and should be incorporated into transitional and aftercare programming for inmates who are released from incarceration. States and the federal system should commit adequate and long-term funding for intermediate sanctions and consider the privatization of intermediate sanctions.

Programs should enhance treatment and rehabilitative components found to be effective in reducing reoffending.

Surveillance and control is not enough to reduce reoffending. Programs should incorporate treatment and other programming to become more effective. A multiple modality approach with treatment designed according to offenders' individual treatment needs combined with surveillance may be most promising. This would include vocational and educational components as well as cognitive and behavioral programming. Participants in intermediate sanctions programs should be evaluated as to their treatment needs and then provided with access to services, such as programs designed to help offenders develop prosocial attitudes and behaviors, deal with anger and hostility, become better at problem-solving, and overcome substance abuse addictions. For any treatment to work, the program environment must be supportive and staff dedicated to treatment. There is ample evidence that treatment works. Research has identified principles of effective treatment (See Andrews, 1994; Bonta, 1997; Gendreau, 1993). Correctional programs that are structured and focused on specific criminogenic needs of offenders, use multiple treatment modalities, focus on the development of skills, and which use behavioral methods have been shown to be most effective at reducing reoffending. The National Institute of Corrections (2000) reports that the most successful types of treatment models include programs such as (1) social learning (ex. anti-criminal modeling and skills development); (2) cognitive behavioral (problem solving, self-control skills, anger management, personal responsibility, attitudinal change, moral reasoning, social perspective taking); (3) and family based therapies. Intermediate sanctions have great potential in rehabilitating offenders if such principles are incorporated into the foundation of programs.

Intermediate sanctions that are residential and which serve residential populations should incorporate aftercare components to increase the success of higher risk populations.

Programs that provide aftercare in community-based settings for prisoners appear to be effective at reducing offending (Mackenzie, 2000). Evaluations of boot camp programs, for example, suggest that the aftercare component is essential for participant success. Intermediate sanctions such as halfway houses, intensive supervision programs, and day reporting centers can be incorporated into the community supervision and aftercare of jail and prison inmates.

States and the federal government should be engaged in developing community support, information, and guidance.

The legislative position of the American Correctional Association (n.d.) as to the use of intermediate sanctions encourages the involvement of communities in the operation of intermediate sanctions. Intermediate sanctions should be adequately prepared to address needs of offenders and the communities that they service, operated in a manner to provide information to the public and offenders about their operations and their selection and placement processes, and engaged in developing community information, support, and guidance.

REFERENCES

Administrative Office of the Courts. (2001). *Court and community: An information series about US probation and pretrial services—Federal corrections and supervision division*, Administrative Office of the Courts, Probation Division.

Administrative Office of the United States Courts. (1981). Implementing community service: The referral process. *Federal Probation, 53*(1), 3–9.

Allen, G. F., & Treger, H. (1990). Community service orders in federal probation: Perceptions of probationers and host agencies. *Federal Probation 54*(3), 8–14.

Allen, G. F., & Treger, H. (1994). Fines and restitution orders: Probationers' perceptions. *Federal Probation, 58* (2), 34–40.

American Correctional Association. (*n.d.*). *American Correctional Association (ACA) legislative position statement on community corrections and intermediate supervision*. Lanham, MD: American Correctional Association. Retrieved on August 5, 2003, from http://www.aca.org/government/wp_community.pdf

Anderson, D. C. (1997). *Sensible justice: Alternatives to prison*. New York: The New Press.

Andrews, D. A. (1994). *An overview of treatment effectiveness: Research and clinical principles (Draft)*. Washington, DC: National Institute of Corrections.

Andrews, D. A., Bonta, J., & Hoge, R. D. (1990). Classification for effective rehabilitation: Rediscovering psychology. *Criminal Justice and Behavior, 17* (1), 19–52.

Austin, J. M., Jones, M. & Bolyard, M. (1993). *The growing use of jail boot camps: The current state of the art.* Washington, DC: National Institute of Justice.

Austin, J., Camp-Blair, D., Camp, A., Castellano, T., Adams-Fuller, T., Jones, M., et al. (2000). *Multi-Site evaluation of boot camp programs, final report.* Washington, DC: National Council on Crime And Delinquency.

Beccaria, C. (1983). *An essay on crimes and punishments.* Brookline Village, MA: Branden Press Inc. (Translated and reprinted from *Dei delitti e delle pene,* (4th ed.), 1775, London: F. Newberry).

Beck, A. J. & staff (1999). *Correctional populations in the United States, 1996.* Washington, DC: National Institute of Justice.

Beck, A. J. (2000). *Prison and jail inmates at midyear 1999.* Washington, DC: Office of Justice Programs.

Beck, A. J., & Harrison, P. M. (2001). *Prisoners in 2000.* Washington, DC: Bureau of Justice Statistics.

Beck, A. J., Karberg, J. C., & Harrison, P. M. (2002). *Prison and jail inmates at midyear 2001.* Washington, DC: Bureau of Justice Statistics.

Beck, J. L., & Klein-Saffran, J. (1990). Home confinement and the use of electronic monitoring with federal parolees. *Federal Probation, 54*(4), 22–33.

Belenko, S., Winterfield, L., Phillips, M., Grant, A., & Caligiuri, R. (1995). *Estimating the displacement effects of Alternative to Incarceration Programs: Final report of the Jail Displacement Study Phase II.* New York: Criminal Justice Agency.

Bennett, L. A. (1995). Current findings on intermediate sanctions and community corrections. *Corrections Today, 57* (1), 86–89.

Berry, B. (1985). Electronic jails: A new criminal justice concern. *Justice Quarterly, 2,* 1–22.

Bonta, J. (1997). *Offender rehabilitation: From research to practice.* Public Works and Government Services Canada.

Boone County Jail. (n.d.). *Community service program.* Kentucky Department of Corrections, Division of Local Facilities. Retrieved November 11, 2002, from http://www.boonecountyky.org/jail/community_service.htm

Bowers, D. M. (2000). Home detention systems. *Corrections Today, 62*(4), 102–106.

Bureau of Justice Assistance. (1996). *How to use structured fines (Day Fines) as an intermediate sanction.* Washington, DC: Bureau of Justice Assistance.

Bureau of Justice Assistance. (1997). *Improving the nation's criminal justice system: Findings and results from state and local program evaluations.* Effective Programs Monograph No. 1. Washington, DC: US Department of Justice, Bureau of Justice Assistance.

Bureau of Justice Assistance. (2000). *Creating a new criminal justice system for the 21st century: Findings and results from state and local program evaluations.* Effective Programs Monograph. No. 2. Washington, DC: U.S. Department of Justice, Bureau of Justice Assistance.

Bureau of Justice Statistics. (2001). *Federal criminal case processing, 2000: With trends 1982-2000.* Washington, DC: Bureau of Justice Statistics.

Byrne, J. M., Lurigio, A. J., & Baird, C. (1989). The effectiveness of the new intensive supervision programs. *Research In Corrections, 2*(2), 1–48.

Camp, C. G., & Camp, G. M. (2000). *The corrections yearbook 2000: Adult corrections.* Middletown, CT: Criminal Justice Institute.

Canning, K., & Harrigan, K. (2002). Violators face tough civil, criminal fines. *Pollution Engineering, 32* (2), 3.

Cappillino, C. (1993). Role of community service in reducing jail population in Ulster County. *The IARCA Journal on Community Corrections, 5* (5), 13–14.

Caputo, G. A. (2000). Why not community service? *Criminal Justice Policy Review, 10* (4), 503–519.

Caputo, G. A. (2002, November). Community service in Texas. Paper presented at the meeting of the American Society of Criminology, Chicago.

Caputo, G. A. (2004). Treating sticky-fingers: An evaluation of treatment and education for shoplifters. *Journal of Offender Rehabilitation, 38* (3), 49–68.

Caputo, G. A., Young, D., & Porter, R. (1998b). *An evaluation of New York City's Alternative to Incarceration Programs: First interim report.* New York: Vera Institute of Justice.

Caputo, G. A., Young, D., & Porter, R. (1998c). *Community service for repeat misdemeanor offenders in New York City.* New York: Vera Institute of Justice.

Carranza, E., Liverpool, N. J. O., & Rodriguez-Manzanera, L. (1994). Alternatives to imprisonment in Latin America and the Caribbean. In U. Zvekić (Ed.), *Alternatives to imprisonment in comparative perspective* (pp. 384-438) United National Interregional Crime and Justice Research Institute. Chicago: Nelson-Hall Publisher.

CASES. (1994a). Research on the Court Employment Project. *Review of Research.* New York: Center for Alternative Sentencing and Employment Services.

CASES. (1994*b*). Establishing empirically-based intake criteria for the Court Employment Project. *Review of Research.* New York: Center for Alternative Sentencing and Employment Services.

Challinger, D. (1994). Alternatives to imprisonment in Australia and New Zealand. In U. Zvekić (Ed.), *Alternatives to imprisonment in comparative perspective* (pp. 253-266) United National Interregional Crime and Justice Research Institute. Chicago: Nelson-Hall Publisher.

Clark, C. L., Aziz, D. W., & MacKenzie, D. L. (1994). *Shock Incarceration in New York: Focus on treatment.* Washington, DC: National Institute of Justice.

Clear, T. R., & Cole, G. F. (2003). *American corrections (5ᵗʰ Ed.).* Belmont, CA: Wadsworth.

Clear, T. R., & Dammer, H. R. (2000). *The offender in the community.* Belmont, CA: Wadsworth.

Clear, T. R., & Hardyman, P. L. (1990). The new intensive supervision movement. *Crime and Delinquency, 36* (1), 42–60.

Cohen, M. A. (2000). Measuring the costs and benefits of crime and justice. *Criminal Justice, 4,* 263–315.

Courtright, K. E., Berg, B. L., & Mutchnick, R. J. (1997). The cost effectiveness of using house arrest with electronic monitoring for drunk drivers. *Federal Probation, 61*(Sept.), 19–22.

Courtright, K. E., Berg, B. L., & Mutchnick, R. J. (2000). Rehabilitation in the new machine? Exploring drug and alcohol use variables related to success among DUI offenders under electronic monitoring—Some preliminary outcome results. *International Journal of Offender Therapy and Comparative Criminology, 44,* 293–311.

Cowles, E. L., & Castellano, T. C. (1996). Substance abuse programming in adult correctional boot camps: A national overview. In D. L. MacKenzie & E. E. Hebert (Eds.), *Correctional Boot Camps: A Tough Intermediate Sanction* (pp. 207–232). Washington, DC: National Institute of Justice.

Coyne, P. (1996). On the home stretch. *New Statesman and Society, 9* (Feb. 9), 30-31.

Craddock, A. (2000). *An exploratory analysis of client outcomes, costs, and benefits of day reporting centers—Final report.* Terre Haute, IN: Indiana State University, Department of Criminology.

Crew, R. E., & Vancore, M. (1994). Managing victim restitution in Florida: An analysis of the implementation of FS 775.089. *The Justice System Journal, 17* (2), 241–248.

Crocker, K. W. (2003). In Nashville, jail programs turn around lives. *Sheriff, 55* (3), 38–39, 62–63.

Cromwell, P. F., & del Carmen, R. V. (1999). *Community based corrections (4th Ed.)*. Belmont, CA: West/Wadsworth.

Cronin, R. C. (1994). *Boot camps for adult and juvenile offenders: Overview and update*. Washington, DC: National Institute of Justice.

Davis, R. C., & Bannister, T. M. (1995) Improving collection of court-ordered restitution. *Judicature, 79* (1), 847–869.

del Carmen, R. V., & Vaughn, J. B. (1986). Legal issues in the use of electronic surveillance in probation. *Federal Probation, 50* (2), 60-69.

Department of Justice, Sentencing Team, Policy Programs and Research Sector. (1994). Intermediate Sanctions in Canada. In U. Zvekić (Ed.), *Alternatives to imprisonment in comparative perspective* (p. 323-348) United National Interregional Crime and Justice Research Institute. Chicago: Nelson-Hall Publisher.

Diggs, D. W., & Pieper, S. L. (1994). Using day reporting centers as an alternative to jails. *Federal Probation, 58* (1), 9–12.

Ditton, P. M., & Wilson, D. J. (1999). *Truth in sentencing in state prisons*. Washington, DC: Bureau of Justice Statistics.

Durose, M. R., & Langan, P. A. (2001). *State court sentencing of convicted felons, 1998 —Statistical tables*. Washington, DC: Bureau of Justice Statistics.

English, K., Pullen, S., & Colling-Chadwick, S. (1996). *Comparison of intensive supervision probation and community corrections clientele: Report of findings*. Denver: Colorado Division of Criminal Justice. Retrieved on July 23, 2003, from http://dcj.state.co.us/ors/docs7.htm

Evans, D. G. (1996). Ontario changes direction. *Corrections Today, 58*(Feb), 30, 32.

Finckenauer, J. O. (1982). *Scared straight! And the panacea phenomenon*. Englewood Cliffs, NJ: Prentice-Hall, Inc.

Finn, M. A., & Muirhead-Steves, S. (2002). The effectiveness of electronic monitoring with violent male parolees. *Justice Quarterly, 19*, 293–312.

Finn, P. (1998). *Chicago's Safer Foundation: A road back for ex-offenders*. Washington, DC: U.S. Department of Justice, National Institute of Justice.

Flowers, G. T., Carr, T. S., & Ruback, R. B. (1991). *Special alternative incarceration evaluation*. Atlanta: Georgia Department of Corrections.

Fulton, B., & Stone, S. (1995). Achieving public safety through rehabilitation and reintegration: The promise of a new ISP. In J. O. Smykla & W. L. Selke (Eds.), *Intermediate sanctions: Sentencing in the 1990s* (pp. 115–134). Cincinnati: Anderson Publishing Co.

Fulton, B., Latessa, E. J., Stichman, A., Travis, L. F., Corbett, R. P. Jr., & Harris, M. K. (1997). A review of research for practitioners. *Federal Probation, 61* (4), 65–75.

Gainey, R. R., & Payne, B. K. (2000). Understanding the experience of house arrest with electronic monitoring: An analysis of quantitative and qualitative data. *International Journal of Offender Therapy and Comparative Criminology, 44*, 84–96.

Gendreau, P. (1993). The principles of effective intervention with offenders. Paper presented at the International Association of Residential and Community Alternatives Conference, Philadelphia.

Georgia Department of Corrections (2001). *Probation in the new century, FY 2001 Year End summary.* Georgia Department of Corrections, Probation Division.

Georgia Department of Corrections. (2000). *Alternatives to prison offer broader range of sanction.* Georgia Department of Corrections. Retrieved November 14, 2002 from http://www.dcor.state.ga.us/PublicRelations/PressReleases/html/2000feb16.html.

Gilliard, D. K. (1999). *Prison and jail inmates at midyear 1998.* Washington, DC: Office of Justice Programs.

Glaze, L. E. (2002). *Probation and parole in the United States, 2001.* Washington, DC: Bureau of Justice Statistics.

Gordon, M. A., & Glaser, D. (1991). The use and effects of financial penalties in municipal courts. *Criminology, 29* (4), 651–676.

Gould Publications of Texas, Inc. (2002). *Texas criminal law and motor vehicle handbook 2002 edition.* Longwood, FL: Gould Publications of Texas, Inc.

Gould Publications, Inc. (2002). *California penal code handbook 2002 edition.* Longwood, FL: Gould Publications, Inc.

Gowdy, V. B. (1993). *Intermediate sanctions.* Washington, DC: National Institute of Justice.

Gowen, D. (1995). Electronic monitoring in the southern district of Mississippi. *Federal Probation, 59*(1), 10–13.

Great Britain Home Office. (1992, June). *Statistics on community service orders.* Great Britain Home Office. Research and Statistics Department. United Kingdom. Retrieved November 11, 2002, from http://www.homeoffice.gov.uk/rds/pdfs2/hosb1392.pdf

Greek, C. E. (2002). Tracking probationers in space and time: The convergence of GIS and GPS systems. *Federal Probation, 66*(1), 51–53.

Greene, J. A. (1990). *The Staten Island day fine experiment.* New York: Vera Institute of Justice.

Greene, J. A. (1993). *The day fine system: A tool for improving the use of economic sanctions.* New York: Vera Institute of Justice.

Greenwood, P. W., with A. Abrahamse. (1982). *Selective incapacitation: Report prepared for the National Institute of Justice.* Santa Monica, CA: Rand Corporation.

Haas, S., & E. J. Latessa. (1995). Intensive supervision in a rural county: Diversion and outcome. In J. O. Smykla & W. L. Selke (Eds.), *Intermediate sanctions: Sentencing in the 1990s* (p. 153–69). Cincinnati: Anderson Publishing Co.

Hanley, R. (1996, Nov. 19). Faced with prison, ex-prosecutor flees home in New Jersey. *New York Times wire.*

Harding, B. G. (2000). *Directory of community-based programs for women offenders.* Longmont, CO: National Institute of Corrections Information Center.

Harper, A. G. (1997). After more than ten years, New Jersey ISP is still thriving. *The New Jersey Corrections Quarterly, 13,* 2. Retrieved November 13, 2002, from http://www.corrections.com/njaca/PastQuarterlys/June97_ Quarterly/After_ten_years.htm

Harrison, P. M., & Karberg, J. C. (2003). *Prison and jail inmates at midyear 2002.* Washington, DC: Bureau of Justice Statistics.

Hartland, A. T. (1998). Defining a continuum of sanctions: Some research and policy development implications. In J. Petersilia (Ed.), *Community Corrections: Probation, Parole, and Intermediate Sanctions* (pp. 70–79). New York: Oxford University Press.

Hartmann, D. J., Friday, P. C., & Minor, K. I. (1994). Residential probation: A seven-year follow-up study of halfway house discharges. *Journal of Criminal Justice, 22*(6), 503–515.

Hillsman, S. T. (1990). Fines and day fines. In M. Tonry & N. Morris (Eds.), *Crime and justice: A review of research, Vol. 12* (pp. 49-98). Chicago: University of Chicago Press.

Hillsman, S. T., & Greene, J. A. (1987). *Improving the use and administration of criminal fines: A report of the Richmond County, New York, Criminal Court Day-Fine Planning Project.* New York: Vera Institute of Justice.

Hillsman, S. T., & Greene, J. A. (1992). The use of fines as an intermediate sanction. In J. M. Byrne, A. J. Lurigio, & J. Petersilia (Eds.), *Smart sentencing: The emergence of intermediate sanctions* (pp. 123–141). Newbury Park, CA: Sage Publications.

Hillsman, S. T., Sichel, J. L., & Mahoney, B. (1984). *Fines in sentencing: A study of the use of the fine as a criminal sanction.* New York: Vera Institute of Justice.

Hinds, L. (1999). The gross violations of human rights of the apartheid regime under international law. *Rutgers Race & the Law Review, 1*, 231–317.

Hinzan, G. (2000). The effective use of electronic monitoring. *Journal of Offender Monitoring, 13*(2), 12–13.

Immarigeon, R. (1986). Community service sentences pose problems, show potential. *The National Prison Project Journal, 10*, 13–15.

Jefferson County Community Supervision and Corrections Department. (n.d.) *The Jefferson County, Texas Restitution Center #1.* Texas Department of Criminal Justice, Jefferson County Community Supervision and Corrections Department. Retrieved November 14, 2002 from http://www.co.jefferson.tx.us/cscd_residential_services/jcrc1.htm.

Johnston, W. (2001). Boston area program integrates electronic monitoring with substance abuse treatment for women. *Journal of Offender Monitoring, 14*(3), 20–21.

Jones, M. (1995). Predictors of success and failure on intensive probation supervision. *American Journal of Criminal Justice, 19*(2), 239–254.

Jones, R. K., & Lacey, J. H. (1999). *Evaluation of a day reporting center for repeat DWI offenders.* Washington, DC: US Department of Transportation, National Highway Traffic Safety Administration.

Jones, W. L. (2000). *Community supervision in Texas: Summary statistics.* Austin, TX: Texas Department of Criminal Justice, Community Justice Assistance Division.

Joutsen, M., & Bishop, N. (1994). Noncustodial sanctions in Europe: Regional overview. In U. Zvekić (Ed.), *Alternatives to imprisonment in comparative perspective* (pp. 279–292) United National Interregional Crime and Justice Research Institute. Chicago: Nelson-Hall Publisher.

Joutsen, M., & Zvekić, U. (1994). Noncustodial sanctions: Comparative overview. In U. Zvekić (Ed.), *Alternatives to imprisonment in comparative perspective* (pp. 1–42) United National Interregional Crime and Justice Research Institute. Chicago: Nelson-Hall Publisher.

Keenan, J. P. (1996). Programming in Georgia's boot camps. In D. L. MacKenzie & E. E. Hebert (Eds.), *Correctional boot camps: A tough intermediate sanction* (pp. 93–106). Washington, DC: National Institute of Justice.

Keenan, J. P., & Barry, R. (1994). Measuring the military atmosphere of boot camps. *Federal Probation, 58* (1), 67–71.

Klein-Saffran, J. (1995). Electronic monitoring vs. halfway houses: A study of federal offenders. *Alternative to Incarceration*, Fall, 24–28.

Klein-Saffran, J. (1996). Bureau of Prisons: Expanding intermediate sanctions through intensive confinement centers. In D. L. MacKenzie & E. E. Hebert (Eds.), *Correctional boot camps: A tough Intermediate sanction* (pp. 107–117). Washington, DC: National Institute of Justice.

Knapp, K., & Burke, P. (1992). *Residential community corrections facilities: Current practice and policy issues*. Washington DC: U.S. Department of Justice.

Ko, M. (2001). If you're not in jail, you're free. *Report/Newsmagazine, 28*(15), 32–33.

Ko, M. (2002). Keeping tabs on dangerous parolees. *Report/Newsmagazine, 29*(3), 27.

Krajick, K. (1982). Community service: The work ethic approach to punishment. *Corrections Magazine – New York, 8* (5), 6–16.

Kramer, R., & Porter, R. (2000). Alternative-to-incarceration programs for felony offenders: progress report and preliminary findings from a recidivism analysis. New York: Vera Institute of Justice.

Langan, P. A., & Cunniff, M. A. (1992). *Recidivism of felons on probation, 1986–1989*. Bureau of Justice Statistics Special Report. Washington, DC: Bureau of Justice Statistics.

Larivee, J. J. & O'Leary, W. D. (1990). *Managing the development of community corrections*. Washington, DC: U.S. Department of Justice, National Institute of Corrections.

Larivee, J. J. (1995). Day reporting in Massachusetts. In M. Tonry & K. Hamilton (Eds.), *Intermediate sanctions in overcrowded times* (pp. 128–130). Boston: Northeastern University Press.

Latessa, E. J., & Allen, H. E. (1982). Halfway houses and parole: A national assessment. *Journal of Criminal Justice, 10* (2), 153–163.

Latessa, E. J., & Allen, H. E. (1999). *Corrections in the community (2nd Ed.)*. Cincinnati: Anderson Publishing Company.

Latessa, E. J., & Travis, L. F., III (1991). Halfway house or probation: A comparison of alternative dispositions. *Journal of Crime and Justice, 14*(1), 53–75.

Latessa, E. J., & Travis, L. F., III (1992). Residential community correctional programs. In J. M. Byrne, A. J. Lurigio, & J. Petersilia (Eds.), *Smart sentencing: The emergence of intermediate sanctions* (pp. 116-181). Newbury Park, CA: Sage Publications.

Lawrence, R. (1990). Restitution as a cost-effective alternative to incarceration. In B. Galaway & J. Hudson (Eds.), *Criminal justice, restitution, and reconciliation* (pp. 207–216). Monsey, NY: Criminal Justice Press.

Lee, S. (1974, January). Jackal and the Punisher. *Spiderman*, Volume 1, issue 140 (storyline author: Gerry Conway).

Lilly, J. R., & Ball, R. A. (1992). The Pride Inc., program: An evaluation of 5 years of electronic monitoring. *Federal Probation, 56*(4), 42–47.

Lilly, J. R., Ball, R. A., Curry, G. D., & McMullen, J. (1993). Electronic monitoring of the drunk driver: A seven-year study of the home confinement alternative. *Crime and Delinquency, 39,* 462–484.

Lowenkamp, C. T., & Latessa, E. J. (2002). *Evaluation of Ohio's community based correctional facilities and halfway house programs, final report.* Cincinnati: University of Cincinnati, Division of Criminal Justice, Center for Criminal Justice Research.

Lurigio, A. J., & Petersilia, J. (1992). The emergence of intensive probation supervision programs in the United States. In J. Petersilia (Ed.), *Community corrections: Probation, parole, and intermediate sanctions* (pp. 3–17). New York: Oxford University Press.

Lutze, F. E., & Brody, D. C. (1999). Mental abuse as cruel and unusual punishment: Do boot camp prisons violate the Eighth Amendment? *Crime & Delinquency, 45* (2), 242–255.

MacKenzie, D. (1997). Criminal justice and crime prevention. In L. W. Sherman, D. Gottfredson, D. MacKenzie, J. Eck, P. Reuter, & S. Bushway (Eds.), *Preventing crime: What works, what doesn't, what's promising! A report to the United States Congress* (Ch. 9, pp. 1–59). Washington, DC: National Institute of Justice.

MacKenzie, D. (2000). Evidence-based corrections: Identifying what works. *Crime & Delinquency, 46* (4), 457–471.

MacKenzie, D. L. (1990). Boot camp prisons: Components, evaluations, and empirical issues. *Federal Probation, 54* (3), 44–52.

MacKenzie, D. L. (1994). Results of a multisite study of boot camp prisons. *Federal Probation, 58* (2), 60–66.

MacKenzie, D. L. (1995). Boot camps—A national assessment. In M. Tonry & K. Hamilton (Eds.), *Intermediate sanctions in overcrowded times* (pp. 149–160). Newbury Park, CA: Sage Publications, Inc.

MacKenzie, D. L., & Shaw, J. W. (1993). The impact of shock incarceration on technical violations and new criminal activities. *Justice Quarterly, 10* (3), 463–87.

MacKenzie, D. L., & Brame, R. (1995). Shock incarceration and positive adjustment during community supervision. *Journal of Quantitative Criminology, 11* (2), 111–142.

MacKenzie, D. L., & Parent, D. G. (1992). Boot camp prisons for young offenders. In J. M. Byrne, A. J. Lurigio, & J. Petersilia (Eds.), *Smart sentencing: The emergence of intermediate sanctions* (pp. 103–119). Newbury Park, CA: Sage Publications.

MacKenzie, D. L., & Souryal, C. (1994). *Multi-site study of shock incarceration.* Washington, DC: National Institute of Justice.

MacKenzie, D. L., Brame, R., McDowall, D., & Souryal, C. (1995). Boot camp prisons and recidivism in eight states. *Criminology, 33* (3), 327–357.

MacKenzie, D. L., Gould, L. A., Riechers, L. M., & Shaw, J. W. (1990). Shock incarceration: Rehabilitation or retribution? *Journal of Offender Counseling, Services, & Rehabilitation, 14* (2), 25–40.

MacKenzie, D. L., Shaw, J. W., & Gowdy, V. B. (1993). *An evaluation of shock incarceration in Louisiana.* Washington, DC: National Institute of Justice.

MacKenzie, D. L., Wilson, D. B., & Kider, S. B. (2001). Effects of correctional boot camps on offending. *The Annals of the American Academy, 578,* 126–43.

Mair, G. (1995). Day centers in England and Wales. In M. Tonry & K. Hamilton (Eds), *Intermediate sanctions in overcrowded times* (pp. 131–138). Boston: Northeastern University Press.

Majer, R. D. (1994). Community service: A good idea that works. *Federal Probation, 58* (2), 20–23.

Marciniak, L. M. (1999). The use of day reporting as an intermediate sanction: A study of offender targeting and program termination. *The Prison Journal, 79* (2), 205–225.

Marciniak, L. M. (2000). The addition of day reporting to intensive supervision probation: A comparison of recidivism rates. *Federal Probation, 64* (1), 34–39.

Martin, C., Olson, D. E., & Lurigio, A. J. (2000). *An evaluation of the Cook County Sheriff's day reporting centerp program: Rearrest and reincarceration after discharge.* Chicago: Illinois Criminal Justice Information Authority.

Martin, M., Choate, J., Johnson, T., & Willett, J. (1998). *Community Supervision and Corrections Department Tarrant County shock incarceration facility local boot camp process evaluation.* Austin, TX: Texas Department of Criminal Justice, Research, Evaluation, and Development Unit.

Maruschak, L. M. (1999). *DWI offenders under correctional supervision. Bureau of Justice Statistics Special Report.* Washington, DC: U.S. Department of Justice, Bureau of Justice Statistics.

Maryland Division of Parole and Probation. (n.d.). *Adult offender court-ordered community service program.* State of Maryland, Division of Parole and Probation. Retrieved November 11, 2002, from http://www.dpscs.state.md.us/pnp/acocsgp.shtml

McBride, D., & VanderWaal, C. (1997). Day reporting centers as an alternative for drug using offenders. *Journal of Drug Issues, 27* (2), 379–398.

McCarthy, B. R., McCarthy, B. J., Jr., & Leone, M. C. (2001). *Community-based corrections (4th Ed.).* Belmont, CA: Wadsworth.

McDevitt, J., & Miliano, R. (1992). "Day reporting centers: An innovative concept in intermediate sanctions," in J. M. Byrne, A. J. Lurigio, & J. Petersilia (Eds.), *Smart sentencing: The emergence of intermediate sanctions.* Newbury Park, CA: Sage Publications.

McDonald, D. C. (1986). *Punishment without walls: Community service sentences in New York City.* New Brunswick, NJ: Rutgers University Press

McDonald, D. C. (1992). Punishing labor: Unpaid community service as a criminal sentence. In J. Byrne, A. Lurigio, & J. Petersilia (Eds.), *Smart sentencing: The emergence of intermediate sanctions* (pp. 182–193). Newbury Park, CA: Sage Publications.

McEwen, T. (1995). *National Assessment Program: 1994 survey results.* Washington, DC: National Institute of Justice.

McGarigle, B. (1997, May). Satellite tracking for house arrest. *Government Technology Magazine.* [Available at: http://www.govtech.net/1997/maytoc/maytoc.phtml]

McIvor, G. (1990). Community service and custody in Scotland. *Howard Journal of Criminal Justice, 29* (2), 101–113.

McIvor, G. (1993). Community service by offenders: The Scottish experience. *The IARCA Journal on Community Corrections, 5* (5), 15–17.

Mercer, R., & Brooks, M. (1999). Judge fails test to outwit gps tracking system. *Correctional compass: The official newsletter of the Florida Department of Corrections,* October, p. 5.

Mercer, R., Brooks, M., & Bryant, P. T. (2000). Global positioning satellite system: Tracking offenders in real time. *Corrections Today, 62*(4), 76–80.

Meyer, J. & Grant, D. (2003). *The courts in our criminal justice system.* Upper Saddle River, NJ: Prentice-Hall.

Meyer, J., & Jesilow, P. (1997). *"Doing justice" in the people's court: Sentencing by municipal court judges.* Albany, NY: State University of New York Press.

Mezghani, R. (1994). Alternatives to imprisonment in Arab countries. In U. Zvekić (Ed.), *Alternatives to imprisonment in comparative perspective* (pp.

69–79) United National Interregional Crime and Justice Research Institute. Chicago: Nelson-Hall Publisher.

Michigan Department of Corrections. (n.d.). *Community residential programs.* Retrieved July 15, 2003 from http://www.michigan.gov/corrections/0,1607,7-119-1435-5035—,00.html

Miller, G. (2000). A SMART solution to jail crowding: Offender reintegration without compromising community safety. *Corrections Today, 62*(4), 72–74.

Montana Department of Corrections (1998). *Performance audit.* Legislative Audit Division, Montana Department of Corrections.

Morash, M., & Rucker, L. (1990). A critical look at the idea of boot camp as a correctional reform. *Crime & Delinquency, 36,* 204–222.

Morris, N., & Tonry, M. (1990). *Between prison and probation: Intermediate punishments in a rational sentencing system.* New York: Oxford University Press.

Mullaney, F. G. (1988). *Economic sanctions in community corrections.* Washington, DC: National Institute of Corrections.

National Institute of Corrections. (2000). *Promoting public safety using effective interventions with offenders.* Washington, DC: National Institute of Corrections.

National Institute of Justice. (1996). *Inventory of aftercare provisions for 53 boot camp programs.* Washington, DC: National Institute of Justice.

National Law Enforcement Corrections Technology Center. (1999). *Keeping track of electronic monitoring.* Washington, DC: National Law Enforcement Corrections Technology Center.

Nellis, M. (1991). The electronic monitoring of offenders in England and Wales. *British Journal of Criminology, 31,* 165–185.

New York State Department of Correctional Services & Division of Parole. (1998). *The tenth annual shock legislative report 1998.* Albany, NY: New York State Department of Correctional Services & Division of Parole

New York State Division of Probation and Correctional Alternatives (n.d.) *Community service standards.* New York State Division of Probation and Correctional Alternatives. Retrieved November 11, 2002, from http://dpca.state.ny.us/nysdpca/pdfs/ccstand.pdf.

Odekunle, E. (1994). Alternatives to imprisonment in Africa: An overview. In U. Zvekić (Ed.), *Alternatives to imprisonment in comparative perspective* (pp. 45–52) United National Interregional Crime and Justice Research Institute. Chicago: Nelson-Hall Publisher.

Orchowsky, S., Lucas, J., & Bogle, T. (1995). Evaluation of the Fairfax day reporting center (FDRC), final report to the governor and the General Assembly of Virginia. Richmond, VA: Virginia Department of Criminal Justice Services.

Outlaw, M. C., & Ruback, R. B. (1999). Predictors and outcomes of victim restitution orders. *Justice Quarterly, 16* (4), 847–869.

Papy, J. E., & Nimer, R. (1991) Electronic monitoring in Florida. *Federal Probation, 55,* 31–33.

Parent, D. (1989). *Shock incarceration: An overview of existingpPrograms.* Washington, DC: National Institute of Justice.

Parent, D. (1990). *Day reporting centers for criminal offenders: A descriptive analysis of existing programs.* Washington, DC: National Institute of Justice.

Parent, D. (1990b). *Recovering costs through offenderfFees.* Washington DC: National Institute of Justice.

Parent, D. G. (1995). Day reporting centers. In M. Tonry & K. Hamilton (Eds), *Intermediate sanctions in overcrowded times* (pp. 125–127). Boston: Northeastern University Press.

Parent, D. G. (1996). Boot camps and prison crowding. In D. L. MacKenzie & E. E. Hebert (Eds.), *Correctional boot camps: A tough intermediate sanction* (pp. 263–274). Washington, DC: National Institute of Justice.

Parent, D. G., & Barnett, L. (2002). *Transition from prison to community initiative.* Cambridge, MA: Abt Associates, Inc.

Parent, D. G., & Corbett, R. P., Jr. (1996). Day reporting centers: An evolving intermediate sanction. *Federal Probation, 60* (4), 51–54.

Parent, D., Byrne, J., Tsarfaty, V., Valade, L., & Esselman, J. (1995). *Day reporting centers: Volume 2.* Washington, DC: U.S. Department of Justice, National Institute of Justice.

Payne, B. K. & Gainey, R. R. (2000). Is good-time appropriate for offenders on electronic monitoring?: Attitudes of electronic monitoring directors. *Journal of Criminal Justice, 28,* 497–506.

Pearson, F., & Harper, A. G. (1990). Contingent intermediate sentences: New Jersey's intensive supervision program. *Crime & Delinquency, 36* (1), 75–86.

Pease, K. (1985). Community service orders. In M. Tonry & N. Morris (Eds.), *Crime and justice: An annual review of research,* Volume 6 (pp. 51–94). Chicago: University of Chicago Press.

Peters, E. M. (1995). Prison before the prison: The ancient and medieval worlds. In N. Morris & D. J. Rothman (Eds.), *The Oxford history of the prison: The practice of punishment in western society* (pp. 3–47).

Petersilia, J. (1990a). When probation becomes more dreaded than prison. *Federal Probation, 54* (1), 23–27.

Petersilia, J. (1990b). Conditions that permit intensive supervision programs to survive. *Crime & Delinquency, 36* (1), 126–145.

Petersilia, J. (1998). A crime control rationale for reinvesting in community corrections. In J. Petersilia (Ed.), *Community corrections: Probation, parole, and intermediate sanctions* (pp. 20–28). New York: Oxford University Press.

Petersilia, J. (1999). A decade of experimenting with intermediate sanctions: What have we learned? *Perspectives, 23*(1), 39–44.

Petersilia, J., & Turner, S. (1993). *Evaluating intensive supervision probation/ parole: Results of a nationwide experiment.* National Institute of Justice Research in Brief. Washington, DC: National Institute of Justice.

Petersilia, J., Turner, S., Kahan, J., & Peterson, J. (1985). *Granting felons probation: Public risks and alternatives.* Santa Monica, CA: RAND Corporation.

Poole, C., & Slavick, P. (1995). Boot camps: A Washington State update and overview of national findings. Olympia, WA: Washington State Institute for Public Policy.

Porter, R., Lee, S., & Lutz, M. (2002). Balancing punishment and treatment: Alternatives to incarceration in New York City. New York: Vera Institute of Justice.

President's Commission on Law Enforcement and Administration of Justice. (1967). *Task force report: The courts.* Washington, DC: U.S. Government Printing Office.

Rackmill, S. J. (1994). An analysis of home confinement as a sanction. *Federal Probation, 58*(1), 45–52.

Ramirez, R. (n.d.). *Community service restitution and victim restitution report: Fiscal years 2000 and 2001 (Draft).* Texas Department of Criminal Justice, Community Justice Assistance Division.

Renzema, M. (1992). Home confinement programs: Development, implementation, and impact. In J. M. Byrne, A. J. Lurigio, & J. Petersilia (Eds.), *Smart sentencing: The emergence of intermediatesSanctions.* London: Sage.

Renzema, M. (2000). Tracking GPS: A third look. *Journal of Offender Monitoring, 13*(2), 6–8, 27.

Renzema, M., & Skelton, D. T. (1990). *Use of electronic monitoring in the United States: 1989 update.* Washington, DC: National Institute of Justice.

Restitution Incorporated. (n.d.) *National death row inmate restitution artsShow.* Chapel Hill, NC: Restitution Incorporated. Retrieved on November 14, 2002 from http://www.restitutioninc.org/

Roberts-Van Cuick, K. (2000). Supervising the sex offender: Contact with children. *Corrections Today, 62* (7), 106–109.

Rothman, D. J. (1995). Perfecting the prison: United States, 1789-1865. In N. Morris & D. J. Rothman (Eds.), *The Oxford history of the prison: The practice of punishment in western society* (pp. 111–129).

Rowley, M. (1990). Comparison of recidivism rates for delinquents processed in a restitution-diversion program to a matched sample processed in court. In B. Galaway & J. Hudson (Eds.), *Criminal justice, restitution, & reconciliation* (pp. 217–225). Monsey, NY: Criminal Justice Press.

Roy, S. (2002). Adult offenders in a day reporting center—A preliminary study. *Federal Probation, 66* (1), 44–50.

Schmidt, A. K. (1991). Electronic monitors: Realistically, what can be expected? *Federal Probation, 55*(2), 47–53.

Schneider, P. R. & Finkelstein, M. C. (1998). *RESTTA.* Bethesda, Maryland: Pacific Institute for Research and Evaluation.

Schwitzgebel, R. K., Schwitzgebel, R. L., Pahnke, W. N., & Hurd, W. S. (1964). A program of research in behavioral electronics. *Behavioral Science, 9,* 233–238.

Spelman, W. (1994). *Criminal incapacitation.* New York: Plenum Press.

Stephan, J. J. (1999). *State prison expenditures, 1996.* Washington, DC: Bureau of Justice Statistics.

Stephan, J. J. (2001). *Census of Jails, 1999.* Washington, DC: Bureau of Justice Statistics.

Stinchcomb, J. (2002). Prisons of the mind: Lessons learned from home confinement. *Journal of Criminal Justice Education, 13,* 463-478.

Stinchcomb, J. B., & Terry, W. C., III. (2001). Predicting the likelihood of rearrest among Shock Incarceration graduates: Moving beyond another nail in the boot camp coffin. *Crime & Delinquency, 47* (2), 221–242.

Sugihara, H., Horiuchi, K., Nishimura, N., Yamaguchi, A., Sato, S., Nishimura, I., et al. (1994). An overview of alternatives to imprisonment in Asia and the Pacific Region. In U. Zvekić (Ed.), *Alternatives to imprisonment in comparative perspective* (pp. 95–202) United National Interregional Crime and Justice Research Institute. Chicago: Nelson-Hall Publisher.

Texas Department of Criminal Justice (1999). *Electronic monitoring*, Agency Brief. Austin, TX: Texas Department of Criminal Justice, Community Justice Assistance Division.

Tobolowsky, P. M. (1993). Restitution in the federal criminal justice system. *Judicature, 77* (2), 90–95.

Tonry, M. (1990). Stated and latent functions of ISP. *Crime and Delinquency, 36* (1), 174-191.

Tonry, M. (1996). *Sentencing matters.* New York: Oxford University Press.

Tonry, M. (1997). *Intermediate sanctions in sentencing guidelines.* Washington, DC: National Institute of Justice.

Tonry, M., & Hamilton, K. (1995). *Intermediate sanctions in overcrowdedtTimes.* Boston: Northeastern University Press.

Tonry, M., & Lynch, M. (1996). Intermediate sanctions. In M. Tonry (Ed.), *Crime and justice: a review of research, Vol. 20* (pp. 99–144). Chicago: University of Chicago Press.

Turner, S., & Petersilia, J. (1992). Focusing on high-risk parolees: An experiment to reduce commitments to the Texas Department of Corrections. *Research in Crime & Delinquency, 29* (1), 34-61.

Turner, S., & Petersilia, J. (1996a). *Day fines in four U.S. jurisdictions.* Santa Monica, CA: Rand Corporation.

Turner, S., & Petersilia, J. (1996b). *Work release: Recidivism and corrections costs in Washington State: Research in brief.* Washington, DC: National Institute of Justice.

Turner, S., Petersilia, J., & Deschenes, E. P. (1992). Evaluating intensive supervision probation/parole (ISP) for drug offenders. *Crime & Delinquency, 38* (4), 539–556.

U.S. Congress, Office of Technology Assessment (1988). *Criminal justice, new technologies, and the Constitution.* Washington, DC: U.S. Government Printing Office, OTA-CIT-366.

U.S. General Accounting Office. (1991). Report to the Chairman, Subcommittee on Intellectual Property and Judicial Administration, Committee on the Judiciary, House of Representatives. *Prison alternatives: Crowded federal prisons can transfer more inmates to halfway houses.* Washington, DC: U.S. General Accounting Office.

U.S. General Accounting Office. (1993a). Report to the Chairman. Subcommittee on Crime and Criminal Justice, Committee on the Judiciary, House of Representatives. *Intensive probation supervision: Cost-savings relative to incarceration.* Washington, DC: U.S. General Accounting Office.

U.S. General Accounting Office. (1993b). Report to the Chairman, Subcommittee on Crime and Criminal Justice, Committee on the Judiciary, House of Representatives. *Intensive probation supervision: Crime-control and cost-saving effectiveness.* Washington, DC: U.S. General Accounting Office.

U.S. General Accounting Office. (1993c). Report to the Chairman, Subcommittee on Crime and Criminal Justice, Committee on the Judiciary, House of Representatives. *Intensive probation supervision: Mixed effectiveness in controlling crime.* Washington, DC: U.S. General Accounting Office.

U.S. General Accounting Office. (1993d). Prison boot camps: Short-term prison costs reduced, but long-term impact uncertain. Washington, DC: U.S. General Accounting Office.

U.S. General Accounting Office. (1998). Report to the chairman, Senate Committee on the Judiciary, and the chairman, Subcommittee on Crime, House Committee on the Judiciary. *Fines and restitution, improvement needed in how offenders' payment schedules are determined.* Washington, DC: U.S. General Accounting Office.

U.S. General Accounting Office. (2001). Report to congressional committees. *Prisoner releases: Trends and information on reintegration programs.* Washington, DC: U.S. General Accounting Office.

U.S. National Highway Traffic Safety Administration (2001, January). **Repeat intoxicated driver laws.** Retrieved November 11, 2002, from http://www.nhtsa.dot.gov/people/outreach/stateleg/reseciton.html

U.S. Sentencing Commission. (2000). *Sourcebook of federal sentencing statistics.* Washington, DC: U.S. Sentencing Commission.

Vera Institute of Justice. (1981). *The New York City Community Service Sentencing Program: Development of the Bronx pilot project.* New York: Vera Institute of Justice.

Vigorita, M. S. (2002). Fining practices in felony courts: An analysis of offender, offense and systematic factors. *Corrections Compendium, 27*(11), 1–27.

Vollum, S. & Hale, C. (2002). Electronic monitoring: A research review. *Corrections Compendium, 27*(7), 1–9.

von Hirsch, A. (1976). *Doing Justice.* New York: Hill and Wang.

von Hirsch, A., Wasik, M., & Greene, J. (1989). Punishments in the community and the principles of desert. *Rutgers Law Journal, 20,* 595–618.

Wagner, D., & Baird, C. (1993) *Evaluation of the Florida community control program.* Washington, DC: National Institute of Justice.

Wheeler, G. R., Hissong, R. V., Slusher, M. P., & Macan, T. M. (1990). Economic sanctions in criminal justice: Dilemma for human service? *The Justice System Journal, 14* (1), 63–77.

Whitehead, J. T., Miller, L. S., & Myers, L. B. (1995). The diversionary effectiveness of intensive supervision and community corrections programs. In J. O. Smykla & W. L. Selke (Eds.), *Intermediate sanctions: Sentencing in the 1990s* (pp. 135–152). Cincinnati: Anderson Publishing Co.

Whitfield, D. (2001). *The magic bracelet: Technology and offender supervision.* Winchester, England: Waterside Press.

Wilkinson, R. A. (2000). The impact of community service work on Ohio state prisoners: A restorative justice perspective and overview. *Corrections Management Quarterly, 4*(3), 1–13.

Winterfield, L. A., & Hillsman, S. T. (1991). *The effects of instituting means based fines in a criminal court: The Staten Island day-fine experiment.* New York: Vera Institute of Justice.

Winterfield, L. A., & Hillsman, S. T. (1993). *The Staten Island day-fines project: Research in brief.* Washington DC: National Institute of Justice.

Winterfield, L. A., & Hillsman, S. T. (1995). The Staten Island day-fine experiment. In G. L. Mays & P. R. Gregware (Eds.), *Courts and justice: A reader* (pp.436–448). Prospect Heights, IL: Waveland Press.

Women's Prison Association & Home, Inc. (*n.d.*). *Services.* Retrieved on July 20, 2003, from http://www.wpaonline.org/WEBSITE/services.htm

Worzella, D. (1992). The Milwaukee municipal court day-fine project. In D. C. McDonald, J. Green, C. Worzella (Eds.), *Day fines in American courts: The Staten Island and Milwaukee experiments. Issues and practices in criminal justice* (pp. 61–76). Washington, DC: National Institute of Justice.

Young, D., Porter, R., & Caputo, G. A. (1999). *Community service for repeat misdemeanor offenders in New York City: Final report.* New York: Vera Institute of Justice.

Young, D., Porter, R., & Caputo, G. A. (1998). *Community alternatives for felony offenders: A preliminary assessment.* New York: Vera Institute of Justice.

Zachariah, J. K. (1996). An overview of boot camp goals, components, and results. In D. L. MacKenzie & E. E. Hebert (Eds.), *Correctional boot camps: A tough intermediate sanction* (p. 17–38). Washington, DC: National Institute of Justice.

Zimring, F. E., & Hawkins, G. (1995). *Incapacitation: Penal confinement and the restraint of crime.* New York: Oxford University Press.

INDEX

Note: Page numbers in *italics* indicate charts and graphs.
   Page numbers in **bold** indicate chapters.